C O M M E M O R A T I V E B O O K P L A T E

2006

Ms. Emily D. Meyers
made a gift to the Free Library of Philadelphia

in honor of
Constance Lyford

Louis Lozowick. *Winter Fun.* Lithograph. 1941. Print and Picture Collection, Free Library of Philadelphia

Free
LIBRARY of
PHILADELPHIA

The Rise and Fall of
American Public Schools

The Rise and Fall of American Public Schools

The Political Economy of Public Education in the Twentieth Century

ROBERT J. FRANCIOSI

Westport, Connecticut
London

371.0109
F846r

Library Cataloging-in-Publication Data

Franciosi, Robert J.
   The rise and fall of American public schools : the political economy of public education in the twentieth century / Robert J. Franciosi.
      p.   cm.
   Includes bibliographical references and index.
   ISBN 0–275–97687–4
   1. Education—United States—History—20th century. 2. Public schools—United States—History—20th century. I. Title.
LA212.F73   2004
371.01′0973—dc22   2004003012

British Library Cataloguing in Publication Data is available.

Library of Congress Catalog Card Number: 2004003012
ISBN: 0–275–97687–4

First published in 2004

Praeger Publishers, 88 Post Road West, Westport, CT 06881
An imprint of Greenwood Publishing Group, Inc.
www.praeger.com

Printed in the United States of America

The paper used in this book complies with the Permanent Paper Standard issued by the National Information Standards Organization (Z39.48–1984).

10 9 8 7 6 5 4 3 2 1

For my parents: Julius and Shirley Franciosi

Contents

Illustrations

Figures

Tables

Preface

Subsumed into this book's somewhat sensational title are the many trajectories—rising, falling, and zigzag—that American public schools have followed since their creation. This book traces the paths of both student achievement and resources over the past 100 years, and it offers reasons why the two have not been parallel. It also makes the case that the path schools should follow in the future is greater decentralization of control through parental choice.

This book started as the policy report *No Voice, No Exit: The Inefficiency of America's Public Schools* that I authored for the Institute for Policy Innovation (IPI). I would like to thank the IPI, George Pieler, and Eric Schlecht for starting me on the path that led to this book. During the journey, I perhaps have strayed widely in some areas, and the opinions and conclusions expressed here are solely my own. I would like to thank my editor Jim Dunton, who saw the potential in the IPI report and has patiently helped me along the way. I would also like to thank Michael K. Block, Mary Gifford, and Karla Phillips for their ideas and suggestions. Nothing in this book represents in any way the official policy of the Arizona Department of Education.

Introduction

THE CONTINUING CRISIS

In their defense of modern American public education, David Berliner and Bruce Biddle maintain that much of the present criticism regarding the condition of the nation's schools is, as they state in the title of their book, a "manufactured crisis" (Berliner and Biddle 1995). If so, then the current mound of criticism and reform of public education is merely the latest product of one of the nation's oldest industries. By 1830, a magazine editor was already weary with "a never ceasing ding-dong about reform and change in our public schools" (Reese 1995, 16). Over a century later, Richard Hofstadter summarized the history of commentary on education in America as "a literature of acid criticism and bitter complaint" (Hofstadter 1962). For much of the past 200 years, someone somewhere has found something to grumble about in America's schools.

A 1999 keyword search by Gregory Cizek through ERIC (Educational Resources Information Center—a government-supported database of education and literature) found 4,027 articles published since 1966 that used the word *crisis* in combination with *education, school(s),* or *classroom.* He also found 260 listings of books and other library materials written between the 1930s and the present that contained the keyword *crisis.* Over the past half-century, there have been crises in food service, insurance, scheduling, art education, early-childhood special education, middle-school social sciences, inorganic chemistry, and school psychology. "In every decade since the 1940s, books have described the entire American school system—from elementary schools to universities—as being in crisis" (Cizek 1999).

Many of the issues and problems that are currently the subjects of worry and debate have seemingly always plagued America's public schools. Taxpayers, it seems, have perpetually complained about extravagant spending by local schools, and schools in turn have unceasingly grumbled about a lack of funds. Teachers have been perennially scarce, and those who can be found to teach are invariably unqualified, overworked, and underpaid. Parents are always hostile and suspicious, and the children seem to get surlier every year. For conservatives, schools are forever abandoning the legacy of centuries of scholarship and learning for new and controversial ideas. This apostasy would be more dangerous to society if children were actually learning the stuff, but the schools' ability to teach effectively is also in perpetual decay. For self-styled progressives, on the other hand, bigots, know-nothings, and reactionaries are ever-present obstacles to the adoption of new, scientifically proven methods in teaching and school administration. The difficulties of teaching immigrant children, dilapidated buildings, bureaucracy, inefficiency, and calls for reform—all seem constants in our public schools.

The history of American school policy is the story of repeated waves of reformers, each bemoaning the present state of the schools and offering a list of measures sure to bring improvement. In the mid-nineteenth century, the annual reports of noted education reformer Horace Mann, who was secretary of the Massachusetts Board of Education, were a chronicle of the deficiencies of the state's locally controlled district schools: overcrowded schoolhouses in worse condition than the local jails and sometimes even lacking privies for the students. If outhouses did exist, they could hardly be dignified with the term *privy*, since they offered no privacy and were invariably defaced by coarse and scurrilous student graffiti. The teachers, Mann and other reformers of the time reported, were often uneducated, immoral, and ill bred, and occasionally drunkards. Schools were like this, according to Mann and his associates, because of the shortsightedness and stinginess of the local voters. The solution the reformers sought was increased oversight by state authorities over local schools districts (Nasaw 1979, 38–39).

The quality of sanitary facilities seemingly was and is an important issue in American education. A teacher in Oregon during the state's pioneer days faced a local school board that was balking at paying for the construction of separate privies for boys and girls as mandated by the state. The teacher claimed to have overcome the board's resistance by demonstrating that the total cost for both privies would be only $20 (Tyack 1974, 18). In 1996, a long-time educator, consultant, and lobbyist launched Project CLEAN (Citizens, Learners, and Educators Against Neglect) to prod schools to improve the "prison-like design and poor upkeep" of school restrooms. In keeping with the mores of modern education, simple decency must be girded by social science, so an *Education Week* article describing the work of "Dr. Toilet" contains an inevitable quote from a pediatrician who has witnessed children suffering from infections because they were hesitant to use their schools' facilities (Gewertz 2003).

At the beginning of the twentieth century, another wave of reformers again used the dilapidated physical condition of the schools to dramatize the need for change. Their targets were the local urban political machines and the control the bosses and political hacks had over the local schools. The reformers' goals were to take politics out of the schools, to centralize control, and to institute the efficient management techniques being used by the most modern business enterprises. As part of the effort, the reformers' muckraker allies catalogued the harmful effect of machine graft and patronage on urban school systems. In Philadelphia, they found teachers continually on the lookout to warn students of plaster falling from the ceiling overhead, funds so scarce that teachers had to pay for supplies out of their own pockets, and one principal having to use a pay phone located in the school to make calls (Tyack 1974, 95).

From time to time, American schoolhouses, in addition to being in a continuous state of disrepair, have also ostensibly suffered from a lack of space due to burgeoning enrollment. In the 1920s, school districts had difficulty accommodating an enrollment boom as more and more students continued their education through high school. Schools without enough seats had to operate on double shifts. Furthermore, many school districts had difficulty keeping their buildings at the minimal requirements for health and safety. Thousands of schools at the time did not even meet nineteenth-century standards for school facilities, including basic sanitary amenities. Many schools deferred building in the 1920s, only to be hit by an extreme scarcity of funds during the Great Depression in the following decade (Zilversmit 1976, 260).

Schools enjoyed a respite as enrollment declined due to World War II, but after the war, observers worried about another facilities crisis as the baby boomers were about to engulf the school system. In 1945, an African American teacher, Mrs. Florence Christmas, related to a committee of the U.S. Senate the financial difficulties facing her school. Located on the grounds of a local church, the school was financed and built by teachers, parents, children, and patrons of the school. At the time of Mrs. Christmas's testimony, the school still did not have enough seats for all the children and was trying to raise $12.57 to pay for painting the building inside and out. In 1947, after a six-month cross-country tour to observe the nation's schools, Benjamin Fine, the education editor of the *New York Times*, concluded, "America's public school system is confronted with the most serious crisis in its history." He found that school buildings were in a "deplorable state all over the nation." The United States, Fine also noted, spent less on education than did Great Britain or the Soviet Union (Ravitch 1983, 3, 7).

Not only have American schools suffered from inadequate space and shabby and crumbling buildings; the teachers who have labored in those buildings have apparently been perpetually overworked and underpaid. In her 1880 exposé, writer, teacher, and women's rights advocate Mary Abigail Dodge complained about the "degradation of the teacher" as women teachers lacked opportunity for advancement and had to submit to male supervisors and board members who, although above the teachers in rank, were, Dodge asserted, below the teachers both intellectually and socially. These petty bureaucrats so burdened teachers with requirements for reports and statistics that they had no time left to teach. At the time, women in city schools earned on average only $12 per week, compared to $31 for male school employees. Twenty-five years later, at the beginning of the twentieth century, the National Education Association found little improvement. The annual salary of a teacher was less than $12,000 in today's dollars, and beginning teachers earned less than unskilled laborers. In 1911, a detailed survey of five cities found that teachers made less than many unskilled workers, leaving them with little money to set aside for savings or to support a family. Turn-of-the-century teachers and other observers complained of intense oversight by supervisors and a lack of discretion and influence. In 1919, the turnover rate was 20 percent (Tyack 1974, 62–64, 258–59, 268).

After WWII, Benjamin Fine found schools closing because of a severe teacher shortage. Experienced instructors were leaving due to low pay, and schools were having to hire underqualified teachers. Teacher morale was low. Florence Christmas testified that she earned more in one week making vegetable containers in a factory than she earned in a month as a teacher. Wilma Upchurch, a teacher from Nebraska who testified before the Senate with Mrs. Christmas, stated that pay in her rural district was so low that teacher turnover was 50 percent, and one in five teachers in the entire state had an emergency teaching certificate. This was nothing compared to Utah, where one in four teachers lacked certification, and Colorado, where one-third of teachers were hired on a temporary basis. In Iowa, 800 rural schools did not even have teachers (Ravitch 1983, 3–7).

Inequality of resources among schools has also been an unsolvable problem for American education. In 1857, a group of African American leaders in New York complained that the board of education was spending one cent on school facilities per African American child compared to $16 for a white student, even though proportionally more African American students attended city schools. The result, they told an investigating committee, was that black children attended dingy schools in dangerous neighborhoods while white children went to near-palaces with all the latest comforts and conveniences. Ninety years later, in the middle of the twentieth century, spending across the nation still differed by as much as 60 to 1 (Tyack 1974, 119; Ravitch 1983, 7).

While educators have complained almost constantly of a lack of adequate funds, taxpayers have repeatedly denounced public schools as extravagant, corrupt, and laden with bureaucracy. In the nineteenth century, when high schools offered a relatively small number of students what was then considered an elite education, communities repeatedly balked at spending the significant amount of money needed to run institutions that most children would not attend. Many taxpayers considered high schools antidemocratic, and some opponents of public funding for secondary education likened high schools to "horse leeches" (Reese 1995, 64).

In 1880, Harvey Scott, the editor of the Portland *Oregonian*, embarked on a crusade against the local school system, which he viewed as "cumbrous, complex and costly," run by a new class of professional education bureaucrats. His views were seconded by one of his readers, a self-described defender of the common school, who felt that the local school system had become "superficial, overloaded and overtaxing" (Tyack 1974, 83–84).

In 1889, the U.S. Commissioner of Education reported an average of four supervisors per district in 484 cities surveyed . During the first decades of the twentieth century, the expansion of high-school enrollment, the diversification of curricula, a movement by educators to serve the whole student, and the introduction of science and scientific management to education gave rise to an army of administrators, counselors, nurses, teachers of vocational courses, curriculum directors, and others in school districts across the nation. Between 1890 and 1920, the number of supervisors increased from 9 to 144 in Baltimore, from 7 to 159 in Boston, from 31 to 329 in Detroit, from 58 to 155 in St. Louis, and from 66 to 268 in Philadelphia. These systems were catching up to where New York started. The school system in the Big Apple expanded its bureaucracy from 235 to 1,310 supervisors during the same period (Tyack 1974, 185).

In a nation of immigrants, schools have always struggled with teaching a diverse student body. Students in New York schools at the beginning of the twentieth century spoke 29 different languages and dialects. In the past, ethnic minorities were perhaps even more aggressively trying to get schools to teach their cultures and languages than they are today. In nineteenth-century Cincinnati, German parents boycotted schools they felt did not accord enough respect to German culture. Politicians back then were not above a little multicultural pandering. William Thompson, the mayor of Chicago at the beginning of the Roaring Twenties, encouraged his city's schools to teach about Irish, German, and Polish heroes. No doubt in a bid for the Irish vote, he also threatened to punch King George in the nose (Tyack 1974, 87, 172, 179).

Then as now, parents worried about what was being taught in the classroom. The Scopes trial in the 1920s is well-known, and the teaching of evolution remains controversial today. A concern that predated teaching evolution was the fear that schools were hostile to boys. In the nineteenth century, educators were concerned that boys might be feminized by being taught by too many female teachers. In 1909, Leonard Ayres of the Russell Sage Foundation found that boys were more likely to be held back in school than girls, and that girls were more likely to complete school. The only conclusion, Ayres decided, was that schools were more amenable to girls than to boys (Tyack 1974, 63, 200–201). Nearly 90 years later, the superintendent of a Massachusetts school district found that a disproportionate number of high-school girls were being inducted into the National Honor Society—an example, many believed, of a school environment that was not "boy-friendly" (Galley 2002). Another controversy dating from the first decades of the twentieth century is the teaching of "sex hygiene," as it was called at the time. In San Francisco in the years after World War I, an Irish newspaper warned that the schools were in danger of being taken over by "sex hygienists and birth controllers" (Tyack 1974, 166).

After WWII, schools were inundated with a wave of criticism that was novel in two respects. First, it was national in scope: the American public school system, rather than a city system, was under scrutiny. Second, it focused primarily on academic achievement. Books by Robert M. Hutchins, the chancellor of the University of Chicago, Albert Lynd, a businessman and school board member whose book was titled *Quackery in the Public Schools,* and Arthur Bestor, a historian and educator, took American schools to task for failing their primary purpose. Instead of teaching students reading, mathematics, history, and literature, schools were preoccupied with teaching proper dating etiquette, drivers' education, and the correct way to brush one's teeth. These criticisms were echoed in the popular press and by parents' groups. High school students were unprepared for college, were unable to write simple English sentences or do elementary mathematical calculations, and couldn't find New York or Boston on a map. These concerns were launched through the stratosphere along with *Sputnik* in 1957. The father of the nuclear navy, Admiral Hyman Rickover, criticized the schools for putting the country in danger because they were not producing scientists, engineers, and mathematicians in sufficient quantity and quality to compete with the Soviet Union (Ravitch 1983, 72–75, 228; Berliner and Biddle 1995, 146).

Nearly a quarter of a century later, apparently, little progress had been made. In 1983, the National Commission on Excellence in Education, which had been created by the Reagan administration, published *A Nation at Risk.* The report warned that the United States was in peril of losing its leadership in commerce, science, and technology, and that national security was in danger due to a "rising tide of mediocrity" in the U.S. school system. The report came during an unprecedented time in American education. For 10 years, broad-based indicators of student achievement had been falling in what has come to be known as the "Great Test Score Decline." At the same time, public dissatisfaction with the nation's schools was rising. The criticisms contained in *A Nation at Risk* caused such a detonation that Berliner and Biddle still felt compelled to counter them 12 years after the report was released. The "mother of all critiques," it launched a reform effort that has not lost its vigor after two decades (National Commission on Excellence in Education 1983, 5; Berliner and Biddle 1995, 139).

Efforts to return schools to rigor and the fundamentals are one-half of a debate that has continued for over a century. The other side has been a movement to make the education of American youth less rigid, stultifying, and dull. In 1856, the school committee of Lynn, Massachusetts, criticized the instructional methods of its teachers. "Mechanical drill," committee members worried, was taking the place of "living assimilation," and "parrot-like repetition" was displacing "a real ability to think." During the 1860s, the committee advocated alternative teaching methods called "object teaching" and "oral instruction," with the goal of moving away from recitation and the accumulation of "isolated facts" and toward teacher interaction with students and the stimulation of curiosity, thought, and understanding (Kaestle and Vinovskis 1980, 181).

Later critics, including Harvard president Charles Eliot, Joseph Mayer Rice, a pediatrician who had studied education in Germany, and the aforementioned Mary Abigail Dodge, denounced mass education in the nineteenth century as inflexible and cheerless, teaching children useless trivia. Rice claimed that the results achieved in New York schools were below those of other cities, denounced the methods of instruction as "dehumanizing," and labeled the system as "antiquated" and "pernicious" (Tyack 1974, 81–83, 151).

After 80 years of effort by so-called progressive educators to make schools more child-friendly, critics in the 1960s accused schools of essentially being where they were a century earlier. Barely had schools a chance to get back to basics after *Sputnik* when along came another series of books—this time authored by radical critics of establishment schools. With titles like *Death at an Early Age, Our Children Are Dying, The Way It Spozed to Be,* and *Education and Ecstasy,* this tidal wave of memoirs, exposés, and manifestos formed a radical-leftist critique of American public schools. Despite the mainstream liberal establishment's attempt to improve education for the poor and minorities with the passage of the Elementary and Secondary Education Act in 1965, radicals made a deeper indictment of the school system. This new movement "blamed American society for the persistence of racism and inequality; it blamed the bureaucratic nature of the educational system for failing to respond to children as individuals; it blamed the teaching profession for serving its own interests instead of the interests of children" (Ravitch 1983, 235–36). Over 30 years later, radical critics continue to fault the public education system for the same problems—only these critics are now found on the right end of the political spectrum.

It is difficult to tell from the current polemics which side is currently ascendant and what exactly is going on in America's classrooms. Are children's minds being filled with intellectual mush, or are their souls being crushed by rote memorization, incessant competition, and failure? Nearly a century after John Dewey and his wife Alice opened their Laboratory School at the University of Chicago, some educational liberals still claim that drill and rote memorization of trivia dominate American classrooms. They label as "radical ideas" (*radical* to them being a compliment) an emphasis on problem solving, student-initiated projects, and "self-aware thinking" (Berliner and Biddle 1995, 301–2). Diane Ravitch claims to see a modern synthesis of the two movements: the implementation of a traditional academic curriculum and rigorous standards along with more-innovative teaching methods. However, she believes that the new wave of progressive education is more likely to flourish in private and charter schools than in traditional public schools (Ravitch 2000, 450–52, 464).

Not only have many of the issues confronting public education in the United States remained the same for over 200 years, but the rhetoric of the debates over school policy has remained fairly constant as well. In the nineteenth century, proponents of public funding for high schools characterized their opponents as Jesuits, "Romanists," and wealthy aristocrats who did not want their children brought into contact with the offspring of ditch diggers and mechanics. In an 1883 issue of *Education,* one satirical public school advocate caricatured what he viewed as the typical penny-pinching, shortsighted, and ignorant capitalist, a "Mr. Anthracite Ironsides." A self-made and naturally rather rotund man, Mr. Ironsides had some use but little respect for former schoolmates who went through high school to become schoolmasters, ministers, engineers, and, occasionally, a "literary feller" (Reese 1995, 62–63, 73).

In the following century, according to defenders of public education, religious zealots and the wealthy were still thorns in the side of American schools. In the 1950s, one writer classified critics of public schools as "(a) the 'chronic tax conservationists' who resist every addition to the public expense; (b) the 'congenital reactionaries' who are suspicious of everything that 'isn't like it used to be when I was in school'; (c) numerous tribes of 'witch hunters,' especially those to whom every political and social change since 1900 is 'red'; (d) numerous 'religious tongs' which whet their axes on many forms of prejudice." Another was blunter: the enemies of public schools were "real-estate conservatives, super-patriots, dogma peddlers, and race haters" (Ravitch 1983, 74). Thirty years later, David Berliner and Bruce Biddle alleged the following motives for those responsible for manufacturing the latest crisis: "classical conservatism a la Edmund Burke; 'economic rationalism'; defense of the rich; religious

BLACKWELL'S
BOOK SERVICES

Order Type: 101 Firm Order

Customer
Name: Free Library Of Philadelphia

Customer
Alpha Code
& Number: 119350009

Del
Add: 01

Customer PO-2532-L-7/2007
Ord Nbr:

Dept:
Customer
Order Date: 16-Mar-2007

Fund
Number:

BBS Order
Number: M276723

ISBN: 0275976874   ISBN-13: 9780275976873   List Price 64.95

Title: **THE RISE AND FALL OF AMERICAN PUBLIC SCHOOLS** Author: Franciosi, Robert J.

Sub-Title: **The Political Economy Of Public Education In The Twentieth**

Publisher: Praeger Publishing

Order
Qty: 1

Shipped
Qty: 1

Series Title:

Spine Title:

Volume Number: Publication Year: 2004   No. of Volumes: 001   Format: Hardback

Document Text:

Accompanying Material: .

fundamentalism; suspicion of the federal government; hostility to public education and the academy (in general) and to social research (in particular); and racial, sexist, and ethnic bigotry" (Berliner and Biddle 1995, 132).

The rhetoric of reform has remained as constant as the rhetoric of defense. At the beginning of the twentieth century, business, political, and intellectual leaders called for schools to use the scientific management methods employed by the most modern business organizations. At the start of the twenty-first century, there are still calls for the school system to model itself on the private sector. However, as education historians David Tyack and Larry Cuban point out, while the recommendation has remained the same, what it means to be "run like a business" has changed (Tyack and Cuban 1995, 41). A hundred years ago, the latest business model was that of the giant trusts and corporations: centralization, hierarchy, and management by experts. Today's business model calls for deregulation, decentralization, worker empowerment, and the elimination of middle management. Then as now, advocates claimed a system modeled after the private sector would increase "accountability" (Tyack 1974, 167).

One tool of accountability was and is testing. In 1844, Samuel Gridley Howe, a school reform advocate and friend of Horace Mann, sought to measure the output of Boston schools by giving a uniform written test to the top class. The results, in Howe's view, confirmed the sorry state of Boston's schools. Taking the results of all students together, only 30 percent of questions were answered correctly, and students made a grand total of 35,947 punctuation errors. Howe concluded that there was too much rote learning of facts without an understanding of the principles behind them. Howe's solution was the creation of a new professional executive, a superintendent, to manage the schools (Tyack 1974, 35–36).

Although the school policy debate has seemingly remained the same, public schools themselves have changed. The public education system is quite different today than it was 200, 100, or even 50 years ago. The most obvious difference is that today there is in fact a public school system that serves over 90 percent of American children. The hodgepodge of private academies, charity schools, individual tutors, and parental instruction that saw to the education of American children in 1800 has been almost entirely displaced by a government-run system that has consistently grown more organized, more professional, and more centralized. Secondly, more American children are attending school, and they are staying in school longer. In 1869, 65 percent of children between 5 and 19 were enrolled in school. By the end of the twentieth century, that proportion had increased to over 90 percent (U.S. Department of Education 2002, table 38). Indeed, the United States has been a world leader in the educational attainment of its citizens.

This slight immersion in the history of crises in and complaints about public schooling in the United States is meant to provide some perspective on the dilemmas and problems facing schools today. By their very nature, public schools are creatures of democratic compromise—many times the compromise of very diverse interests. It is no surprise when idealists and ideologues, reformers and radicals are impatient and sometimes outraged over the balance among interest groups that is often struck. It might be depressing that the democratic process has not been able to solve some of the difficulties that seem to perpetually afflict public schools, but it should be noted that despite its schools straying from some optimal path desired by experts and advocates of various shades, the nation has thrived. This gives some indication that, despite the theories and models reformers have put forward for the past 200 years, voters, parents, and taxpayers have proven to have a better understanding of what type of education will benefit their children, and have been willing and able to weigh those benefits against the costs.

THE PURPOSE OF THIS BOOK

The purpose of this book is to evaluate the condition of state-controlled education. It offers an explanation of how schools have come to where they are, and it critically reviews the many reforms that seek to push public schools even farther along various paths. The second major intent of the book is to serve as paean to local control of public schools. The control of neighborhood schools by parents and local communities has been one of the most sacred principles of American education and politics. As William Fischel (2002) has pointed out, Americans have tenaciously tried to hold on to this power against reformers from all sides. They have resisted those who seek to increase the influence of distant, central authorities in the name of equity, efficiency, accountability, or progress, and they have also repeatedly voted down the voucher proposals of school-choice advocates who seek the dissolution of local public schools altogether.

The right of parents and local communities to educate their children as they see fit is deeply ingrained in the American psyche and perhaps requires no defense. However, a decentralized education system governed primarily by local communities has objective benefits as well. The growth of American education that made the nation one of the world leaders in education for over 100 years was aided by the decentralized nature of the American school system. Had education been subject to national control, the political compromise reached regarding funding would no doubt have resulted in investing fewer resources in schools than the wealthier sections of the country would have desired. Decentralized control allowed the more-affluent and innovative states to move ahead in building their education systems. This phenomenon is not unique to the United States. In general, nations with decentralized education systems have devoted more resources to schooling and have had greater educational attainment among their population.

A system of multiple school districts supported by local property taxes has the same incentives to operate efficiently and satisfy the desires of its clients as a market made up of competing private firms. By being able to choose among jurisdictions when selecting homes, families living in regions with several school districts benefit in the same way that consumers do from markets served by several firms. Competition among providers leads to greater efficiency and more consumer-friendly service. Multiple school districts make it easier for families to vote with their feet in selecting schools. The resulting competition leads to lower costs and higher student performance—an outcome that has been repeatedly found to be empirically true.

This is not to say the solutions arrived at by local communities have been universally beneficial. Since school policy is largely decided in the public arena, each resolution is a compromise acceptable to the majority; and the majority in a local community can be more tyrannical than a distant despot. A policy decision can incite among the minority on the losing side anything from mild dissatisfaction to boiling frustration. The minority may find itself the victim of outright oppression. There is no doubt that the results of some of the policies agreed upon by local communities have harmed and offended the minorities on the losing side; African Americans and Catholics are two prominent examples in the nation's history.

In response to the dissatisfaction and oppression of minorities caused by decisions at the local level, reformers have attempted to short-circuit the local, democratic control of schooling. Their efforts have taken the form of centralization of control, greater involvement of ever-higher levels of government, and transfer of power from elected representatives to unelected functionaries such as judges. The result has been schools increasingly shaped not by the popular choice of the local community, but by mandates handed down from officials on high.

It is not the intention of this book to defend every outcome caused by the decentralized system of governance of American public schools. I do point out that the move toward more central, less democratic control has had its costs, and I hope to convince the reader that local control over education continues to have advantages that are worth preserving. This leads to the third major theme of the book: that a system of school choice is the best way to maintain the advantages of local control in the modern education system. As Albert O. Hirschman (1970) outlined, there are two ways of influencing an organization: voice and exit. *Voice* is control through politics, debate, persuasion, and voting. *Exit* is control through the market in which individual customers or members end their relationship with an organization that is failing to satisfy their needs or desires. Although control of education in the United States has been primarily through voice, exit has played an important role as well. Those dissatisfied with local schools have been able to move down the road to a new community with more satisfactory public schools, or they may simply send their children to private schools.

Parents' voices have been eroded by mandates from state and federal legislators, by judicial orders, and by the power of interest groups such as teachers' unions. With uniformity across schools being the explicit goal of many reform movements and the necessary outcome of centralization, parents have seen their neighborhood school grow increasingly like the local franchise of a national fast-food chain. School choice, by giving parents the power of exit as well as of voice, will dramatically tilt the balance of power back to parents. Although the benefits of choice are oversold in terms of their impact on student achievement, choice will enhance parental control, and with it a diversity that has been steadily sapped from public education.

OUTLINE OF THIS BOOK

The numerous modern crises in education can be pigeonholed into two main categories. There are complaints about resources, which are alleged to be perpetually scarce or unjustly distributed; and there are complaints about what those resources produce: children lacking in basic skills or necessary virtues. Chapter 1 examines both resources and achievement in public education over the past century. The two have followed quite different trajectories. In terms of resources, the past 100 years have been consistently good to America's schools. Americans are world leaders in the amount they spend on education. Spending per pupil has risen steadily, even after taking inflation into account. Despite continual concerns over a shortage of teachers, enough have been hired to see the ratio of students per instructor fall almost continuously. Teachers are better paid, better educated, and more experienced than ever before. A more intractable problem is funding equity. Despite over three decades of effort to make school funding more equal, there are still large differences in spending among the nation's schools.

Has the education of children by the public school system over the past century kept pace with the amount of resources poured into the system? In the elite circles of school reform, the debate over the present quality of public education focuses primarily on academic achievement, to wit: (1) Has the quality of American public education declined over the years? (2) Is the level of achievement in American public schools adequate? (3) Is the quality of American public education inferior to that found in other nations? (4) Has the efficiency of American public schools declined; that is, are taxpayers getting less education per dollar now than before?

It is worth noting that, while these questions may be vexing the members of advocacy groups, think tanks, universities, and government agencies, according to the public the main problem with public schools over the past 30 years has been a lack of discipline. In 1999, 18 percent of those surveyed called discipline a major concern. This compares to 9 percent who thought schools suffered from a lack of financial support, 11 percent who thought fighting and gangs were a severe problem, and 4 percent who thought low standards and the quality of education were significant deficiencies. In previous years, the public's worry over lack of discipline has occasionally taken second place to preoccupations about drug use or lack of funds, but even so school discipline has always been a close second in the public's mind. Concerns about standards, curricula, or hiring good teachers have never been held by more than 11 percent of those polled. This is a significant divergence between parents of students and the reformers who wish to change how those students are educated (U.S. Department of Education 2002, table 23).

The first question, the trend in achievement of American students through time, is difficult to answer because we have only begun asking it relatively recently. Ever since the Pilgrims waded ashore and founded the Plymouth colony, the proper education of youth has been seen as crucial to the spiritual salvation, commercial prosperity, or survival of the community and nation. Nevertheless, for most of the nation's history, a student's ability to add, spell, or find France on a map was solely a matter of concern for the student, his or her parents, and the school. Success in school was deemed a function of a student's hard work and talent, and the student was held responsible if he or she failed to learn (Ravitch 2002). A student's moral education was considered as, if not more, important than the cognitive skills that were imparted. Learning the virtues of diligence, punctuality, self-discipline, and temperance was considered as necessary to the public welfare and the individual student's progress in life as learning the three Rs (Randall 1994, 28).

The past 50 years, however, have seen a growing emphasis on cognitive skills, on a model of the school as a type of factory that produces educated individuals, and on quantitative measures of school and student performance. After WWII, several forces led to the increasing centralization of the education system and a greater role for levels of government outside and above the local school district. To evaluate the effects of the myriad state and federal policies put in place at this time, judges, legislators, and agency functionaries naturally focused on measures of school performance that could be easily gathered and manipulated on a large scale. Money was such a measure, and so was the race of the schoolchildren. Student performance on standardized tests was a third.

Of course, examination of student skills has always been a part of education. In the nineteenth century, high schools frequently administered entrance examinations, and one or two innovative school officials had used testing on a districtwide scale to measure the performance of students and teachers. However, the tests were not standardized across school districts or through time. The first decades of the twentieth century saw the beginnings of the scientific education movement, and as in all fields of study aspiring to be sciences, practitioners of scientific education were strong believers in measurement. They created the standardized test that could be administered to students en masse. In spite of this, the first decades of the twentieth century also saw the advent of progressive education. Among the many intellectual initiatives lumped under this blanket were a call for greater deference to educators as professionals and a depreciation of cognitive skills and academic knowledge as important outcomes of schooling. Thus, test results were for the most part considered solely the concern of knowledgeable professionals. Scores were used to guide students into what was deemed the proper vocational track, or to make unfortunate generalizations about racial or ethnic groups. They were not used to inform the public about the effectiveness of their local schools. So for the first half of the twentieth century, broad measures of student performance through time were sparse.

Indicators of student performance during the first half of the twentieth century are limited to indirect measures—the reading level of texts and popular books and magazines, enrollment levels in various subjects, and a handful of studies with limited scope in both geography and time. These indicators provide mixed evidence for trends in achievement. The textbooks used in American schools have unquestionably become less difficult, but the difficulty of popular reading materials has remained constant. Enrollment rates in academic-level courses dropped from the beginning of the twentieth century, when the high schools were opened up to a broader population of students. Finally, the handful of then-and-now studies are so fraught with problems that the authors of the most comprehensive review of these studies conclude that they can draw no conclusion (Stedman and Kaestle 1991a, 89). The ambiguous results of the studies are demonstrated by the fact that they are simultaneously cited as evidence for both the steady improvement and the stagnation of learning in American schools (Rothstein 1998, ch. 3; Coulson 1999, 178–79).

After WWII, when the schools became a matter of national concern, an increasing federal role in education led to the creation of a national standardized test to measure student achievement: the National Assessment of Educational Progress (NAEP). With the rollout of the NAEP in the late 1960s, partisans on both sides of the debate finally had hard numbers representing all American students. During the 1970s, the NAEP showed a decline in student performance that is also seen in other less-representative measures of performance such as the Scholastic Aptitude Test (SAT, now called the Scholastic Assessment Test). More recently, student achievement in reading as measured by the NAEP has remained flat, while math and science scores have risen, to the point where most of the losses suffered in the early 1970s have been regained.

Evidence regarding the adequacy of student achievement in the United States and of how American students compare to their peers abroad is more conclusive. The two questions are related; one benchmark of the adequacy of the skills of American students is the performance of students in other nations. On international comparisons of student achievement, American students regularly place in the middle of the pack, with relative performance falling the higher the grade level. That is, while American students in lower grades tend to be above the international average, American high-school students tend be below average. There are other indications that the education received by American students falls short. Colleges and businesses spend significant amounts of money on remedial training. Of the subjects tested by the NAEP, only in reading do more than 30 percent of students perform at a level considered proficient or better. Richard Murnane and Frank Levy (1996, 34–35) estimate that nearly 50 percent of high-school graduates do not have skills adequate enough to earn what is considered a middle-class wage.

The examination of student achievement and school resources in the first chapter aspires only to be thorough. It does not claim to be balanced, since balance lies as much in the eye of the reader as in the claims of the author. I attempt to represent all points of view, but readers may disagree about the weight I give each argument or the conclusions I draw. Even though readers may not value the conclusions in chapter 1, it is hoped that they at least value the chapter as a resource for further study, and find in the cited references authors with more agreeable viewpoints.

Fluctuating or flat output that is combined with a steady increase in inputs implies a reduction in efficiency; taxpayers are getting less learning per dollar spent. Chapter 2 focuses on the efficiency of American public education. Whether American public education is rising or falling in this area is a matter of hot dispute. The effectiveness of inputs such as spending per pupil, class size, and teacher training has been the subject of constant argument since the release of the *Equality of Educational Opportunity* Report—commonly known as the Coleman Report—in 1966 (Coleman et al. 1966). Despite many attempts to declare the matter settled, the question of whether money and other resources matter remains open after nearly 40 years of research and debate. Something must be going on in the schoolhouse that is not commonly found in other sectors of the economy. It would not take 40 years of sophisticated statistical research and reams of studies to determine whether more money could obtain a higher-quality automobile, personal computer, or hotel room, or whether a better-trained workforce increased productivity.

Teachers are the most expensive and most important input into education, and numerous researchers have looked at the teaching corps for explanations of trends in costs and student performance over the past decades. With respect to teachers, three reasons have been cited to account for the fact that achievement has not matched the increase in resources: (1) the creation of greater job opportunities for women outside of education, (2) the rise of teachers' unions, and (3) the inherent nature of teaching students that has prevented the use of labor-saving technology. The availability of other jobs for women has meant that schools have had to face greater competition for well-qualified teachers. This is exacerbated by the fact that wages in other sectors rise due to increases in productivity spurred by technological improvement. Video, computers, and Internet hookups have not enabled teachers to gain similar improvements in productivity. Stagnant productivity in teaching and greater opportunities for women elsewhere imply that schools must pay the same wages for less-able teachers, or try to maintain teacher quality by paying more. Either way, the cost per unit of quality will rise.

Costs can also rise due to the greater bargaining power of teachers who are organized in unions. Workplace rules gained through collective bargaining can also limit the ability of administrators to run their schools efficiently. The difficulty presented by union pay schedules and seniority rules makes it difficult to reward the able, cull the incompetent, and place teachers where they may be more effective. All this can lead to an adverse effect on student achievement. The evidence is that teachers' unions have a modest effect on student achievement. There is much clearer indication that unions have led to increased costs. So again, modest changes in achievement along with increased cost result in lower efficiency.

The ambiguous results regarding school inputs and student achievement do not imply that schools and teachers do not matter. There is strong evidence that teachers and schools do have a significant effect on learning (Hanushek, Kain, and Rivkin 1998). More properly stated, the conclusion arrived at by the research reviewed here is that inputs *as conventionally measured* by spending, teacher credentials, or class size have an effect that is small or unclear. This has significant implications; it implies that the policy levers most favored by legislators, governors, union officials, and advocates have only a tenuous connection to school performance. The implications of the limits on what policymakers can effectively accomplish—what I call the policy frontier—will be discussed further in chapter 5.

Finally, chapter 2 turns to an examination of private schools. The nation's private schools have been put forth as examples of more-effective educators and more-efficient users of resources. Among supporters of school choice, this is credited to the need for private schools to actively compete for students. Doubters attribute the apparent advantages of private schools to their being more selective. The overall consensus of the research is that once student traits are taken into account, student performance in private schools—as measured by test scores—is only marginally superior, with the impact being most marked for minority children. However, test scores measure only one aspect of a school. There are other school characteristics that parents value as well: safety, diversity, and common values, for example. In addition, private schools are undoubtedly more efficient. Thus, although school choice is perhaps oversold as a way to raise the educational level of all American students, it still presents advantages.

Chapters 3 and 4 examine two additional explanations for the present condition of public education. They look at two phenomena that roughly divide the history of American public education over the past century. In both cases, public education has followed a distinct path, but whether that path has been upward or downward depends upon the point of view of the observer.

Chapter 3 discusses the central event of the first half of the twentieth century up to the beginning of WWII: the great high-school boom. During this time, a greater proportion of Americans obtained a secondary education, and the United States became a world leader in the educational attainment of youth. The question of what sort of education all these students were to receive sparked a debate that echoes to this day. High schools were once elite institutions that trained students for college or for certain white-collar positions. Their curriculum was heavily focused on traditional academic subjects. In response to competitive pressure from alternative schools that were offering a more practical and vocational education, high schools began expanding their curricula at the end of the nineteenth century, adding courses in industrial arts, home economics, and life skills. The new curricula received strong support from the academy. Several new movements converged into a call for schools to move away from traditional subjects and teaching methods toward a more practical, holistic, and student-friendly education. The result was that, unlike other nations in which vocational and academic secondary education were provided in separate institutions, in the United States students following academic and vocational tracks attended school in the same building. Thus, the modern American high school was created.

The new high school adopted a somewhat laissez-faire attitude toward learning that has been likened to a shopping mall (Powell, Farrar, and Cohen 1985). Students entered and selected a course of study from a variety of scholastic "shops." It has been argued that the openness, practicality, and flexibility of the shopping-mall high school is better suited to a highly mobile and democratic society like the United States. However, to its critics, the modern American high school is a story of democracy betrayed and opportunity denied. According to the critics, the new mass of students entering America's high schools were shunted by aptitude tests and guidance counselors into weak, nonacademic courses that offered no upward mobility. Depending on the critics' political beliefs, all this was done at the behest of industrialists seeking a well-trained, pliable workforce, or well-meaning social engineers wanting to improve society through rational planning.

Of course, the authors of books and articles denouncing the lax academic standards of the new high schools tend to be people who have succeeded in traditional academic subjects like mathematics, science, English, or history. They see taking students out of Latin and algebra to teach them bookkeeping, sewing, or personal hygiene as educational decline. However, the thrust of chapter 3 is a play on the major theme of this book: American public education is in its current condition largely because the public has chosen it to be that way. The American high school was a response to a market demand for a broader, more practical education. Despite its rather lax academic standards, it received much popular support, at least during the first half of the twentieth century. In the second half of the century, criticism of poor academic standards in public schools grew and gained greater public attention. The increasing importance of a college education and the increasing return to cognitive ability seem to be moving the nation toward a greater emphasis on academic skills.

Chapter 4 discusses the central phenomenon of school policy during the second half of the twentieth century: the increasing power of central authorities over the traditionally locally controlled public schools. The struggle between the center and the edges has been perennial throughout the nation's history, but it accelerated rapidly after WWII. Chapter 4 begins by delving into our nation's past to show the origins of the system of local control. It then outlines various struggles between parents defending their power and successive waves of reformers. The education policies agreed upon within local communities have perpetually dissatisfied both insiders and outsiders. Before the Civil War, reformers thought the locals too stingy, backward, and parochial. Fifty years later, the local system was inefficient and corrupt. In the second half of the twentieth century, local control over the neighborhood school came under a sustained assault that led to the unparalleled centralization of control. In the name of greater equity, justice, and adequacy, several interests groups sought greater intervention by state and federal authorities in order to alter the school policies agreed to by local majorities. The most prominent and wrenching intervention has been, of course, the racial desegregation of public schools. The saga of desegregation merits a book in itself. Here I concentrate on other movements toward centralization that are less emotionally charged, but still have been a significant shock to the system.

After racial desegregation, the most notable centralizing reform has been the push for reform of state school finance systems. At the end of the 1960s, a growing movement sought to equalize school resources through litigation. Advocates arranged for parents and teachers to sue local districts and state governments, alleging that existing systems of school finance were unconstitutional. Their success in the courtroom brought major overhauls of school finance systems, leading states to take more responsibility for school funding. At the same time, other groups using the advocacy model pioneered by the civil rights movement turned to the federal government for programs to correct perceived injustices toward girls, the disabled, and the poor.

Setting aside the benefits these initiatives had for those they were intending to help, centralization of school control has had tangible effects on schools. The most significant, as has already been touched upon, is the quantification of schooling. Legislators, state and federal bureaucrats, judges, and others responsible for implementing the new wave of reforms required measures to gauge the progress of their initiatives. These measures had to be uniform across children, schools, and states and relatively easy and inexpensive to compile and analyze. It was natural to use quantitative measures—such as test scores or data on the racial makeup of schools—that can be easily summarized in graphs and pie charts. In policy debates, the complex multiple purposes of schooling have been neglected as attention has focused on spending, test scores, or the proportion of white and black children in a classroom.

Greater centralization can potentially weaken competition among schools. Why vote with one's feet if the school in the next neighborhood uses the same books, spends the same amount of money per student, and implements the same mandated policies as your children's present school? Weakened competition can cause costs to rise and achievement to fall. Loss of control to higher authorities can alienate parents, causing them to send their children to private schools. Finally, alienation of parents can erode taxpayer support of public schools, causing spending on education to fall. Research has linked these outcomes to increased centralization over the past 40 years, and it is perhaps no coincidence that surveys find confidence in public schools falling.

Chapter 5 turns to a survey of the myriad plans, schemes, and proposals to improve public schools that are currently being put forward. Rather than undertaking the formidable task of examining the evidence regarding the effectiveness of each reform, I examine the proposals through the prism of the major theme of this book: central versus local control of education. I ask what effect each proposed reform has on the governance of schools: does it preserve the tradition of local control, or does it increase the momentum toward central control? In one sense, the answer to this question is universal to all the proposals considered. It is the nature of advocates of a reform to believe that they have an answer to the problems of schools everywhere. Although they may start at the grass roots, they dream of arriving at the top of the tree, where they will have the power to enable children in every corner of the nation to benefit from their vision.

I argue in chapter 5 that the universal dreams of reformers are misguided; that policymakers at every level of government—from the district board through the U.S. Congress—are constrained to a feasible set of effective policies. The boundaries of this set are determined by information, more specifically by the difficulty policymakers have in obtaining information. The higher a person is in the tree, the harder it is for that person to see what is happening on the ground. Also, the higher the person is, the more difficult it is to transfer his or her will downward through those sitting on lower branches. This, too, is a problem of information. People on the lower branches may not be entirely frank with those above them regarding events on the ground or their own actions. Consequently, what a policymaker can effectively and properly do varies with where he or she sits in the tree, and the number of feasible options gets smaller the higher the person sits.

Chapter 5 classifies reforms into two broad categories based on their premise regarding the nature of school governance. The vast majority of reforms I lump into the first category, which I refer to as "establishment reforms." Establishment reforms contain no major criticism of the way schools are governed or of the incentives for principals, teachers, students, or others in the system. Modest establishment reforms simply call for boosting the public education system as it is presently constituted: more funding, smaller classes, better technology, and higher teacher pay. More ambitious proposals want new curricula or teaching methods. I also classify as establishment reforms efforts to make school funding more equitable or more adequate. To be sure, these reforms can lead to root and branch transformation of the organization of public education and to seismic shifts in power between local districts and higher levels of government. However, these effects are only incidental to the intent of the reform. The reforms are based on the premise that improving schools requires altering the level or distribution of resources rather than changing how schools operate. I also include under establishment reforms proposals for prohibiting bilingual education, mandating the teaching of reading through phonics or equal time for creation science, requiring students to begin the day with the Pledge of Allegiance or a prayer, and other similar regulations. Again, these reforms are not based on the supposition that there are basic flaws in the way public schools are controlled, but rather on the belief that control has fallen into the wrong hands.

Although not directly aimed at affecting the control of schools, establishment reforms often contain impulses that lead to greater centralization. The universalist nature of reformers is one such impulse. Successfully having the school board require phonics is good; a state rule that all schools use phonics is better; and a federal mandate is best. Establishment reforms that call for greater resources also tend to look toward higher authorities because they have deeper pockets.

In contrast to establishment reforms are what I refer to as "accountability reforms." Accountability reforms are based on the premise that public schools suffer from a fundamental organizational flaw. Proponents of accountability reforms believe that, because schools are public agencies, administrators, principals, teachers, and even students lack sufficient incentives to teach effectively, learn diligently, or spend money wisely. Consequently, accountability reformers believe that policies need to be put in place that give the actors within schools the incentive to perform well.

Accountability reforms are further subdivided into centralizing and decentralizing reforms. Centralizing accountability reforms are policies, such as high-stakes testing and incentive payments, through which district, state, or federal policymakers directly attempt to provide incentives that induce those below them in the education hierarchy to perform effectively. Centralizing accountability reforms make schools more accountable to central authorities either at the state or federal level. The central authorities set the standards that schools must meet and determine the benchmarks against which school performance is measured. By contrast, decentralizing accountability reforms are policies, such as vouchers, that seek to make the education establishment more accountable to parents. Under decentralizing accountability systems, parents set the standards schools must meet, evaluate progress toward meeting expectations, and exit to sanction schools deemed to be nonperforming.

The school reform movement is large enough to contain the proponents of both centralizing and decentralizing accountability reforms. Advocates are able to cohabit happily and condemn the "educrats," lax standards, pedagogical fads, and waste of the current public education system. Chapter 5 argues for a separation of the two camps. Although accountability reforms of both types show promise in boosting student achievement, centralizing accountability reforms run the danger of exacerbating one of the most adverse trajectories in public education over the past decades: the increasing centralization and bureaucratization of schooling in the United States.

CHAPTER 1

A Century of Progress?
Resources and Outcomes in
Public Education

THE CONTINUING EXPANSION

The United States spends more on public schools than on any other government service—federal, state, or local—except Social Security. In 1998, public schools in the United States spent an estimated $318 billion. In contrast, that same year all the state and local governments combined spent $50 billion for police protection, $20 billion for fire protection, $87 billion for highways, and $22 billion for parks and recreation. The federal government in 1998 spent $270 billion on national defense, $193 billion on Medicare, and $379 billion on Social Security. Money spent by Washington on foreign aid and other international programs totaled a mere $13 billion (U.S. Census Bureau 2002, 133, 267, 303).

A boom in high school attendance at the beginning of the twentieth century was the beginning of a massive investment by American communities in public education. For the next hundred years, all the measures of material resources invested in schools have moved in a positive direction: more money per student, smaller class sizes, more-educated teachers, and a longer school year. Figure 1.1 shows inflation-adjusted yearly spending per student in American public schools from the end of WWI to the end of the century. During this time, spending per pupil increased from $440 to $8,194—an increase of over 1700 percent, or an average yearly rate of 5.8 percent—an impressive rate of growth. It is faster than the growth rate of the U.S. economy as a whole, which grew at an average inflation-adjusted rate of 3.6 percent per year from 1930 to 2001. Spending, as might be expected, was relatively flat during the Great Depression and

Figure 1.1
Inflation-Adjusted Per-Pupil Spending in Public Schools (2000–2001 Dollars)

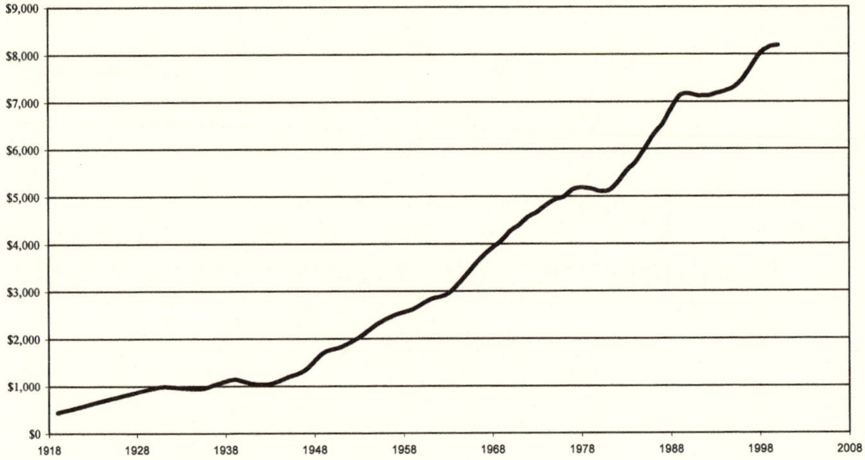

Source: U.S. Department of Education (2002).

WWII. The growth in education spending came primarily after WWII, with two modest dips during the recessions of the early 1980s and 1990s.

An alternative measure of the resources devoted to education is the share of national resources allotted to schools. Figure 1.2 shows elementary and secondary education's share of the gross domestic product (GDP) after WWII. GDP is the value of all goods and services produced in the United States during a year, so Figure 1.2 is in effect showing education's share of the postwar economic pie. If one thinks of the nation as a single family, this is the share of the family's budget given over to schooling; it can be considered a measure of national effort. Clearly evident are two dramatically different chapters in the story of the resources the United States has chosen to devote to education. From the immediate postwar period through the mid-1970s, education spending as a share of GDP grew rapidly: from 2.3 percent in 1949 to a high of 4.6 percent in 1975. Since then, education's share of national output has held relatively steady. Statistical analyses confirm what ocular inspection suggests: for individual states as well as for the entire nation, over the past 30 years, education spending rose steadily with income so that the ratio of the two remained nearly constant (Poterba 1996; Fernandez and Rogerson 1997). Before this, education spending rose faster than income, leading to the sharp rise shown in Figure 1.2.

The same studies show that, over the past 30 years, education spending across states has been independent of the size of the student population. That is, the amount a state spends on education depends on the income

Figure 1.2
K–12 Expenditures a Percentage of Gross Domestic Product

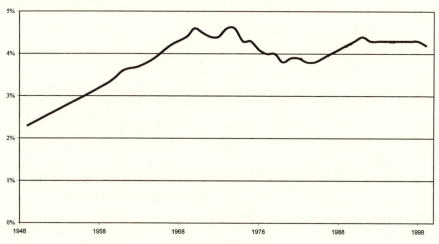

Source: U.S. Department of Education (2002).

of its residents, not on the number of students it must educate. Thus, if the ratio of income to education spending remains constant, per-pupil spending can only grow if income rises at a faster rate than the school population. From 1971 to 1984, total enrollment fell from 51 million students to 45 million (U.S. Department of Education 2002, table 3), so spending per student was still able to increase, even though the country as a whole was spending a slightly smaller fraction of its economic resources on education. However, enrollment has increased since 1984, and now there are more children than ever in America's elementary and high schools. Education's share of GDP climbed back above 4 percent but has since remained almost flat at around 4.3 percent. Between 1990 and 2000, the American GDP grew by 55 percent, while the number of Americans between 5 and 19 years of age grew by 16 percent (U.S. Census Bureau 2002, 13, 422). As long as this pattern holds and the economy grows faster than the school-age population, we can expect per-student spending to keep rising.

Another measure of the amount of effort a nation is making in support of education is spending per pupil as a fraction of per capita GDP or income—that is, if national income were divided equally among every man, woman, and child, the fraction of each person's income that would be needed to pay to send one child to school. Very rich countries may have high per-pupil spending yet have a relatively light education burden if schools consume a small fraction of national income. Total education spending as a fraction of GDP does not take into account student population. Two equally wealthy countries that devote the same fraction of their GDP to education can spend vastly different amounts per student if the sizes of their young populations are different. Per-pupil spending as a fraction of per capita income accounts for both a nation's wealth and the size of its student population. By this measure as well, the U.S. commitment to education has increased over the century. Per-pupil spending as a fraction of per-capita personal income has doubled from 15 percent in 1929 to 31 percent in 1998 (U.S. Department of Education 2002, table 38).

The United States is among the top nations globally in the amount spent on education. Table 1.1 compares per-pupil spending in the United States to seven other peer nations and to the average for the developed countries as a whole. U.S. per-student spending is above average, and among the developed countries the United States ranks behind only Denmark, Austria, Norway, and Switzerland in the amount of money it spends per student. In terms of the share of national economic resources devoted to education, the United States is slightly below average for the advanced nations. (The figures in Table 1.1 are for public education only, while the numbers in Figure 1.2 are for public and private education. Hence the percentage point difference.) Since the U.S. economic pie is so large, the nation is able to give education a smaller slice and still spend more per student than most of the rest of the world. In terms of effort as measured by per-pupil spending divided by per-capita GDP, the effort of the United States is equal to the average of its peer countries (OECD 2000, table B4.2).

The increase in resources devoted to education has allowed American public schools to improve along several dimensions. First, it has allowed schools to lengthen the school year. The average school year in 1869 was

Table 1.1
Per Pupil Expenditures on Public and Private Education 1997

	(US $'s)	
	Primary	Secondary
Australia	3,633	5,570
France	3,621	6,564
Germany	3,490	6,149
Japan	5,202	5,917
Korea	3,308	3,518
Switzerland	6,237	9,045
United Kingdom	3,206	4,609
United States	5,718	7,230
Average for Developed Countries	3,851	5,273

Source: OECD (2000).

132 days, approximately six months, and the average student was present for 60 percent of that time. The average school year now is 50 percent longer, nine months, and the average student is in his or her seat 90 percent of the time (U.S. Department of Education 2002, table 38).

The increase in per-pupil spending has also allowed schools to hire more teachers and decrease the number of pupils per teacher. Since the 1950s, the number of pupils per teacher in public schools has dropped nearly 40 percent: from 26.9 to 16.2 (U.S. Department of Education 2002, table 65). Despite the need for more teachers, the quality of teachers as measured by experience and credentials increased in the last four decades of the twentieth century. In 1961, 14.6 percent of teachers did not have bachelor's degrees; by 1996, this had dropped to less than 1 percent. At the same time, the proportion of teachers with master's, doctoral, and other higher degrees jumped from 23.4 percent to well over 50 percent. Also, more than half of the teaching force has over 15 years of experience—up from 11 years at the beginning of the 1960s (U.S. Department of Education 2002, table 70).

Inflation-adjusted teacher pay also increased by 45 percent from 1959 to 1998 (U.S. Department of Education 2002, table 75). After a steady rise in the 1960s, teacher pay started to lag behind inflation in the 1970s and early 1980s due to high inflation rates—administratively set salaries could not keep up—and because the graduation of the baby boomers reduced the demand for teachers. The decline in enrollment meant that schools could pay teachers less, let the teaching force erode slightly, and still reduce class size. The increase in enrollment since the mid-1980s has led to the hiring of more teachers and to an increase in real salaries to above the peak at the end of the baby boom. Inflation-adjusted salaries have since held steady: the average U.S. teacher now makes over $40,000 per year.

One of the few aspects that has not improved for teachers is job satisfaction. Over 20 percent of those teaching in 1996 said that they would definitely or probably not teach if given the choice again. Although this is an improvement in morale compared to the 36 percent who said the same in 1981, it is nearly double the level in 1961 (U.S. Department of Education 2002, table 70).

Although U.S. education spending has been increasing steadily, a major area of concern has been how spending is distributed across the nation's children. Table 1.2 shows the average revenue per student for schools with various characteristics: location, the share of nonwhite students, and the fraction of students in poverty. The third column shows actual revenue per student, while the fourth column adjusts revenue for cost and need. The cost adjustment is based on a teacher cost index that measures how much it would cost to hire an equally qualified teacher in different geographic locations. The need adjustment assumes that it costs different amounts to educate different types of students. For example, the need

Table 1.2
Revenue Inequality among Public Schools

	Percent of all students enrolled	Revenue per Student	
		Actual	Cost- and need-adjusted
Metropolitan status			
Urban	26.9	$5,781	$4,593
Suburban	48.8	5,748	4,730
Rural	24.3	4,894	4,597
Revenues by minority enrollment			
Less than 5%	21.5	5,425	4,739
50% or more	27.0	5,797	4,574
Revenues by school-age children in poverty			
Less than 8%	22.2	6,266	5,080
25% or more	26.6	5,600	4,554

Source: National Research Council (1999b, table 2-5).

adjustment assumes that it costs 130 percent more to educate a special education student, and 20 percent more to educate a student with limited English skills (National Research Council 1999b, table 2-5).

As Table 1.2 shows, per-pupil revenue is actually higher in urban districts and in districts with large nonwhite populations. This is due in part to the fact that central city districts, which tend to have large nonwhite populations, are relatively rich in property, giving them a large tax base per student. Also, nonwhite districts are more eligible for federal aid. Once adjusted for cost and need, per-pupil revenue is higher in rich, white, suburban districts: 11.5 percent higher in rich versus poor districts, 3.6 percent higher in white compared to nonwhite districts, and 3.0 percent higher in suburban over urban districts.

Since payroll is by far the largest expenditure for schools, the cost adjustment was made using a teacher cost index constructed by Jay Chambers (1995). The index measures the cost of hiring comparable teachers for districts located in areas with different characteristics. For example, it costs more to hire teachers in both urban and rural areas. Other things equal, districts in sparsely populated counties (50 persons per square mile) need to pay 2.7 percent more to attract teachers. Similarly, districts in very dense urban areas (10,000 persons per square mile) have to pay their teachers 5.7 percent more. It also costs more to attract teachers to work in schools in violent communities. Chambers found that the average teacher would accept a 1.5 percent cut in pay to work in a county in which the rate of violent crime was 9 per 10,000 compared to a county with a crime rate of 58 per 10,000 (Chambers 1995, 45).

Taking only the difference in costs into account actually makes revenue more equal across districts. According to the unadjusted figures, average spending per child in a district with less than 8 percent of children in poverty is only 12 percent greater than in the average district with 25 percent or more poor children. After adjusting for cost, affluent districts have only a 5 percent edge. The greater cost of attracting teachers to urban districts reduces the revenue advantage these districts enjoy.

Not included in Chambers's teacher cost index are features of the working environment, such as the level of school violence, teachers' feelings of support, their ability to influence policy, and their job satisfaction, even though he found that some of these factors do affect teacher pay. For example, the average teacher would be willing to give up 0.70 percent of his or her income for an improvement equal to a standard deviation in the index of violent student behavior.[1] Taking the average annual teacher's salary in 1998, this is equal to a $284 yearly pay cut to move to a less-violent school. Similarly, the average teacher would be willing to take a 0.31 percent pay cut—$377 using the average 1998 annual salary—for a standard deviation improvement in the support they receive in their work environment.

Chambers did not include these attributes in his teacher cost index for two reasons. First, they are subjective measures by teachers; second, they are school-level characteristics, while hiring tends to be done at the district level. This demonstrates one of the shortcomings of the districtwide salary schedules typically used by public schools. Pay schedules that do not reflect the work environment of individual schools limit the ability of rough schools to attract and keep quality teachers. Whether these factors should be omitted from cost adjustments is unclear. To the extent that urban, predominantly nonwhite, poor school districts are more likely to have teaching environments made disagreeable by student violence, self-destructive behavior, and family problems, omitting these characteristics from the index understates revenue inequality across districts. Districts with adverse characteristics have to pay more than districts with more pleasant working conditions to attract equally qualified teachers. On the other hand, incorporating these factors into the index implies that the solution to these problems is simply a matter of giving schools more funding, whereas the real solution is to implement policies that ameliorate adverse conditions.

Accepting the need-based adjustment as valid requires assuming that the classification of students is uniform across district types. That is, if District A reports having more special education or limited-English children than District B, the difference reflects actual student characteristics rather than the willingness of District A to classify students as having special needs. It is well known that public schools classify a disproportionate number of poor and nonwhite students as having learning disabilities. In 1992, African American children made up 16 percent of the U.S. school population, but 32 percent of children in programs for mild mental retardation, 29 percent of children in programs for moderate mental retardation, and 24 percent of students in programs for serious mental disturbance. The U.S. Department of Education's Office of Civil Rights found regional patterns in the tendency of schools to diagnose minority children as having learning disabilities, with the greatest difference in the South. In Virginia, African Americans are 20 percent of the student population, but represent 51 percent of students labeled educable mentally retarded (Ladner and Hammons 2001). This bias would cause a need-based index to overestimate inequality between white and nonwhite districts.

Matthew Ladner and Christopher Hammons found that race is by far the largest factor in determining the proportion of students in a school district who are enrolled in special education programs. However, they found that nonwhite enrollment has a *negative* effect on special education enrollment. That is, other things equal, the higher the percentage of African American or Hispanic students, the lower the fraction of students labeled as having learning disabilities. Predominantly white districts have a greater tendency to classify African American or Hispanic students as having learning disabilities. If nonwhite districts underestimate their special education population and predominantly white districts overestimate the fraction of their nonwhite students who require special education, need-adjusted figures will understate revenue inequality between white and nonwhite districts.

Table 1.3 looks at changes in the inequality in education spending during a period in which activists, judges, and legislatures tried to equalize state-by-state school spending. The first and second rows show inequality in education spending and income in the United States as measured by the Gini coefficient. A metric used by economists to gauge inequality, the higher the coefficient, the greater the inequality in spending or income. During the entire twentieth century, education spending has been much more equal than the distribution of income. Also true for the past hundred years is that inequality in school spending has remained relatively stable (Hoxby 1998b). As Table 1.3 indicates, after twenty years inequality had fallen by only a fraction. On the other hand, since inequality did not grow

Table 1.3
Inequality in School Expenditures

	1972	1977	1982	1987	1992
Inequality					
Education spending	16.3	15.0	13.8	15.8	15.5
Median household income	40.1	40.2	41.2	42.6	43.3
Inequality decomposition					
Within states	32.2	41.5	47.5	32.8	35.3
Between states	67.8	58.5	52.5	67.2	64.7

Source: Murray, Evans, and Schwab (1998).

worse, we can infer that poor districts also saw their flow of resources increase over the past century.

Table 1.3 also breaks down spending inequality among and within states. As can be seen, education spending in the United States is greater among the different states than within them. In 1992, 64.7 percent of the difference in spending among school districts was due to differences in spending among states, while 35.3 percent of spending inequality was due to differences in spending by districts within a state. Despite decades of equalization efforts by most states, the fraction of overall spending inequality that can be attributed to differences within states has actually risen. Thus, any hope of substantially equalizing spending would require the transfer of money between states.

The tables and charts in the preceding pages have shown that, in terms of resources, the American commitment to education has increased substantially over the past century. Taxpayers have spent more per student, even after accounting for inflation, allowing schools to reduce class sizes and hire better-paid and more-educated teachers. American children attended school more days each year. Still, any demonstration of increasing material effort will do little to calm the maelstrom of controversy over spending that surrounds American public education. The facts given above provide no guidelines about whether the level of spending has been adequate. Has inflation-adjusted per-pupil spending increased by 586 percent since WWII? Some would say it should have increased by 1,000 percent. Do urban districts spend $33 more per pupil on average than suburban districts? Many believe that, given the special needs of their students, urban districts should spend even more. Others would assert that schools already receive too much money, given the terrible job they do with what they already receive.

Almost everyone can agree that American public schools should be safe and clean and should impart enough knowledge and skills to enable their graduates to be self-sufficient. How much funding it takes to meet these goals is a matter of hot dispute in school board meetings, legislatures, and courtrooms across the nation. Education is considered a public good. Advocates for increased school funding have always sought to coax money from taxpayers by selling education as an antidote to crime or social unrest; but at what point do the costs of schooling outweigh the benefits to society? The eighth grade? College? Setting aside this deeper question, consensus regarding spending often gets caught on the more mundane fence that divides necessities from frills. In one school, parents may be unhappy that their children attend class in portable buildings, while in another school, parents would be happy if the roof did not leak. High-speed Internet access, lighted playing fields, and PDAs for the entire teaching staff may seem like necessities to some, but local taxpayers might disagree.

Second, school funding is traditionally determined through the political process. Legislators do not use finely tuned cost-benefit analyses to set goals and divide up funding among those goals. Rather, they split an always finite amount of resources among competing interests through political negotiations that often involve parochial interests, political heft, emotional pleas, and vague social priorities. In 2000, a federal judge ruled that the state of Arizona's method for determining funding to educate limited English proficient children was "arbitrary and capricious" (*Flores v. Arizona* 2000). The same might be said of almost any appropriation decision in any legislature.

Legislators' task is not made any easier by the fact that there is no rigorous, proven way of relating spending to educational goals. Several methods have been developed to help guide policymakers in their deliberations on school funding (Augenblick, Myers, and Anderson 1997). In the "expert design" method, education experts design the ideal school system from the ground up. States that have adopted this approach have typically found that the resulting school costs substantially more than what is currently spent or politically feasible. The "successful school" method surveys actual schools that have evident success and derives a funding level based on these schools, adjusted for local circumstances. The "econometric method" uses sophisticated statistical analysis to develop input-output models of schools. The advantage of this approach is that it can produce estimates of marginal impacts per dollar: how much test scores can be expected to rise given one more dollar in per-pupil spending. The disadvantage of this method, as we will see in chapter 2, is that the models created do not always find a relationship between conventionally measured inputs and outputs. In addition, all three methods can be thwarted by local circumstances, the uncertain, and the unforeseen.

The conceptual, procedural, and technical problems of determining an adequate level of education spending has not stopped policymakers from attempting to set an adequacy standard. The New Jersey State Supreme Court, in the landmark school funding case *Robinson v. Cahill* (1973), tried to lend operational substance to the state constitution's requirement that public schools be "thorough and efficient." In its decision, the court flirted with an output-based standard: the state should provide a school system that ensured all children some minimal level of education. However, rather than determining what that level was or whether the state should expend the resources to guarantee that even the most disadvantaged children—those with physical or mental handicaps—would reach that level, the court backed away and used an input-based, spending-per-pupil standard. It concluded that whatever the minimal level should be, only the greatest of coincidences would make it equal to the spending in the state's lowest spending districts (Van Geel 1976, 104–6). In 2002, a New York appeals court fended off a challenge to the state's system of school funding, citing the state's contention that only an eighth-grade education was necessary to serve on a jury, read a newspaper, or follow a political debate. The court held that the state was not required to "guarantee some higher, largely unspecified level of education, as laudable as that goal might be" (Gehring 2002). Despite the efforts of judges, legislators, and education experts, a definitive answer about how much should be spent on educating America's youth has yet to be determined.

THE UPS AND DOWNS OF STUDENT ACHIEVEMENT

Textbooks

Since mass testing of American students is a phenomenon of only the past 30 or so years, we must turn to indirect measures of student achievement. One such indicator is the reading level of textbooks and other material. During the 2000 presidential election, the Internet site *yourdictionary.com* published a brief comparison of political discourse over the past 200-plus years with the loaded title "Presidential Debates Mirror Long-term School Decline." The authors, Dr. Robert Beard and Paul J. J. Payack (2002), claimed to find a recent decline in the level of American political rhetoric. According to Beard and Payack, the complexity of the language used by American politicians was roughly constant over the first 140 years of the Republic. George Washington's 1796 Farewell Address had a 12.0 grade reading level as measured by the Flesch-Kincaid reading scale. The seven speeches made by Stephen Douglas during his debates with Abraham Lincoln in 1858 had an average reading level at grade 11.9. Lincoln, the possessor of a more common touch, delivered speeches at a slightly lower 11.2 grade level. Franklin Roosevelt's declaration of war following Pearl Harbor in December 1941 had a grade level of 11.5.

The seeming decline in the rhetorical skill by those aspiring to be president of the United States appeared after WWII. During their 1960 debate, both Kennedy and Nixon spoke at below the tenth-grade level. Jimmy Carter and his opponents returned the level of discourse back above the tenth grade during their debates, but there has been a steady decline since then. President Clinton's statements during debates with his opponents were slightly above the eighth-grade level. His opponents—George H. W. Bush and Ross Perot in 1992 and Bob Dole in 1996—failed to surpass the seventh-grade level. During the 2000 election debates, the statements of both George W. Bush and Al Gore averaged below the eighth-grade level. By comparison, the typical discussion on the public affairs show *Meet the Press* averages at an 8.5 grade level.

Beard and Payack's study is an interesting, if minor, commentary on the current level of political eloquence. Despite its title, it cannot be used to conclude anything definitive about the state of education over the 204 years it covers. The study does not examine the language level of other political figures or other forms of communication, such as letters, memoranda, or books. It compares spoken and somewhat spontaneous remarks made during television debates to more-carefully drafted speeches. Farewell addresses and declarations of war can be expected to contain a higher level of rhetorical flourish than other, more common political communications. The study also compares some of the most inarticulate presidents and candidates to one of the most skilled wordsmiths to ever hold the office of president: Abraham Lincoln. Finally, any decline in the level of political speech can be attributed to numerous factors besides education. In his famous essay "Politics and the English Language," George Orwell complained about the state of the English language, political and otherwise, without once mentioning schools. Still, Beard and Payack's analysis is worth citing for its title alone. It is telling that from among the conditions that could have been accused of causing the rot of political language—television, the Internet, popular culture—Beard and Payack chose education, so common is the belief in the decline of America's schools.

For more definitive, but still imperfect and indirect, evidence of decline in American education during the first half of the twentieth century, it is more helpful to study the reading levels of textbooks. Diane Ravitch (2000) and Andrew Coulson (1996) have claimed to find stronger evidence in textbooks of a fall in the quality of schooling. In 1930, the Elson readers introduced the trio of Dick, Jane, and their dog Spot to American children: "Come, Dick. Come and see. Come, come. Come and see. Come and see Spot. Look, Spot. Oh, look. Look and see. Oh, see" (*Fun with Dick and Jane* 1996, 8–9). In spite of their limited vocabulary and repetitive manner of speaking, Dick and Jane could convey a sense of urgency and enthusiasm. Still, compare this passage to the more somber maunderings of Edgar Allan Poe in the pages of an earlier Elson reader:

It was during one of my lonely journeyings, amid a far distant region of mountain locked within mountain, and sad rivers and melancholy tarns writhing or sleeping within all—that I chanced upon a certain rivulet and island. I came upon them suddenly in the leafy June, and threw myself upon the turf, beneath the branches of an unknown odorous shrub, that I might doze as I contemplated the scene. I felt that thus only should I look upon it—such was the character of phantasm which it wore. (Elson and Keck 1910, 389)

The two passages are not directly comparable since Dick and Jane are intended for the beginning reader while the extract from Poe, which has a college-equivalent reading level, is intended for seventh graders. Nevertheless, the stark contrast between the two serves as a metaphor for the steady simplification of the language in textbooks that began between the two world wars and continued to the 1960s (Chall, Conard, and Sharples 1991, 11–14).

The analysis of the reading difficulty of textbooks began in the early 1920s as part of the new science of education. Textbooks, along with other aspects of learning, were measured and quantified, and the results were fed into the formulas and theories psychologists and educators were developing at the time. Psychologist Edward L. Thorndike laid the foundation for the study of textbook language by publishing lists of how frequently given words appeared in print and offering recommendations for the grade in which specific words should be taught. In 1923, Bertha Lively and S. W. Pressey used Thorndike's word lists and other text characteristics, such as the number of new words per thousand words of text, to develop the first readability formula that ranked the language difficulty of textbooks. In 1930, A. I. Gates conducted experiments to link reading difficulty with how well students learned. He estimated that the average first-grade student needed to see a word repeated 30 to 35 times before mastering it. A student with an above-average IQ needed 20 repetitions; a below-average student 40 (Chall, Conard, and Sharples 1991, 11–14).

Several factors prompted investigations into the readability of textbooks. First was the advent of a new way of teaching reading, called the whole-word or look-say method. In contrast to the traditional phonics method, which emphasized reading by decoding the constituent sounds of individual words, the look-say method emphasized recognizing entire words by sight and contextual meaning. Books using the look-say method included limited, simple vocabularies that students could quickly recognize and master. This requirement, backed with the findings of Gates's study, was the theory behind Jane's repeatedly urging Dick to come and see Spot.

In addition to new-fangled theories percolating down from education scientists, teacher concern also motivated studies of textbook difficulty. Despite the literary qualities of Edgar Allan Poe and fellow writers populating elementary school texts, teachers found the books of the time too hard for their students. Lively and Pressey's study was done at the urging of a group of junior high school science teachers worried about the difficulty of their textbooks (Chall, Conard, and Sharples 1991, 11). This concern about textbook difficulty grew out of the need for American schools to cope with a larger, more diverse student body. High school textbooks in use at the time had been written for the more select group of students traditionally served by high schools. The wave of students that flooded American high schools after WWI had, on average, a weaker academic background than had the typical high-school student in the past. Thus, there was a mismatch between the level of the textbooks and the ability of the majority of students. Furthermore, although elementary school attendance had been nearly universal for some time, Chall and her coauthors suggest that an influx of children from immigrant families with limited English language skills during the 1920s also helped prompt educators to examine textbook difficulty.

To address the needs of teachers and incorporate the new research and theories on teaching, first-grade reading textbooks grew ever simpler, introducing students to fewer new words and repeating more often the words that were taught. By the end of the 1930s, most texts met the specifications suggested by Gates. The trend in simplification of reading textbooks continued until the 1960s, when it began to be reversed, and the increasing popularity of decoding-based or phonics teaching methods caused the number of different words in reading texts to increase. The simplification of other types of textbooks both started and ended later than the simplification of reading texts. Between the 1940s and the 1970s, textbooks used for social studies, literature, grammar, and composition became increasingly less challenging as measured by reading level scores, maturity level, the difficulty of questions included, and the ratio of pictures to text. Since the beginning of the 1970s, the difficulty of textbooks has remained the same or improved modestly. Social studies and science textbooks issued between 1974 and 1989 were written at or slightly above the grade level of the intended audience. The readability levels of textbooks remained constant between 1974 and 1989, except for high school social studies texts, which dropped two grade levels in difficulty on average (Chall, Conard, and Sharples 1991, 13, 14, 62).

The trend of decline in textbook difficulty through the 1960s is confirmed by work done by Donald P. Hayes of Cornell University and his colleagues Loreen T. Wolfer and Michael F. Wolfe (1996). They examined 800 elementary, middle, and high school readers published between 1919 and 1991 using the LEX measure. The LEX measure is based on the empirical observation that the distribution of words used by a speaker or writer invariably follows a log-normal distribution, with different individuals simply having different parameters of the same statistical distribution. So, for example, the frequency of word use in a scientific paper would follow a log-normal distribution with technical words like *lognormal distribution* being used more often. Less-specialized communications, like newspaper articles, would be more likely to use less-technical, more widely known words like *newspaper*.

The higher a text's LEX score, the more specialized its vocabulary, and hence, the more complicated it is. Newspapers have an average score of 0. The most complex article found by Hayes and his coauthors, a scientific article on transhydrogenase, had a score of 58.6. The typical work of American fiction has a score of −15.8. Interestingly, the language used in television cartoon shows is more complex as measured by LEX score (−28.6) than the typical television program shown in prime time (−36.4). Hayes and his colleagues found that the readers used after WWII to teach

American children were less difficult than prewar textbooks. From 1919 to 1945, the LEX score of a first-grade reader was −47.3. From 1946 to 1962, the average LEX score was −59.7. By way of comparison, a first-grade equivalent reader for the British schools during the immediate post-war period had a LEX score of −44.4.

Although the postwar period was probably the high noon of what is called the progressive education movement—the umbrella label given to a grab bag of education reforms that in general sought to make education less scholarly and academic—it is not the sole reason for the dumbing down of textbooks. Americans, for some reason, have generally simplified their textbooks after major wars; the complexity of schoolbooks fell after both the Civil War and WWI (Hayes, Wolfer, and Wolfe 1996). The backlash against the weakening of educational rigor during the 1950s led to a reversal in the trend toward simplification for texts in the lower grades until the early 1990s, when reading levels had nearly reattained their prewar levels. The level of texts for higher grades, however, continued to plunge until the average seventh-grade reader in the early 1990s had the language complexity of a fifth-grade text before WWII. In addition to shrinking the vocabulary, publishers also shrank sentence length, with the average sentence in a fourth-grade reader losing six words.

Hayes and his coauthors also conducted a smaller survey of the texts used by a high school in Ithaca, New York. They found that the English books differed little by grade level or by curriculum track. The vocabulary in the average English text, including texts used for honors classes, was less complicated than the vocabulary of the average newspaper. As might be expected, science texts were more complicated than English texts, with the books used for advanced placement classes scoring in the positive range.

Along with the change in style in textbooks came a change in content. The authors who filled the pages of the old-style readers—Aesop, Shakespeare, Longfellow, Tennyson, Dickens, Hawthorne, and Whittier—did not have sufficiently limited vocabularies or the monotonously repetitive writing styles needed to conform with the new teaching theories. They also lacked, according to the thinking of the time, sufficient realism and relevance to the modern world. Education experts in the 1920s and 1930s believed that modern research in psychology and learning showed the value of less fantasy, imagination, sentimentality, and romanticizing of the past. They also believed that children should learn practical facts and information about the present. Out should go the folktales, fables, legends, histories, and myths, to be replaced by stories that followed the making of a pair of child's pajamas from the cotton fields to the child's bedroom. In 1920, literary selections made up 80 percent of a second-grade reader. By 1935, this was cut to 40 percent, and it was as low as 2 percent in some textbooks (Ravitch 2000, 254–55). Instead of reading literature created by writers or traditional stories handed on by generations, children had to trek through texts that were manufactured via scientific algorithms. Dick and Jane were the Depression-era equivalents of the virtual characters inhabiting modern video games.

The result of greater simplification is that American textbooks were increasingly failing to broaden students' vocabulary and expose them to the more particular language they would need to master various skills. Hayes and his coauthors, and others like E. D. Hirsch (1987), point to findings from the fields of artificial intelligence and psychology indicating that knowledge of words and facts are inseparable from mastering skills. Hayes and his coauthors give the example of a catcher yelling "squeeze bunt!" during a baseball game. The speed and dexterity a player is blessed with is useless unless he can instantly recall what a squeeze bunt is and the strategy the team has for countering it. (Of course, the reader might have trouble making sense of this example without knowing what baseball and a squeeze bunt are. Even communication at a moderate level of complexity assumes a set of shared references.) Similarly, a student cannot master history, biology, or auto repair without knowing the language of that specific domain. Hayes and his coauthors posit that the dumbed-down textbooks used by the baby boomers are responsible for their dismal performance on the SAT.

A study done by Chall, Conard, and Harris (cited in Chall 1996) for the Advisory Panel on the Scholastic Aptitude Test Score Decline (sponsored by the College Board and Educational Testing Service) discovered a strong link between texts' becoming easier and the notorious fall in SAT scores in the 1960s and early 1970s. They found that students who had used more challenging texts in the first grade performed better on the SATs 10 years later. The relationship between SAT scores and the quality of texts used by students in the sixth and eleventh grades was not as strong. Still, Chall and her colleagues found an unequivocal decay in textbook quality:

The sixth grade reading textbooks, for example, had a lower percent of original selections from literature, more stories written specifically for the readers, a lower ratio of expository to narrative prose—all indices of a decrease in challenge. . . . In general, the sixth grade history textbooks in use during the declining years seemed almost to change their purpose. From books that were meant to be read, they seem to have become encyclopedic magazines intended to be used for browsing or for reference. (Chall 1996)

Although, by some measures, the reading level of textbooks has improved somewhat since the 1960s, the quality of textbooks has continued to decline in other aspects. Contrary to criticisms and recommendations, textbooks became longer and more copiously illustrated. Textbooks from the 1970s examined by Chall ranged from 300 pages for fourth graders to thousand-page behemoths intended for high-school students. The typical book in their survey gained from 29 to 180 pages between 1974 and 1982. The books' tremendous size was due to their ambitious scope—an affliction that affected social studies books the most. One fourth-grade book in the sample sought to incorporate history, geography, civics, economics, and sociology in 10 chapters with titles such as "Living on Planet Earth" and "Learning to Live in Peace." Such breadth raises the danger of "mentioning" or briefly touching on topics without any in-depth discussion or explanation. Chall, Conard, and Sharples did find that textbooks had improved in this aspect since the early 1980s, providing more text per concept, more cohesion, and greater depth. They also found that textbooks increasingly used summary statements, listings of learning goals, and outlines of content to help students determine what precisely they should pull out from reading the text (Chall, Conard, and Sharples 1991, 51).

Chall and her colleagues did not intend to investigate the factual accuracy of the books they surveyed, but they did find occasional inconsistencies among them: the number of members of the Lewis and Clark expedition, for example, and precisely when the expedition left St. Louis. The content of recent textbooks has been found to be even more abysmal. A survey led by John L. Hubisz, a physics professor at North Carolina State University, examined middle school science texts published during the late 1980s and the 1990s. It is even more damning of textbook quality than the readability studies of Chall and Hayes. Hubisz and his colleagues found books that contained much material that had little to do with science and texts rife with scientific errors, irrelevant photographs, "experiments that could not possibly work, and diagrams and drawings that represented impossible situations" (Hubisz n.d. 3). Examiners found "East" and "West" transposed on a compass; the Equator drawn through Tucson, Arizona; the Statue of Liberty with the wrong arm upraised; and singer Linda Ronstadt "described as a silicon crystal doped with an arsenic impurity" (Hubisz n.d. 58). They concluded that not one of the books examined achieved scientific accuracy (Hubisz n.d. 90).

Hubisz and his colleagues found books that, like the Dick and Jane readers, had been manufactured rather than written. The "authors" were not authors in the conventional way of thinking. When the reviewers contacted those listed as authors, none claimed the responsibility of authorship, and some did not know that they were even credited as helping with the writing. Whereas Dick and Jane had been created by professors steeped in the latest pedagogical theories, the books reviewed by Hubisz and his colleagues were assembled by editors at publishing companies. Those listed as authors frequently only reviewed parts of the entire book; some had criticized the material they were given, but had heard or seen no evidence that the publisher had acted on their comments.

History textbooks suffer from the same factual problems that Hubisz and his fellow surveyors found in science texts. The history books considered by the Texas Board of Education for the 1992–93 school year contained 231 factual errors, including the assertion that the United States settled the Korean War by "using the bomb." In addition to this nuclear detonation unnoticed at the time by the world at large, the books moved events forward in time. Thus, the assassinations of Robert Kennedy and Martin Luther King, Jr., were moved from the administration of Lyndon Johnson to that of Richard Nixon. Similarly, the Bush-Dukakis election was moved from 1988 to 1989 (Henry 1994, 42–43).

The list of errors found in history books was compiled by conservative critics with more fundamental objections to the content of the books. Hence, for their ideological opponents, criticisms over simple factual accuracy became just another arrow to deflect. When one school board member questioned the wisdom of spending $20.2 million on error-laden history books, she was attacked by some colleagues, scholars, and others for playing politics, "nitpicking," and minimizing the broader, more important issues that the books were trying to address (Henry 1994, 42–43).

Textbook adoption by the Texas State Board of Education has long been an arena of ideological combat, identity politics, and pandering to interest groups across the political spectrum. Religious conservatives, Hispanic advocates, and libertarians scrutinize proposed books for passages they take as offensive or believe are inaccurate. Publishers, eager to see their books adopted, are swift to remove offending material. In the 2002 selection round, a publisher changed "millions of years" to "over time" in a passage discussing glacial movement in order to steer clear of conflicts with the biblical creation story. These decisions are of national importance. Since Texas is the second largest purchaser of books in the nation, its choices affect the textbooks available to schools in other states (Manzo 2002). This selection process demonstrates the diversity of values parents and other members of the community expect schools to impart to the children in their care. Not only must schools teach the three Rs, but they must also ensure that the heroes of the various groups are honored and a broad range of values are respected. The necessary compromise among interest groups shows the drawbacks of the political-voice approach of governing schools. The result is textbooks widely viewed as pap.

The American Textbook Council (2000) also in part blames identity politics for the poor quality of textbooks. Figures such as Alexander Hamilton, Thomas Edison, Martin Luther, and Napoleon are marginalized or have disappeared. Christopher Columbus, George Washington, and Thomas Jefferson are treated as problematic and ambivalent figures. Others such as Mansa Masu, Anne Hutchinson, and Rigoberta Menchu have taken their place on pedestals. The council also worries that graphs, pictures, and activities have replaced "clear, fluent" written narrative in textbooks, so that children do not practice how to learn through reading.

It is compelling to infer that a decline in textbook quality over the past century caused a similar trend in the quality of American education. We have seen that textbook quality has been linked to the decline in SAT scores. However, there is little evidence to confirm such a decline through the 1950s. The reading level of popular magazines, best-selling novels, and military manuals remained constant through the middle of the twentieth century (Stedman and Kaestle 1991a, 114–15). For more concrete evidence of prewar trends, we turn to what are called then-and-now studies.

Then-and-Now Studies

The question of whether current students were receiving the same education as their grandparents has continually motivated researchers. In 1906, John Riley gave the entire ninth-grade class in Springfield, Massachusetts, tests in spelling, arithmetic, and geography identical to the ones given to the city's ninth-graders 60 years before. He found that Springfield students at the beginning of the twentieth century performed better than had their earlier peers (Stedman and Kaestle 1991a, 80).

Lawrence Stedman and Carl Kaestle (1991a) surveyed 13 similar then-and-now studies using local samples of students that examined changes in such reading skills as speed, comprehension, and vocabulary. The studies covered periods spanning 10 to 36 years between 1916 and 1964. Four of the studies showed unambiguous improvement in reading skills. Three of them covered periods during the 1920s, 1930s, and 1940s. The latest of these four studies compared students in 1932 and 1952. The improvements ranged from two to eight months in reading ability—that is, less than one grade level. Three other studies found positive but statistically insignificant improvement; and 2 found unambiguous decreases in ability. The remaining 4 found mixed results. For example, a study that compared the achievement of students in Grand Rapids, Michigan, between 1916 and 1949 found improvement in comprehension of what they read, but no change in their oral reading ability or silent reading speed. A study with one of the larger samples, 115,000 students in six communities in seven states, found improvement in comprehension but a decline in vocabulary level.

Stedman and Kaestle also found 6 other then-and-now studies with statewide samples that tested changes in reading and other subjects: 2 showed gains in achievement, 2 showed declines, and 2 had mixed results. A study looking at pass rates on the New York Regents examination found an increase from 71 percent passing in 1915 to 84 percent in 1947. However, a later study of students entering the University of Minnesota in 1978 found that their reading skills were poorer than those of first-year students and high-school seniors in 1928. The reading skills of freshmen at the University of Michigan underwent a similar decline between the 1930s and the 1980s. Iowa students showed improvements and declines depending on the year, subjects, and grade levels looked at by researchers. While the reading skills of elementary students improved between 1940 and 1965, high-school students did worse in algebra, reading, science, English, and history in 1954 than in 1934.

Of 4 more then-and-now studies with national samples surveyed by Stedman and Kaestle, 2 showed positive changes, 1 negative, and the third had mixed findings. So of a total of 23 studies examining achievement over the first three-quarters of the twentieth century, 8 showed a clear improvement, 5 found a decline, and 10 had mixed results. Overall, the then-and-now studies showed no definite trend in the quality of American education. This finding is consistent with a more recent study not included in Stedman and Kaestle's survey. Looking at what American students know about their country's history, Dale Whittington (1991) found little change from the 1930s through 1987. Of course, this does not mean that American students' mastery of history was ever what it should have been.

The studies surveyed by Stedman and Kaestle are uneven in quality, and several factors limit the conclusions that can be drawn from them. First, the samples included in many studies are small—35 students in one investigation in rural California—and are unrepresentative of the nation as a whole. Second, changes in education policy influence the nature of the samples. The dropout rate declined throughout the century, which implies that later samples tested many students who would have been dropouts at the time the earlier tests were administered. Presumably, they would have been low-achieving students, which would bias a then-and-now study toward showing a decline in achievement. Third, schools historically had tougher promotion standards. This means that, for example, an eighth-grade class in 1934 would be older, on average, than an eighth-grade class in 1974. The question, then, is whether it is preferable to compare the achievement of 14-year-olds or the achievement of eighth graders. Many of the studies examined by Stedman and Kaestle do not make this adjustment. However, Coulson (1999, 179) cites the longer school year as an indication of a decline in the efficiency of education over this period. Despite more time in school, he contends, the then-and-now studies find no definite improvement in achievement.

Two more aspects of then-and-now studies are worth examining, since they shed light on the larger debate surrounding education policy. First, longitudinal analyses of educational achievement have to account for shifts in underlying social and economic factors. One study in Stedman and Kaestle's survey that looked at reading achievement in Indiana between 1944 and 1976 observed that more of the state's population lived in cities, worked in service rather than laboring jobs, were better educated, and were African American or Hispanic. Although a student's social and economic background does influence achievement, it is hard to say whether the combination of such factors made the school's job tougher or easier. The possible effects of socioeconomic trends continue to play a role in current debates over public education. Defenders of public schools use the changing nature of the student population and society at large to explain disappointing results (Berliner and Biddle 1995, 29, 274–79).

Second, what students need to know has changed. In developing his alpha intelligence test for the U.S. Army during WWI, Robert M. Yerkes, who was a Harvard University professor and president of the American Psychological Association, believed that asking about the nature of Rosa Bonheur's contribution to the arts and whether the Wyandotte was a chicken or a horse were valid measures of intelligence (Stedman and Kaestle 1991a, 87). The continually changing definition of what knowledge is important calls into question the relevance not only of then-and-now studies, but also of centrally controlling what schools teach through standardized tests and state and national curricula.

Test Scores: The Great Test Score Decline

A legacy of the scientific education movement is the standardized test: the instrument of choice for some education reformers, the bane of teachers and students, and a boon to researchers wanting to track educational achievement. The plethora of standardized tests taken by American students makes it much easier to follow trends in student achievement after WWII. The data that are available show an improvement in student ability from the 1950s through the mid-1960s. From 1940 through 1966, scores of Iowa students on the Iowa Test of Educational Development (ITED) for ninth and twelfth graders and the Iowa Test of Basic Skills (ITBS) for fourth and eighth graders rose steadily, with dramatic increases after the launch of *Sputnik*. The rate of gain was 0.023 standard deviations per year for high-school graduates. An improvement in student achievement can be found in other states as well: between 1958 and 1966, high-school juniors in Minnesota gained 0.39 standard deviations on that state's scholastic aptitude test (Bishop 1989).

The mid-1960s saw the beginning of the so-called Great Test Score Decline. From the mid-1960s through the late 1970s, student performance on a wide range of standardized tests grew steadily worse. The most famous decline is that of average scores for the SAT, the Scholastic Assessment Test—then called the Scholastic Aptitude Test (Figure 1.3). SAT scores started falling in 1963, and although math scores have recovered to near their former levels, verbal scores remain near their historic lows. The drop in verbal SAT scores was equivalent to 0.48 standard deviations. Those researchers who play with standard deviations conventionally regard any change of less than 0.20 standard deviations as small, changes between

Figure 1.3
SAT Scores

Source: U.S. Department of Education (2002).

0.20 and 0.80 standard deviations as modest, and changes greater than 0.80 standard deviations as large. To provide some perspective, the average 20-year-old American male is 5 feet 9 inches tall. Losing 0.48 of a standard deviation in height would be equivalent to shrinking 1.2 inches.

A common explanation by defenders of the education system is that the decline was due to the massive increase in the number of students seeking to enter college, leading to a less selective group taking the SAT, and hence to a drop in average scores. Closer examination of the data, however, reveals several inconsistencies. First, the greatest expansion in the population of students taking the SAT came in the years before the decline. From 1952 to 1963, the proportion of high-school seniors taking the test increased from 5 percent to 50 percent, yet during this time the scores remained relatively stable (Herrnstein and Murray 1996, 426; Hayes, Wolfer, and Wolfe 1996, 490).

Second, weakening admission standards for state universities during the 1960s actually led to a decline in the number of white students taking the SAT. Even though the pool of students was shrinking, from 1963 to 1976 the scores of white students fell 34 to 44 points on the verbal test and 15 to 22 points on the math section (Herrnstein and Murray 1996, 427). Between 1971 and 1976, the proportion of total high-school students taking the SAT fell, and the proportion of seniors taking the test at the end of the decline was still slightly smaller than it was 10 years before (Koretz 1992).

Third, if the decline in test scores was due to more test takers bringing down the average, then the upper level of students should have remained unaffected. However, the period of decline saw a shift in the entire distribution of verbal test scores. There was both a proportional and absolute decline in those scoring at the highest levels. Even as the number of test takers was expanding, the number of students scoring over 700 (old scale) on the verbal test fell from 17,500 in 1972 to 10,000 in 1993; 35 percent fewer scored over 600. Finally, from 1963 to 1973, the SAT verbal test actually became easier by 8 to 13 points (Hayes, Wolfer, and Wolfe 1996).

Between the early 1960s and 1980, the fall in SAT scores was mirrored by declines in student performance on other standardized tests for almost all subjects and grade levels. Table 1.4 shows the magnitude of the decline for the SAT, ITED, ITBS, and American College Test (ACT). The table shows the parts of the test that had the largest and smallest declines (in the case of the ACT science test, scores actually increased), and the size of the decline in standard deviations and percentile ranks.

Similar declines occurred in the Illinois decade study (0.28 standard deviations), the Preliminary Scholastic Aptitude Test (0.24 standard deviations), the California Achievement Test (0.22 standard deviations), the Metropolitan Achievement Test (0.42 standard deviations), the Stanford Achievement Test (0.33 standard deviations), the Comprehensive Test of

Table 1.4
Magnitude of the Test Score Decline

Test	Subject	Total Decline	
		Standard Deviations	Percentile Equivalent
SAT			
Largest	Verbal	0.48	0.18
Smallest	Mathematics	0.28	0.11
ITED Grade 12			
Largest	Reading	0.40	0.16
Smallest	Mathematics	0.27	0.11
ITED Grade 10			
Largest	Reading	0.32	0.13
Smallest	Natural Science	0.25	0.10
ITBS Grade 8			
Largest	Mathematics	0.47	0.18
Smallest	Vocabulary	0.26	0.10
ITBS Grade 6			
Largest	Mathematics	0.38	0.15
Smallest	Vocabulary	0.10	0.04
ACT			
Largest	Social Studies	0.55	0.21
Smallest	Science	-0.06	0.02

Source: Congressional Budget Office (1986).

Basic Skills, the National Assessment of Educational Progress, the Graduate Record Exam, the Medical College Admissions Test, the Minnesota Scholastic Aptitude Test, and the Graduate Management Admissions Test (Wynne and Hess 1986; Bishop 1989). Test scores improved, however, on the Law School Admissions Test. The decline occurred in private schools and in Canada as well (Koretz 1992).

Stedman and Kaestle (1991b) are skeptical of the decline's significance. They are not willing to completely dismiss the changing characteristics of students taking the tests as a partial explanation of the drop in scores, and they point to the College Board's own research, which estimated that between 67 percent and 75 percent of the decline in the 1960s and 24 to 40 percent of the decline in the 1970s were due to demographic shifts in the pool of test takers. Not only were more students from traditionally low-scoring groups taking SATs, but younger siblings tend to score lower than the first and second born. One study estimated that 4 to 9 percent of the decline in verbal SAT scores during the 1970s was due to a cohort of younger brothers and sisters taking the test. Changes in the student population could also be responsible for the drop in test scores at lower grade levels as well. In addition to more children from lower in the birth order entering school, a falling dropout rate for African American students and increased immigration of Hispanic and Asians caused the fraction of non-white students in American high schools to increase from one-sixth to nearly one-fourth. Furthermore, children entering school at younger ages and automatic promotion policies caused the average age of students at a given grade level to fall. Stedman and Kaestle attribute between 30 and 50 percent of the decline in standardized test scores in the 1970s to changes in the student population. However, this does not account for the decline during the 1960s or explain the fall in rural, largely white Iowa.

Stedman and Kaestle question whether the decline was as widespread as it seemed. They point to several islands of stability and even improvement. During the 1960s, achievement test scores remained stable for high-school students in Alabama and South Dakota. Scores for junior-high students in Michigan and Mississippi were stable in the early 1970s; and scores on the College Board achievement tests for English composition, biology, chemistry, physics, French, and Spanish increased between 1967 and 1976.

Finally, Stedman and Kaestle question the real significance of the drop in scores in terms of actual student skills. Although the declines are large in percentile terms, in some cases they represent a decline equal to one grade level or less. Furthermore, a large fall in test scores may represent only a small decrease in terms of absolute performance. For example, between 1971 and 1987 the Science Research Associates (SRA) test measured a decline in the reading skills of high-school students equal to one-half to one grade level. For twelfth graders, however, this represents correctly answering 68 percent as opposed to 72 percent of test questions.

However, there are indications of a real decline in skills. The broadest and most comprehensive measure of student achievement in the United States, available since the late 1960s, has been the National Assessment of Educational Progress (NAEP). The NAEP, "the Nation's Report Card," administered by the U.S. Department of Education, has regularly tested representative samples of students nationwide in reading, mathematics, science, and civics for three decades and has recently branched into measuring performance in history, geography, writing, and art. Although it caught only the end of the test score decline, the NAEP provides a partial indication of the absolute decay in skills. Between 1972 and 1978, the percentage of questions high-school seniors answered correctly on the NAEP mathematics test fell from 64.0 to 60.4 percent. The percentage of questions answered correctly by seniors on the NAEP science test fell from 45.2 to 42.5 percent between 1969 and 1972 (Congressional Budget Office 1986).

Although the fall in aggregate scores is seemingly small, they mask a decline in higher-order skills, a continued lack of facility in basic concepts, and a worrisome decay in basic knowledge. While overall NAEP reading scores remained unchanged in the 1970s, seniors did significantly worse on questions testing higher-order inferential skills, with the average percentage correct falling from 64 to 62 percent. On the math test, certain skills, though nothing to brag about to begin with, grew even worse. The fraction of seniors able to express 9/100 as a percentage fell from 61 to 53 percent. The fraction who were able to find the cost per kilowatt when given a simplified electrical bill showing 606 kilowatts costing $9.09 fell from 12 percent in 1973 to 5 percent in 1978. On the NAEP civics tests, the proportion of students who knew that the Senate was part of Congress fell from 94 percent in 1971 to 88 percent in 1975. The proportion who were able to identify Congress as part of the legislative branch dropped from 84 percent to 74 percent between 1968 and 1975; during the same time, the share of seniors who could define *democracy* fell from 86 to 74 percent (Congressional Budget Office 1986).

There have been widely diverse explanations of the test score decline. Many consider it to be evidence of decay in American schools: the weakening of standards regarding performance and discipline, the implementation of ineffectual teaching fads, and the adoption of watered-down and diffuse curricula. Others call it a reflection of the overall turmoil in society at the time. No explanation has been able to account for all the evidence, or overcome observers' prejudices about American schools and American society in general. We have already seen how some researchers attributed the fall in SAT scores to a decline in textbook difficulty after WWII. In addition to simpler textbooks, educators also slowed down the pace of instruction, lowered student workloads, and assigned fewer written papers. This was part of a trend that had been continuing for at least a century to make school more accessible to a wider population of students

(Hayes, Wolfer, and Wolfe 1996). Although the timing of this explanation is right for the SATs, it does not explain why scores for other achievement tests rose in the 1950s, when schooling was becoming easier, and then started to fall in the mid-1960s, when textbooks started to become more difficult. High-school students who took the SAT in the first year of decline, 1963, had been in school during the allegedly educationally soft 1950s. However, children who were in fifth grade at the beginning of the decline in ITBS scores, in the mid-1960s, had spent their entire educational careers in post-*Sputnik* schools.

Other studies examined by the College Board's Advisory Panel found little relationship between the drop in scores and what was happening in schools and classrooms. One study that compared two high schools—one where SAT scores remained unchanged and a second where SAT scores fell more than the national average—found little difference between the two. Both had similar educational approaches and similar English curricula and had introduced in equal measure innovations such as pass-fail grading and nontraditional course offerings. Students in both schools took virtually the same number of academic courses. Teachers had grown equally permissive in both schools, and both had seen discipline problems and truancy grow to the same extent. A study by the American Institutes of Research that looked at 30,000 students in nine states found that the extent to which schools implemented some of the educational innovations promoted at the time had no effect on student achievement (Stedman and Kaestle 1991b).

The nearly sudden and universal onset of the decline—across the nation, in Canada, in public and private schools, over all grade levels—indicates a cause outside the schools. It is difficult to imagine what types of deleterious education practices could spread so rapidly through America's decentralized school system. Indeed, the 1960s saw American youth increasingly engaging in behavior worse than performing poorly on standardized tests. The 1960s also saw a rise in homicide and suicide rates for adolescents and young adults, a jump in arrest rates for those between 18 and 24, and an increase in the reported frequency of sexual intercourse by adolescents (Wynne and Hess 1986). There were other, milder forms, of social transformation as well. The 1960s saw the onset of a decline in the proportion of eligible adults outside the South voting for president, a fall in association membership—including the PTA, a downward trend in church attendance, a drop in philanthropic giving, and the now-infamous decline in participation in male league bowling (Putnam 2000). (Female league bowling actually increased through the 1960s and peaked in the late 1970s.)

The end of the Great Test Score Decline followed a generational pattern. The drop in test scores came to a halt, and in cases reversed itself, starting in the lower grades first as the post–baby boom generation progressed upward through school. This pattern implies an improvement in the quality of education starting in the late 1960s. We have seen that textbooks started to grow more challenging at this time. By the mid- to late 1970s, schools were returning to teaching the basics and attempting to end social promotion, and statewide competency tests were becoming more in vogue. This improvement in achievement with the promotion from grade to grade of the post-boom generation is consistent with a cumulative model of learning. Reforms in schooling were too late for older students who did not receive a solid educational foundation on which to build.

Test Scores: After the Fall

Since the end of the 1970s, scores on a variety of tests have shown an improvement in student performance. In 1987, J. J. Cannell authored a notorious study finding that all of the states in the Union were reporting that their elementary school students were performing above the national average. Linn, Graue, and Sanders (1990) found that the states were comparing themselves to averages that were four to five years old. At the time, publishers of norm-referenced tests renormed their tests—that is, calibrated them to determine what the performance norm was—only every seven years or so. Thus, schools were comparing the achievement of their students to the achievement of students several years in the past. Nevertheless, the barrel of cautions and qualifications that apply to using standardized tests to measure achievement on the way down also apply to measuring achievement on the way up. Significant changes as measured by standard deviation or percentile rank may be small in terms of actual skill. The equating studies used to renorm tests suffer from various problems, including small and unrepresentative samples, and some test publishers caution against using them to infer national trends (Stedman and Kaestle 1991b). In addition, upward trends in student performance may be caused by students becoming accustomed to the tests, or even teachers teaching to the tests (Koretz 1992). However, students who had taken the tests previously did only marginally better than those who had seen them for the first time; hence, Linn, Graue, and Sanders dismiss any familiarization effect as probably miniscule.

For the most comprehensive measure, we turn to the NAEP. Figure 1.4 shows performance on the NAEP for high-school seniors in all American schools, public and private, during the last three decades of the twentieth century. The math and science scores just capture the end of the Great Test Score Decline. Since the early 1980s, when scores reached their lowest point, math and science achievement has generally improved. The improvement, however, has been modest. Since 1982, science scores for 17-year-olds increased by 0.25 standard deviations. Math scores have risen by 0.31 standard deviations. Math scores were better at the end of the 1990s than in the entire 30-year history of the test; science scores, however, still have not reattained the achievement levels of the late 1960s; and read-

Figure 1.4
NAEP Scores (Age 17)

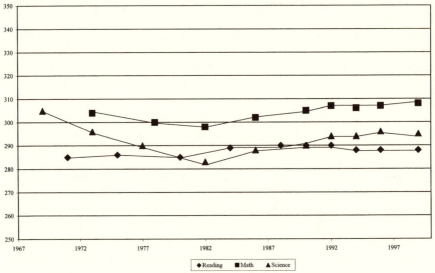

Source: Campbell, Hombo, and Mazzeo (2000).

ing scores have remained flat. Scores for fourth and eighth graders follow a similar pattern, with slightly more impressive gains, for all three subject areas (Loveless and Diperna 2000).

The NAEP, the SAT, and the rest of the alphabet soup of standardized tests indicate that the math skills of American students have improved since the early 1980s, while reading skills have remained unchanged. This phenomenon was noted by Herrnstein and Murray, who believed that mathematics were more resistant to a general decline in educational standards. While the great writers of world literature may be exiled from textbooks by the latest pedagogical fad on teaching reading, the solution to the quadratic equation remains unchanged. In addition, there is an indisputable hierarchy of math skills, while the ranking of authors is most definitely disputable—taking into account not only subject matter, vocabulary, and talent, but also the writer's sex and skin color. Hence, according to Herrnstein and Murray, while schools have found it relatively easy to implement tougher standards for mathematics, the literate subjects—literature and history—remain a swamp inhabited by various politically correct and intellectually feeble monsters (Hernnstein and Murray 1996, 430–33). However, mathematics has not been safe from disputes over the proper way to teach it to students (Hoff 2002).

Alternatively, it may be that, while mathematics is a subject largely learned in school, reading is a skill that is learned outside as much as inside the classroom. So while advancing schools can take credit for progress in mathematics, an increasingly decadent society must take the blame for Johnny's, or Jane's, inability to read. A cursory look at the data seems to back this up. Between 1978 and 1999, the proportion of seniors whose highest math course taken was calculus or precalculus doubled from 6 percent to 13 percent, while the proportion taking prealgebra or general mathematics fell from 20 percent to 7 percent. Over the same period, the proportion of seniors who spent three to five hours in front of the television jumped from 26 percent to 37 percent; while from 1984 to 1999, the proportion of seniors who read daily or weekly for fun dropped from 64 percent to 53 percent (Campbell, Hombo, and Mazzeo 2000, 36, 77–78). This circumstantial evidence, however, is not solid proof. This school versus society explanation was also offered as an explanation of the fall in test scores, but it is not clear that performance in reading and other so-called indirect subjects deteriorated any more than performance in mathematics (Congressional Budget Office 1986, 49–53). In any case, if this view is true, the inability of students to learn outside of school reflects poorly on the schools' claims that they are creating lifelong learners.

The lackluster undulations of aggregate test scores over the past decades hide substantial improvements in achievement by African American and Hispanic students (Figure 1.5). For African Americans, performance in reading and mathematics peaked in the late 1980s and has

Figure 1.5
NAEP Reading Scores (Nonwhite, Age 17)

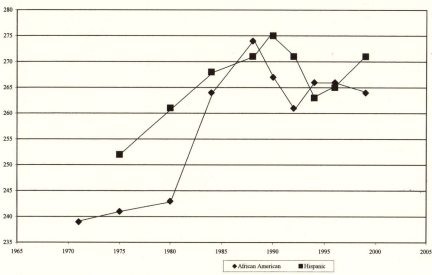

Source: Campbell, Hombo, and Mazzeo (2000).

since dropped somewhat. Only the decrease in reading achievement is statistically significant; and in both subjects performance at the end of the 1990s is significantly better than at the beginning of the 1970s. In science, the performance of African American students has mirrored that of whites. The achievement of Hispanic students improved significantly in all three subjects over the time covered. The drop in reading scores in the 1990s is not statistically significant.

Nevertheless, the performance gap between white and nonwhite students remains huge. In 1999, the average white 17-year-old scored 1.1 standard deviations higher than his or her black counterparts on the NAEP math test, and 1.3 standard deviations higher in science. In math, the average black student scored lower than 75 percent of all white students. The gap is somewhat smaller for Hispanic students: approximately 0.76 standard deviations in both math and science.

Are Schools Good Enough?

We have seen that over the 50 or so years in which the scholastic ability of American students has been measured on an extensive and consistent basis, student performance rises, falls, and rises again by modest amounts. Is this a matter of concern? If the academic capability of the average American student falls from superlative to merely outstanding, it may be worthy of note, but not of grave concern. On the other hand, if average performance rises from abysmal to merely mediocre, that is nothing to crow about. As with spending, the trends in achievement over time tell us little about whether the levels attained at the peaks or troughs are satisfactory.

Determining what level of education can be considered adequate is a bar that is continually moving upward. Functional literacy, as originally defined during the Depression by the Civilian Conservation Corps, was pegged at three to four years of education. This was enough, it was felt, for a person to cope with the reading material essential for day-to-day life. In WWII, the Army raised the definition to a fourth-grade education. After the war, the government steadily raised the level of education it felt was needed to function in society from fifth, to sixth, to eighth grade. By the 1970s, some experts felt that a high-school education was essential (Stedman and Kaestle 1991a, 92). *A Nation at Risk* warned of a workforce inadequately educated to fill future high-skilled jobs. Others argued that work in America was being "de-skilled," that white-collar jobs were being "proletarianized," and that corporate America was not creating enough high-skilled jobs to employ the graduates of American schools. However, most evidence shows the increasing importance of skill in the workplace. The wages of high-school graduates have fallen, while the earnings of college graduates have risen. This is because well-paying manufacturing jobs are being replaced by jobs flipping hamburgers or doing dry cleaning.

Wages for high-school graduates declined across all sectors of the economy: between 1979 and 1987, earnings fell 13.3 percent in the construction industry, 10.9 percent in manufacturing, and 6.9 percent in wholesale and retail trade. During this time, the earnings of college graduates rose by 10.2 percent, 10.5 percent, and 0.4 percent in those same industries, and the number of college graduates working in the manufacturing sector rose by 33 percent (Levy and Murnane 1992).

One measure of the adequacy of education is whether it sufficiently prepares students for the workplace or to pursue further study. We have seen that college professors and business owners alike have complained about ill-prepared graduates for at least the past 50 years. The most comprehensive survey to date of remedial education in colleges and universities was conducted in 1995 by the National Center for Education Statistics (U.S. Department of Education 1996b). It found that 63 percent of private institutions, 81 percent of public colleges and universities, and 100 percent of two-year schools offered at least one course in remedial reading, writing, or mathematics. Twenty-nine percent of freshman had taken one remedial course. Over the previous five years, enrollment in remedial courses stayed the same in 47 percent of the schools offering such help; 39 percent had seen enrollment increase, and 14 percent experienced a decrease in the number of students taking such classes over the same period.

A 1999 survey of college freshmen found that 12.7 percent had taken a remedial course in mathematics while in high school, and 5.1 percent had taken a remedial course in a foreign language—all time highs for the history of the 30-year survey. The proportion that had taken a remedial science class (5.1 percent) was at a 20-year high; with 9-year highs in English (6.3 percent), reading (5.6 percent), and social studies (4.0 percent). Since 1982, the percentage of college freshmen who had taken at least one remedial class in high school had increased from 12 percent to 18.3 percent (Sax et al. 1999).

In 1993, nearly 50 percent of the freshmen entering the California State University system needed remedial help in English or math. By 1999, that percentage had increased to 68 percent of freshmen, while 48 percent of sophomores still had not completed their remedial work (Manno 1995). In 1999, the California State Universities expelled 1,440 students, or 5 percent of their freshmen classes, due lack of skills; 1,259 students needing remedial work left on their own; and 1,300 were given a final chance as sophomores to complete the necessary remedial courses in the fall semester. The California State Universities estimated that remedial help for students costs $10 million a year. The University of California estimates that it spends $1.6 million annually to help academically unprepared students (Weiss 1999). In fall 1995, data obtained by the *Boston Globe* showed that 13 percent of freshmen at the Amherst and Boston campuses of the University of Massachusetts, 44 percent of the freshmen at Fitchburg State, and 20 percent of entering students at Worcester State were taking at least one remedial class (Dembner 1996). A 2001 report by the Ohio Board of Regents found that a third of students entering that state's universities were inadequately prepared for college-level math and English courses. Forty-one percent of high-school graduates entering Kent State University in 2000 required remedial math classes—mostly basic arithmetic and algebra at the seventh-grade level (Galbincea 2001).

In summary, remedial education is widespread, although the burden falls more heavily on certain schools. Most private institutions and nearly all public institutions offer such classes, and approximately 20 to 30 percent of freshmen need remedial help in at least one subject—although in some schools the percentage is much higher. The cost of remedial training for institutions of higher education is difficult to estimate. College administrators and faculty do not wish to brag that they offer such programs, and expenditures on the programs are typically buried deep within the budget and included in other instructional funding. Very rough estimates put the cost of remedial education for colleges and universities at about $1 billion per year (Breneman 1998).

Evidence is even more sparse for the cost of inadequately prepared workers. A 2000 survey by *Training Magazine* found that 30 percent of businesses and other organizations offered remedial training (Business Wire Inc. 2000). Thirty-five percent had a remedial program for mathematics, 28 percent for writing, and 28 percent for reading. The National Association of Manufacturers estimated that half of small companies and three-quarters of large companies had programs to upgrade the skills of their workers, for a total cost of $40 billion (*New York Times* 1994). A study by the Mackinac Center estimated that more than a third of Michigan students left high school with inadequate skills in mathematics, reading, and writing. The study calculated that unprepared students cost Michigan businesses and colleges $601 million per year. This implies that inadequately prepared students cost the United States as a whole $16.6 billion per year (Greene 2000b).

The NAEP attempts to give normative significance to student performance on the tests by labeling the scores as basic, proficient, and advanced. Figure 1.6 shows the proportion of high-school seniors whose performance was less than basic and the proportion whose performance was proficient in the most recent administrations of the NAEP. In all seven subjects, at least one student in five failed to attain basic proficiency. In history, particularly, American students continued a long tradition of appalling performance. Only in reading do more than 30 percent of students perform at a proficient level or better; however, the proportion of students with less than basic reading proficiency rose from 20 to 23 percent during the 1990s. On the positive side, the trend in mathematics was in the op-

Figure 1.6
Fraction of 17-Year-Olds at Each NAEP Achievement Level

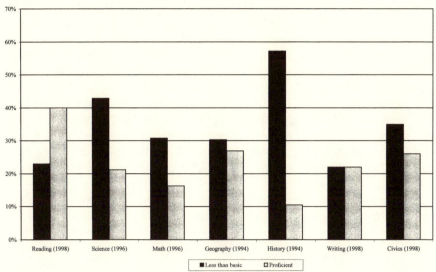

Source: NAEP (various years).

posite direction: the percentage of students with less than basic proficiency fell from 41.9 percent in 1990 to 30.8 percent in 1996.

The normative standards of the NAEP have been criticized as inaccurate and fundamentally flawed (National Research Council 1999a; Rothstein 1998). Setting aside the advanced, proficient, and basic labels, what do the different performance levels imply? For the NAEP reading test, students were given an actual federal income tax form and instructions. Students were to read the information and then answer a question about the purpose of the tax tables. Fifty-nine percent of seniors at the basic level chose the correct answer "to help you determine the amount of tax you owe." By contrast, 84 percent of seniors with proficient reading skills answered the question correctly. In 1990, only 55 percent of high-school seniors knew that a measurement expressed in cubic inches represented the volume of a rectangular box. Ninety-four percent of students performing at the proficient level answered the question correctly compared to 34 percent of students scoring below the basic level. In the 2001 history test, only 48 percent of high-school seniors could identify the Soviet Union as an ally of the United States during WWII. Eighty-six percent of students performing at the proficient level knew the correct answer compared to 35 percent of students performing below the basic level. So although it may be debated whether a high-school graduate should know the identity of former allies of the United States or the difference between volume and length, the performance levels do represent significant differences in knowledge.

Murnane and Levy (1996) estimate that a high-school graduate would have to score 300 on the NAEP reading and mathematics tests to qualify for a job paying a middle-class wage. In math, this means being able to use fractions, decimals, and percentages; recognizing geometric shapes; solving simple equations; and using moderately complex reasoning. In reading, a 300 score signifies the ability to find, understand, summarize, and explain relatively complicated information. In 1999, 60 percent of 17-year-olds met this standard in math, while only 40 percent achieved a 300 in reading. Thus, these authors estimate, in the absence of obtaining further education, learning a skilled trade, or making it big as a rock star, nearly 50 percent of high-school graduates cannot earn enough to make it to the middle class.

Finally, some critics believe that, although the public school system does fine by the average student, it fails students with certain characteristics. This is to be expected from a system governed through politics (voice). Political decisions are compromises to satisfy the majority, or the average person, rather than to satisfy those with unusual or unique needs or wants. We have already seen the large gap between the performance of white and minority students on the NAEP. Stedman (1996) argues that schools are failing the students at the lower end of the talent spectrum. He estimates that 15 to 30 percent of Americans cannot read well enough to fully comprehend everyday material such as newspaper articles, maps, report cards, coupons, recipes, and medicine directions. This cannot be solely attributed to the reading problems of minorities, the elderly, and high-school dropouts; 16 to 20 percent of high-school graduates and 14 to 16 percent of whites surveyed by one literacy study had problems understanding common reading matter. Herrnstein and Murray, on the other hand, contend that, while the typical student in an American public school performs as well now as at any time in the past, public education, as demonstrated by low SAT scores, neglects the academically gifted child (1996, 417–18).

International Comparisons

Another benchmark by which we can gauge the academic skills of American students is to compare them to their peers in other countries. For over 40 years, researchers have conducted large-scale comparisons of student achievement across countries. The findings of the major studies appear in Table 1.5. In general, the Asian countries that participate—Japan, South Korea, Singapore, and Taiwan—are always found at the top of the list, while developing countries are always at the bottom. The rest of the nations that usually participate—the European nations, the United

Table 1.5
International Tests of U.S. Academic Performance

Test	Number of systems[†] participating	Number of systems[†] scoring significantly better than the U.S.
IEA First Mathematics Study 1963-1964[a]		
Age 13 core test	12	9
Last-year secondary—math students	12	10
Last-year secondary—non-math students	10	7
IEA Second Mathematics Study 1980-1982[a]		
Age 13-arithmetic	20	5
Age 13-algebra	20	7
Age 13-geometry	20	10
Age 13-measurement	20	17
Age 13-statistics	20	2
Last-year secondary—number systems	15	9
Last-year secondary—algebra	15	11
Last-year secondary—geometry	15	10
Last-year secondary—calculus	15	10
IEA First Science Study 1966-1973[a]		
Age 10 core test	17	1
Age 14 core test	19	5
Last-year secondary core test	19	10
IEA Second Science Study 1983-1986[a]		
Age 10 core test	15	5
Age 14 core test	17	10
Last-year secondary—biology	14	12
Last-year secondary—chemistry	14	9
Last-year secondary—physics	14	7
First International Assessment (IAEP) 1988[a]		
Age 13—mathematics	12	10
Age 13—science	12	8
Second International Assessment (IAEP) 1991[b]		
Age 9—mathematics	10	5
Age 9—science	10	1
Age 13—mathematics	14	10
Age 13—science	14	5
IEAP Geography—age 13 1991[c]	9	2
IEA International Reading Literacy Study 1991[d]		
Age 9	27	1
Age 14	31	1

(continued)

Table 1.5 (*continued*)

TIMSS 1994-1995[e]		
Fourth grade—mathematics	26	7
Fourth grade—science	16	1
Eighth grade—mathematics	41	20
Eighth grade—science	41	9
Final-year secondary—mathematics general knowledge	21	14
Final-year secondary—science general knowledge	21	11
TIMSS-R 1999[f]		
Eighth grade—mathematics	38	14
Eighth grade—science	38	14
IEA Civic Education Study—age 14 1999[g]		
Civic knowledge	28	0
Civic content	28	6
Civic skills	28	0
PISA 2000[h]		
Age 15—reading literacy	31	3
Age 15—mathematics literacy	31	8
Age 15—science literacy	31	7

[†]For some tests, language groups or provinces in certain countries—e.g., Flemish Belgium or German-speaking Switzerland—are counted as separate systems.

Sources: [a]Medrich, Elliot A., and Jeanne E. Griffith. 1992. "International Mathematics and Science Assessment: What Have We Learned?" Washington, D.C.: U.S. Department of Education, National Center for Education Statistics, NCES 92-01126, p. 26. [b]U.S. Department of Education. 1996. *Digest of Education Statistics, 1996.* Washington, D.C.: National Center for Education Statistics, NCES 96-133. pp. 428, 439, 441, 442, 444. [c]U.S. Department of Education. 2002. *Digest of Education Statistics, 2001.* Washington, D.C.: National Center for Education Statistics, NCES 2002-130. Table 398. [d]U.S. Department of Education. 1996. *Reading Literacy in the United States: Findings from the IEA Reading Literacy Study.* Washington, D.C.: National Center for Education Statistics. [e]U.S. Department of Education. 1996. *Pursuing Excellence.* Washington, D.C.: National Center for Education Statistics, NCES 97-198; and U.S. Department of Education. 1996. *Pursuing Excellence: A Study of U.S. Twelfth-Grade Mathematics and Science Achievement in International Context.* Washington, D.C.: National Center for Education Statistics, NCES 98-049. [f]Martin, Michael O., et al. 2000. *TIMSS 1999 International Science Report.* Boston, Mass.: International Study Center, Lynch School of Education, Boston College, 2000; and Mullis, Ina V. S., et al. 2000. *TIMSS 1999 International Mathematics Report.* Boston, Mass.: International Study Center, Lynch School of Education, Boston College. [g]Baldi, S., et al. 2001. *What Democracy Means to Ninth-Graders: U.S. Results from the International IEA Civic Education Study.* Washington, D.C.: U.S. Department of Education, National Center for Education Statistics, NCES 2001-096. [h]Lemke, Marianne, et al. 2001. *Outcomes of Learning: Results from the 2000 Program for International Student Assessment of 15-Year-Olds in Reading, Mathematics, and Science Literacy.* Washington, D.C.: U.S. Department of Education, National Center for Education Statistics, NCES 2002-115.

States, Canada, Australia, and New Zealand—are typically found trading places in the middle of the pack. For the most part, the performance of American students does not reach the world-leading level of U.S. education spending. American students do perform respectably in some areas, leading the world in reading. Conversely, U.S. students' performance in math and science is middling. American students also tend to do better at younger ages compared to their peers in other countries, but as they advance through the system, they tend to fall farther behind the pack. According to the Third International Mathematics and Science Study (TIMSS) conducted in 1994–95, American fourth graders performed above the international average in math and science; eighth graders were still above average in science but had fallen to average in math; and twelfth graders performed below average in both math and science (U.S. Department of Education 1998c).

The International Association for the Evaluation of Educational Achievement (IEA) math tests—the first administered in 1964, the second carried out in the early 1980s—spanned the period of the Great Test Score Decline. The IEA studies find some evidence of a decline in U.S. educational performance during this time. The fraction of American high-school seniors taking a math-intensive curriculum as preparation for college or for other future training fell from 26 percent to 15 percent. Other countries experienced drops in the share of seniors taking math-intensive curricula as well: for example, Japan from 14 to 13 percent, and England and Wales from 42 to 35 percent. For most countries, however, these drops were due to significant increases in high school enrollment. In 1964, 70 percent of American youths old enough to be seniors in high school were in fact enrolled. This is in contrast to the much lower rates in many other countries, such as 57 percent in Japan and 12 percent in England and Wales. Twenty years later, the United States still had one of the highest enrollment rates for high-school seniors, although other nations had closed the gap. The enrollment rate for youths old enough to be seniors was 92 percent in Japan and 17 percent in England and Wales. We can correct for the jump in enrollment rates by looking at the number of seniors taking a significant amount of mathematics as a fraction of their entire age group, whether in school or not. By this measure, the fraction of American youths in a math-intensive program fell from 18 percent to 12 percent. In 1964, the same ratio for countries where results from both tests are reported was less than in the United States—typically 4 to 8 percent. By the time of the second IEA test 20 years later, this fraction had risen for most nations, and for several it was equal to, or greater than, the U.S. proportion. During this time, too, IEA data show that American schools de-emphasized calculus, while schools in other countries stressed the subject more (Robitaille 1990).

Nevertheless, watering down of standards is not evident in test score trends. Performance by seniors in the calculus part of the IEA test improved in the United States and for most other countries as well. Algebra test scores for 13-year-olds also jumped internationally and in the United States. This is not to say that American seniors gave a stellar showing. In the second IEA test, the average student answered a mere 23 percent of the calculus anchor items correctly, as compared with 66 percent for the average Japanese student and 55 percent for the average English student. (Anchor items are questions from the first test included in the second, specifically aimed to track changes in achievement.) The average score in algebra of 42 percent correct for American 13-year-olds was more respectable; it edged out the 41 percent scored by English students, but was still lower than the 60 percent score of French students and the 61 percent score attained by the Japanese (Robitaille 1990).

We have seen that, as measured by the NAEP, science achievement by American students fell in the 1970s. This worsening of achievement is found among American 10- and 14-year-olds by the first two IEA studies as well. From 1970 to 1984, aside from a very modest drop by Australian students, science achievement increased for all other participating nations for which comparisons can be made (Keeves and Soydhurum 1991, 276). We have also seen that NAEP reading scores have remained flat for the past 30 years. However, according to analysis of international tests, reading performance by American students dropped between 1971 and 1991. For the seven countries for which the tests allow comparisons to be made, achievement improved in Finland and Hungary, stayed constant in Sweden, and dropped for four others, including the United States (Lietz 1996, 181–82).

Myriad explanations have been offered about why American students do not perform as well as might be expected or desired compared to students in other nations. We have seen that it cannot be due to a lack of resources—the United States spends more per student than most other nations. Nor can it be attributed to American schools' being uniquely disorderly or easygoing places—for the lower grades at least. Sixty-one percent of fourth-grade students internationally had teachers who reported that the different academic abilities of their students limited their teaching quite a lot or a great deal. By contrast, only 41 percent of American students had teachers with a similar complaint. Similarly, American teachers said they were less limited by high student-teacher ratios, equipment shortages, and disruptive students than their peers in other countries. American students in fourth grade spent more time each week learning about math and science and were assigned more homework. For eighth graders, U.S. teachers were more likely to complain of apathetic students and parents and low student morale, but their colleagues in Germany and Japan were more likely to cite differing academic abilities of their students, student-teacher ratios, disruptive students, and even threats to personal safety as limiting their teaching. However, principals in the United States were more likely to have to deal with intimidation, verbal abuse, and physical injury to students and teachers on a daily basis than were principals in German schools. Interestingly, an equal proportion, if not more, of German principals dealt with problems such as possession of weapons, inappropriate sexual behavior, and use of illegal drugs. Compared to their fellow eighth graders in Germany and Japan, American students were equally if not more likely to spend three or more hours playing sports, reading, or studying. They were less likely than Japanese students to spend three or more hours per day watching television (U.S. Department of Education 1996a, 1997).

By the end of high school, however, there is a definite shift in priorities. American high-school seniors are less likely than seniors in other countries to be taking math or science classes, and they do less homework per day. American seniors are more likely to have something stolen or to have been threatened. They spend the same amount of time watching television as their peers in other countries, but are much more likely to be working. Sixty-one percent of high-school seniors in the United States work one or more hours at a paid job on a school day, compared to only 28 percent in the other countries participating in the TIMSS. American students work on average three hours per school day, compared to the international average of 1.2 hours. Still, none these factors have been rigorously linked to the relatively poor performance of U.S. students (U.S. Department of Education 1998c).

The lagging international performance of U.S. students has been attributed to what has been termed opportunity to learn—that is, differences among schools internationally in what students are actually taught. Ian Westbury (1992) compared how the math curricula of eighth graders in the United States and Japan compared to the IEA's second mathematics study. While Japanese students taking the test had, on average, covered 82 percent of the algebra subject matter included in the test, coverage for American students ranged from 37 percent, for students in remedial math classes to 88 percent for students in algebra classes. American students in algebra or enriched math classes—representing 25 percent of U.S. students taking the test—performed worse, but not significantly so, than the top 20 percent of Japanese students. When Westbury compared the performance of only those U.S. seniors who had taken calculus to the performance of Japanese students, the gap narrowed, but still remained large: Japanese students got 69 percent of the calculus items correct on average, compared to 48 percent for American students. Westbury ascribes the differences to the longer exposure of Japanese students to the subjects. Students in Japan had typically seen many of the calculus topics before their twelfth year of schooling. By contrast, American students were first introduced to the material when they were seniors. Simon and Woo (1995) also find that opportunity to learn affected relative performance by nations on the international comparison tests. The opportunity to learn argument merely regresses any education problem back up one level. One is still left with the question of why foreign schools provide their students with greater opportunities to learn.

Another reason advanced to explain the mediocre showing of U.S. students is the diversity of the U.S. population. American elite students, it is held, compare well with their peers; it is populations of low-achieving students that lower the overall average for the United States. Be that as it may, gaps between elite students in the United States and elsewhere were found by the third math and science study (TIMSS). U.S. calculus and advance placement (AP) calculus students scored significantly lower than advanced mathematics students in 6 of the 16 nations participating. One bright spot: if the sample is limited only to students who had taken AP calculus, the advanced math students of only one nation, France, outperformed the U.S. students. America's advanced science students still did poorly compared to advanced students in other nations, scoring last among the 16. Even students who had taken AP physics did significantly worse than the elite science students in 6 other countries (U.S. Department of Education 1998c, 43–45, 51–52).

To the extent this is true, it again moves the question back one level. Why does the U.S. public school system fail students at both ends of the achievement spectrum? On the 1991 IAEP mathematics test, for example, not only did the best in some countries—Germany, Switzerland, and the Netherlands—outscore our best, but their worst did better than our worst. For 13-year-olds, the top 10 percent of Swiss students scored 93.3 out of 100, while the bottom 10 percent scored 50.7. In the United States, by contrast, the top 10 percent scored 89.3, and the bottom 10 percent 32.0 (Nickell and Bell 1996). Nickell and Bell attribute this to the fact that German, Swiss, and Dutch schools set basic standards for all students and ensure that all students meet them.

In addition to macro-level international comparisons, a group of researchers led by Harold W. Stevenson conducted seven micro-level comparisons of student achievement (Stevenson and Lee 1998). This research, known as the Michigan studies, examined primary and secondary student performance in mathematics and reading in schools in four Western nations—the United States, Canada, Hungary, and Germany—and three East Asian countries: China, Taiwan, and Japan. In order to account for opportunity to learn, Stevenson and his team carefully constructed the tests based on the topics students in each country should have been exposed to. The tests were administered individually.

Of course, it was impossible to control for all factors, but many of the reasons used to excuse the performance of American students actually favored the Americans. Parents in the U.S. cities were more educated and wealthier than the Chinese parents; average earnings per family were $778 per year in Beijing and $32,500 in Chicago. In Beijing, 98 percent of fathers and 98 percent of mothers worked, compared to 93 percent of fathers and 51 percent of mothers in Chicago. The Chinese families did have fewer children, and the children were more likely to come from intact families. Students in both countries were introduced to various math concepts and skills at about the same time. Finally, it must be noted, China is a centrally governed dictatorship. while schools in the United States are locally controlled (Stevenson et al. 1990).

The findings of Stevenson and his colleagues generally mirror those of the macro-level tests. In mathematics, the performance of students in the East Asian countries was superior, while the scores of American students were comparable to those of the other Western countries. Again, the difference was not due to a dumbbell-shaped distribution of achievement among American students, with groups of very high and very low performers. The distribution of scores in each country, including the United States, tended to have a single peak. The peak for students in the east Asian countries was centered at a higher score than that for American students. Nor did American students demonstrate superior facility in certain skills or topics.

Compared to Chinese students, for example, American students made a poor showing. They scored lower than their Chinese peers in nearly every skill at both grade levels. In computation, 98 percent of Chinese students performed better than the average American student; similarly, in word problems and number concepts, over 90 percent of Chinese students performed better than the average American. When performance was broken down by school, no American school performed better than the worst Chinese school at the first-grade level, and at the fifth-grade level only one American school had students who did as well as the students in the worst Chinese school. Despite the poor performance of American children relative to their Chinese peers, the research team found what has become a typical result of such studies: American parents have lower expectations and are much more satisfied with their children's performance than are Chinese parents (Stevenson et al. 1990).

American students performed better than their peers in other countries, including the Asian nations, in reading. However, it is worth noting that the variance in student performance both within and among classrooms was greater in the United States than in China. That is, the achievement gaps between the best and the worst students in a class and the averages of the best and worst classrooms were larger in the United States than in China (Stevenson and Lee 1998).

Customer Satisfaction

One final measure of school performance is customer satisfaction. Even though test scores are not as high as they could be, schooling serves other purposes as well. American parents may be perfectly content with the education their children are receiving. There was a brief, shining moment, perhaps, when Americans looked upon their schools and thought them good.

In the middle of the twentieth century, the American public's satisfaction with the education system was great and growing. A 1940 Gallup poll found that 85 percent of adults thought that their children were getting a better education than they had received. In 1943, another Gallup survey found 80 percent of parents happy with their children's schools; by 1946, this had increased to 87 percent. In 1938, over half of those asked in another survey said there was nothing about the local school they would change. Forty percent of respondents in a 1946 survey could think of nothing wrong with the local school (Tyack and Cuban, 1995, 13).

As is widely known, this era of good feelings did not last. The public's confidence in public schools, as measured by Gallup polls, has declined over the past three decades (Gallup International 2000). In 1973, 58 percent of Americans expressed a great deal or quite a lot of confidence in public schools; by 2000, only 37 percent admitted to equal faith. Over the past three decades, public confidence in public schools has been below confidence in the military and organized religion and above confidence in "big business" and Congress. Interestingly, the publication of *A Nation at Risk* in 1983 appeared to have little effect on public attitudes, and schools shared a mild boost upward in public confidence with other parts of the American establishment during the mid-1980s. Apparently in terms of public trust, the mid-1980s really were Morning in America for American institutions.

Public education's 21-point drop between 1973 and 2000 is nearly unique in Gallup polls on confidence in organizations. Congress comes close with an 18 point drop over the same period; and only the presidency saw a larger decline of 30 points during the 1990s. The contrast between the schools and the military is noteworthy. Both are government organizations that are looked on as essential public functions. Both have been extensively criticized (let's not forget wasteful military procurement or the Vietnam War). Yet the military saw its standing with the American public improve. Starting at the same level as public education in 1973, public confidence in the armed forces finished the twentieth century six percentage points higher. Unfortunately, space does not permit speculation on why this is the case.

Americans are happier with their local school than with the generic national version, although not by much. In 1999, parents of public school students gave public schools a grade of 1.97 on a scale of 0 to 4, with 4 being best. This was down slightly from a grade of 2.01 in 1982. Public school parents gave their community schools an average score of 2.56, up from a low of 2.31 in 1983, but still less than the 2.80 grade they gave their local school in 1974. As can be expected, parents of private school children rated public schools nationwide lower, but only marginally so (1.81), in the late 1990s; and they rated local schools much lower (2.20) (U.S. Department of Education 2002, table 22). As letter grades, these are in the B−/C+ range for local schools, and C−/D+ for public schools nationally.

Those who wish to see the public approval glass as half full cite the proportion of parents, typically over 50 percent, who give the public schools their children attend an A or B (Berliner and Biddle 1995, 112). How does this compare with the consumer satisfaction rates of other sectors of the economy? For most of the 1990s, according to the American Consumer Satisfaction Index, customer satisfaction with the goods and services purchased from private businesses ranged from a low of 2.83 in 1997 to a high of 2.97 in 1994. Americans were least satisfied with airlines (2.44) and most satisfied with the producers of household appliances (3.28), cosmetics (3.32), and food for themselves and their pets (both 3.28). They gave the federal government a grade of 2.84, local government 2.63, and the Post Office 2.80. So public education fares better than the airlines in terms of consumer satisfaction, but worse than most other industries, including other government agencies.[2]

CONCLUSION

We have seen public education in the United States follow several different trajectories. In terms of resources, the path has been steadily upward: more spending per student, more teachers per student, and better educated teachers. Student achievement has not kept pace. The best indicators show that student performance has risen, fallen, and risen again by modest amounts. By contrast, public confidence in American public education has fallen steadily. Berliner and Biddle allege that the present belief in a crisis in American public education is manufactured by industrialists, government officials in the Reagan and Bush administrations, and the "far right" (Berliner and Biddle 1995, 132–38, 147, 150). However, their book was released 13 years after the publication of *A Nation at Risk* had launched yet another movement of evaluation, criticism, and reform. As of this writing, 7 more years have passed, and interest in education reform is still sufficiently strong to occupy a growing number of think tanks, institutes, and advocacy groups; impel the passage of major new education legislation at the state and federal levels; and sustain the research programs of respected scholars in universities dotting the nation.

Clearly, given President Lincoln's observation on the feasibility of fooling the public for an extended period of time, something must be going on. I a offer three possibilities.

First, parents and taxpayers, comparing the increasing amount of resources devoted to education with the relatively flat level of student performance, have grown frustrated with the system. The weak link between spending and test scores will be further discussed in chapter 2.

Second, the consensus that has surrounded the goals of public schools has disintegrated over time. Where schools were once places for flag salutes, sports, proms, and the three Rs, disputes over sex education, the place of Ronald Reagan in history, and equal resources for boys' and girls' sports have arisen. Some of these arguments are new; some are old but have tapped into modern communications and methods of activist organizations to gain national resonance. The local school has become too small to contain the values of an increasingly diverse community. Furthermore, the increasing importance of cognitive skills for success has made the old shopping mall high school, with its indifferent academic program, outmoded. The rise and fall of the American high school is the subject of chapter 3.

Finally, increasing centralization of school governance has alienated local communities from their schools. As the Gallup polls show, Americans do not like large, remote organizations like Congress, "big business," or big labor unions. Public opinion of the U.S. Congress mirrors that of U.S. schools. Americans dislike the remote, abstract organization, but are more favorably inclined to its local representative. As public schools have increasingly had to serve various groups of stakeholders, judges, and state and federal agencies, members of the public may increasingly view public education as a remote entity over which they have little control. This leads to a growing lack of confidence. The increasing centralization of public schooling is the subject of chapter 4.

Chapter 5 will argue that the remedy for these three trends—increasing inefficiency, diverse values, and growing centralization—is allowing greater parental choice.

NOTES

1. For those not initiated into the mysteries of statistics, using standard deviations allows us to describe the magnitude of effects without having to worry about the units in which a particular characteristic is measured or about its dispersion. A standard deviation of improvement is the equivalent of moving from the average to the 84th percentile. So, for example, the average violent crime rate for counties nationwide is 58 per 10,000 inhabitants. Counties with a violent crime rate of 9 per 10,000 have a lower crime rate than 84 percent of the counties in the United States.

2. The American Consumer Satisfaction Index is reported on a scale of 0–100. I have converted the scores to the 0–4 scale based on the formula ASCI/100 $\times$ 4.

CHAPTER 2

The School Productivity Puzzle

A CLOSE LOOK AT THE DECLINE IN SCHOOL PRODUCTIVITY

The fact that student achievement as measured by test scores has not, in general, kept pace with the resources devoted to education has led many observers to conclude that there has been a decline in the productivity of American schools. In terms of NAEP scores per dollar, Caroline Hoxby (2002c) estimated that the productivity of American schools fell 35 to 42 percent over the last 30 years.

"Where has all the money gone?" has been used as the title of more than one study on the growth of education spending over the past century. Hanushek and Rivkin (1997), in their look at the components of spending growth in the hundred years between 1890 and 1990, found that the major reason for the growth was the increasing price of teachers. Even before WWII, growth in teacher salaries accounted for 44 percent of the growth in expenditures for instructional labor, including not only teachers but also other school staff, such as principals, counselors, psychologists, and librarians. An increase in the student population was the second largest contributor to spending growth, accounting for some 20 to 30 percent.

When the hundred years is broken down into segments, a more interesting picture emerges. Although growth in the price of instructional labor was the most important cause of growth for every subperiod examined, there was a dramatic change after 1970. Between 1970 and 1990, Hanushek and Rivkin estimate, a fall in the typical student-teacher ratio was the second major cause of the increase in spending. This was a small golden age in terms of school resources: enrollment was falling after the baby boom, so schools were able to use a greater share of resources to reduce class size; meanwhile, the teaching force was growing in experience at a time when the nation could actually spend a somewhat smaller fraction of its resources on education.

Lankford and Wyckoff's (1995) examination of spending growth in New York schools during the 1980s found that most schools actually increased staffing during this time, even though enrollment was falling. Increases in expenditures for teaching accounted for 68 percent of budget growth. Much of this growth, they estimate, was due to increased spending on special education.

Special education—the programs and procedures mandated by the federal government that schools must follow in educating the physically and mentally disabled—has been cited both as a reason for spending growth and as a reason why spending remains inadequate. From 1978 to 1990, while overall enrollment fell, the number of students classified as needing special education increased 24 percent. The number of teachers, aides, and staff hired to teach special education students increased nearly 60 percent. It can cost from two to four times as much to educate a special education student as a regular student. Rothstein and Miles's (1995) in-depth study of spending in nine school districts found that special education took a large chunk of the typical school's budget: 17 percent in 1991, compared to 3.7 percent in 1967. Nevertheless, per-pupil spending for regular education increased by 28 percent on average over this period. Lankford and Wyckoff (1996) estimated that 33 percent of the increase in school spending in New York schools was due to special education. After adjusting for inflation, they calculated that per-pupil spending for special education students grew 40 to 54 percent between 1980 and 1993, compared to 30 to 40 percent per regular student. In their analysis, Hanushek and Rivkin attribute 18 percent of spending growth in the 1980s to special education. Thus, although the growing burden of special education can account for about 20 to 30 percent of the spending growth, it did not eat up all the resources added to education.

Bloated bureaucracy and frills also did not account for the additional resources. Instruction remains the largest single item in school budgets: 76 percent by Rothstein and Miles's calculation, 60 percent by Lankford and Wyckoff's. Other items in school budgets—administration, athletics, bilingual education, counseling, and security—have grown by modest amounts, and individually remain relatively small fractions, typically less than 10 percent, of overall spending.

In conclusion, although a significant share has been diverted to special education and other school functions, a large portion of the past century's growth in school resources has flowed straight into the classroom. Thus, the modest gains in achievement compared to the larger increase in resources indicates a real decline in school productivity.

DOES MONEY MATTER?

Ever since the release of the Coleman report (Coleman et al. 1966) in the mid-1960s, which found that school characteristics had little impact on student achievement, the effectiveness of school inputs has been hotly debated. Since the Coleman report, many more studies have tried to determine the link between inputs such as school spending, class size, and the pay, experience, and training of teachers and outputs such as test scores and the income of graduates once they enter the labor force. David Monk characterized the results of nearly three decades of scholarship as

[A] disappointing area of research that has been plagued by a disconcerting pattern of inconsistent and often insignificant results. Analysts seem satisfied with a highly simplified underlying conceptualization of education production. Instead of challenging the underlying model, these production function researchers have pursued a piecemeal approach that revisits old questions and explores them with modest innovation. Analysts write in apparent ignorance of some of the more serious conceptual difficulties that have been discerned. It is journeyman social science. While it is not bad social science, it is not the kind of analysis that is likely to wrest research from its damning legacy of inconsistent and largely insignificant results. (Monk 1992)

Others are more optimistic, claiming that a new wave of research employing new data sets and superior statistical techniques is providing solid evidence that school inputs matter (Verstegen and King 1998; National Research Council 1999b, 143). Alan Krueger, referring to the class size reduction pilot program Project STAR, declares that "One well designed experiment should trump a phalanx of poorly controlled, imprecise observational studies based on uncertain statistical specifications" (Krueger 1998). Others have also expressed impatience that the debate over school inputs is still ongoing:

[I]t is time to stop misrepresenting findings which hinders the development of positive new policies. Policy decisions must rely on substantial primary research, not on ideology, supposition, weak interpretations, or secondary reviews. (Achilles 1996)

The most prominent skeptic in academia has been the economist Eric Hanushek. He has been so prolific and undaunted that some have attempted to cast him out of the polite, academic debate (Biddle and Berliner 2002, 7). Hanushek's seminal contribution was a 1986 review of 147 studies of the education production function and a 1997 update that looked at 377 studies (Hanushek 1986, 1997). These studies examined the effect of various education inputs—spending, class size, teacher qualifications, and so on—on student achievement. For all inputs surveyed, a number of studies found a statistically significant positive effect between inputs and output. A smaller number found negative effects. However, the vast majority of studies found no significant effects whatsoever. For example, of 163 estimates (some studies had more than one) of the effect of per-pupil spending on student achievement, 27 percent showed a positive effect, 7 percent showed a negative effect, and the remaining 66 percent showed no effect.[1] In the case of no input, more than 30 percent of the estimates showed a positive and significant effect (Hanushek 1997). We can see what led to Monk's pessimistic evaluation of the entire research effort.

Critics have dismissed Hanushek's methods as crude vote counting and have attempted to recount the votes in ways that they believe are statistically more correct or more representative. Hedges, Laine, and Greenwald (1994) reexamined Hanushek's studies using a statistical method known as meta-analysis. Hanushek's methodology counted the parameters estimated by the studies based on two criteria. The first was whether the estimated parameter was statistically significant. Estimates that were insignificant were counted as no votes. Second, estimates that indicated an effect opposite that of the one commonly supposed—for example, that larger class sizes and inexperienced teachers improved student achievement—were also counted as no votes by Hanushek. Meta-analysis allows the researcher to count the spoiled ballots among the statistically insignificant estimates. If school inputs actually have no effect, the insignificant estimates should be the result of mere chance, with half showing a positive impact and half a negative impact. If the insignificant estimates are predominantly positive, that is an indication that more than chance is involved. Despite the individual insignificance of the positive estimates, in aggregate they may indicate a actual effect.

Hedges, Laine, and Greenwald conducted a meta-analysis on the set of studies examined by Hanushek and on another set of studies they viewed as more sound. They claim to find that inputs such as per-pupil spending, class size, and teacher experience and education have an impact on student achievement. However, their counter to the simple vote count is still not as strong as they and others represent. They find very strong evidence that teacher experience matters, but class size effects are definitive only when a further subsample of their new sample of studies is used. For teacher education, they found unambiguous results only when examining a subset of studies that asked only if a teacher had a master's degree.

Alan Krueger (2002) also criticizes the simple method of counting estimated parameters and proposes two alternative ways to tabulate studies. First, he proposes that votes should be counted by study rather than by the raw number of estimated parameters, as Hanushek does. As an example, consider two hypothetical studies examining the effect of class size in the same school district. Using student-level data, one study estimates a separate class size parameter for white and minority students for six different grades, yielding a total of 12 estimates showing no impact due to class size. A second study with the same data estimates only one class size parameter for the entire district, which shows a positive impact of reducing class size. Hanushek's method would count a vote of 12 estimates against and 1 in favor, while Krueger's tallying method would end in a tie: one study against and one in favor. Krueger also advocates weighting studies by the quality of the academic journals in which they were published. Finally, Krueger questions some of the specific choices made by Hanushek in counting studies.

Krueger's methods of counting results applied to studies of class size still only musters a plurality of approximately 33 percent finding a positive and significant impact of smaller classes. Another 20 to 27 percent find a positive result that is not significant. By further weighting results regardless of significance, Krueger concludes that the preponderance of evidence points to class sizes mattering. Krueger, however, places greatest weight on the results of the Tennessee STAR experiment on lowering class size: its large size and careful methodology make it superior to the vast majority of other studies on class size.

Most of the studies discussed above look at the effect of school inputs on student achievement as measured by scores on standardized tests. However, a vast amount of research has established that the more time spent in school, the higher the person's earnings. The relationship is as close to being a solid fact as one can get in the social sciences. When research by David Card and Alan Krueger found a positive relationship between school inputs and earnings after graduation, hopes were stirred that more solid evidence existed for the positive effect of school resources (Card and Krueger 1992, 1996). However, the effect of class size, teacher training, and spending on earnings remains as much in question as the effect of resources on test scores. A study by Julian Betts found no link between standard measures of resources and earnings. Betts's review of the other studies that have examined this question found some interesting patterns (Betts 1996). First, the effect of resources on earnings tends to be significant for workers educated before the 1960s. Studies tend to find that resources have not had an impact on workers educated since then.

Second, studies using state-level measures of resources—for example, average per-pupil spending or teacher education—tend to find that resources have a significant effect. The impact tends to weaken the more student-specific resource measures become. Studies using inputs measured at the school level tend not to find a link between resources and earnings. Finally, studies that examine young workers tend not to find any impact due to school resources.

Betts also reviewed studies examining the effects of inputs on educational attainment. Class size had the most consistent effect, with 60 percent of the estimates being positive and statistically significant. Only a third of the estimates for per-pupil spending and a quarter of the estimates for teacher salary and length of school year were positive and significant. No studies found a positive impact due to teacher education, and only 8 percent of the estimates found an effect due to teacher experience. As in the case of the resources-earnings link, studies using data aggregated on a higher level tended to find a positive impact. While 100 percent of the studies using state-level data found that smaller class sizes had a positive effect on attainment, only 33 percent of studies using school-level data found the same result.

Reasons why studies that use more disaggregated data tend to find weaker results revolve around technical issues of statistical analysis. One possibility is that measurement error in school-level and district-level data tends to weaken results; however, Betts found evidence that contradicted this hypothesis. Second, disaggregated studies may lack power. *Power*, to statisticians, means the ability to make statistical inferences. For example, suppose you wished to determine whether a coin was "fair," that is, whether it had an equal chance of landing on head or tails when tossed. A statistical test would be to toss it several times and see if a pattern emerged: landing on one side significantly more times than another. A low-powered test would be to toss the coin only a half-dozen times or so. A high-powered test would be to toss the coin a hundred or even a thousand times. Similarly, low-level data may not provide enough observations to tease out any effect of school resources. Betts did find that some school-level studies using recent data did not have the power to detect the effects of teachers' salaries or the length of the school year. However, the data did have the power to determine the effects of class size and teachers' education. While school-level analyses have few technical problems, aggregate analyses done at the state level may suffer from several possible problems—including omitted factors, measurement error of variables, and aggregation—that could bias estimates.

A decline in the productivity of schooling is not peculiar to the United States. In other developed countries, achievement has remained flat while costs have risen (Grundlach, Wossmann, and Gmelin 2001). The weak relationship between inputs and outputs is also found in other developed countries. Figure 2.1 compares per-pupil spending in countries to average scores for eighth-graders on the TIMSS math test. More rigorous studies confirm the general lack of a relationship between spending and other inputs and achievement (Wossmann 2000; Hanushek 2002; Hanushek and Luque 2002). The story is somewhat different in developing countries. A

Figure 2.1
Spending and Student Achievement Worldwide

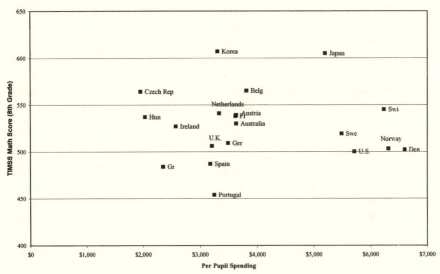

Source: OECD (2000).

majority of studies have found positive and statistically significant impacts from per-pupil spending, facilities, and teacher education in developing countries. However, the fraction of estimates showing a significant
effect due to teacher education or salary or to class size is about the same
as for studies of American schools (Hanushek 2002). Studies of the effect
of school inputs in other developed countries have found the same uncertain results as in the United States.

The inability of researchers to find a definitive link between school inputs and outputs has sometimes been characterized as "schools don't matter." That is, a child's socioeconomic background determines his or her
achievement regardless of the classroom in which the child is placed.
However, even skeptics of the efficacy of input-based reforms hasten to
add that the uncertain empirical link between school inputs as conventionally measured—class size, teacher credentials, per-pupil spending—
does not indicate that schools or teachers do not matter. On the contrary,
research indicates that teachers and schools can have significant effects on
what children learn. The impact of a good teacher can be tremendous. The
differences between a good teacher and a poor one can mean as much as
the equivalent of a year's achievement for students. Whereas 1.0 standard
deviation in class size would improve student achievement by 0.01 to 0.03
standard deviation, 1.0 standard deviation in teacher quality would boost

student performance by 0.11 standard deviation—an effect as much as 10 times greater (Hanushek, Kain, and Rivkin 1998; Hanushek 2002).

What this research implies is that differences in school quality are only weakly linked to inputs as conventionally measured. It is as if there is pedagogical dark matter analogous to the invisible, undetectable cosmic substance that astrophysicists speculate suffuses the universe. The existence of this pedagogical dark matter puts policymakers in an obvious quandary, since if it is beyond their ken, it is beyond their control. The input-based policy levers at their disposal are only loosely attached to the education production machinery.

THE BAUMOL DISEASE

The first response by defenders of the current public education system to the contrast between growth in spending and the lack of growth in achievement is to play down the real increase in funding devoted to education. The spending data reported above were adjusted for inflation using the Consumer Price Index (CPI) calculated by the U.S. Department of Labor. The CPI measures inflation by tracking the cost of a typical basket of goods and services purchased by the average U.S. consumer. Rothstein and Miles (1995), among others, have criticized the use of the CPI to adjust school spending, since it does not take into account the change in the relative price of services—like education—to commodities. Following the analysis first done by Baumol (1967), Rothstein and Miles contend that the labor-intensive nature of teaching causes productivity growth to be slower in education than, say, in manufacturing automobiles. Improvements in technology will allow carmakers to increase output using the same, or even less, labor—leading to lower costs for autos. For labor-intensive services, productivity growth through technology is more difficult. Baumol gives the example of a horn quintet, a composition that will always require five musicians. Even in the Information Age, it still takes one barber to do one haircut. Supposedly, schools also cannot easily substitute robots for teachers, so the cost of education per unit of output remains constant or even increases. Productivity increasing rapidly in one sector while lagging in another means that the cost of output has to rise in the low-productivity sector just to keep quality constant. Thus, using the CPI overstates spending growth in the education sector, since some of the cost increase is necessary to maintain schooling at a constant quality level.

However, as Tyack and Cuban (1995) point out, technology has continually made its way into the classroom to make the task of teaching easier. In 1841, blackboard salesmen claimed that the inventor of their product was "among the best contributors to learning and science, if not among the greatest benefactors of mankind" (Tyack and Cuban 1995, 121).

Among the inventions listed by Tyack and Cuban as making the life of the teacher and student easier are the blackboard, cheap paper to replace slates, inexpensive textbooks that allowed one per child, and ballpoint pens. In addition, more glamorous technologies have been introduced in an attempt to aid or replace the teacher: radio, film, videotape, and personal computers. The failure of repeated waves of new technology to completely replace the teacher has led many to become cynical and dismiss the claims of boosters of the latest new gadgets. Failure, however, has not stopped teachers and school officials from requesting funding to fill their classrooms with the latest technology, up to and including access to the Internet. Indeed, computer-aided instruction with minimal teacher supervision has proven successful for certain types of students (Trotter 2002).

Efforts have been made to use special measures of inflation to adjust education spending to account for what has come to be called the Baumol disease. Note that diagnosing schools with the Baumol disease is admitting that productivity in this sector has been relatively stagnant. A special adjustment is intended to support the case that additional funding has been necessary simply to keep the quality of schooling constant. The problem with using these specially created indices is that the cost of schooling is primarily the cost of teachers. Although the cost of teachers has risen over the past century, so has teacher quality as measured by years of experience and credentials. Consequently, a special index for education inflation runs the risk of understating the quality of education resources that a dollar may buy the same way the CPI overstates it (Hanushek and Rivkin 1997). In the end, even using a cost index that Rothstein and Miles admit is imperfect, inflation-adjusted spending per pupil has still increased by a significant amount: 61 percent from 1967 to 1991.

There is international evidence that the Baumol disease is not the entire story behind the decline in school productivity in developed countries. Grundlach and his coauthors (2001) find that the cost of education in developed countries has risen faster than one would expect if schools were simply suffering from the Baumol disease. Rather, it seems that productivity in schools has fallen instead of remaining stagnant.

CHANGING DEMOGRAPHICS

A second defense of schools has been the claim that schools are doing well by just keeping achievement constant in the face of adverse trends in the larger society (Berliner and Biddle 1995, 178; Tyack and Cuban 1995, 37). We have already noted that the Great Test Score Decline was coincident with an increase in drug use, sexual activity, and criminal activity among adolescents—and with a decrease in bowling by their fathers. In addition, the fraction of families headed by a single parent more than tripled in the postwar years, increasing from 7.4 percent in 1950 to 26.3

percent in 1994. Some problems, although still serious, are not at historical levels. In 2000, 15.6 percent of children lived in poverty, compared to 26.9 percent in 1959. Even though immigration both in numbers and rates is higher than it has been since World War I, it is still lower than at the beginning of the twentieth century. Furthermore, demographic changes over the past decades have not all been bad for children: parents are more educated; real median family income has risen; families are smaller; and more children have spent time in preschool.

A rigorous look at the effect of changing demographics on student achievement found that by far the largest impact was from the education level of parents: on average, the test scores of a child whose mother or father had a college education were a half of a standard deviation higher than the scores of a child whose parents did not graduate from high school. Once other factors were controlled for, the achievement gap between white and nonwhite students was of a similar magnitude. Other characteristics of the child's environment—family income, number of siblings, having a working mother, coming from a single-parent family—had smaller impacts (Grissmer et al. 1994). Grissmer and his coauthors found that, given demographic trends, American children in 1990 should score higher on achievement tests than their 1970 counterparts. The positive effect of more-educated parents and smaller families outweighed the negative trends over the period they examined. In fact, once demographic changes are taken into account, non-Hispanic white children should be scoring higher on the NAEP than they actually are—a strong indication of a decline in school productivity.

On the other hand, black and Hispanic children do better on the NAEP, controlling for demographic changes. This is a possible indication that policies aimed at helping minorities may have had a positive impact. Hanushek (2001) found that that integration and desegregation had the greatest effect on minority achievement. This is not only a result of active government policy, but also of an increase in the standard of living of African American families that allowed them to move to the suburbs. Hanushek estimated that greater integration caused the NAEP test score gap between black and white children to close by 0.4 to 0.5 standard deviations. This is larger than the actual reduction in the gap of 0.3 standard deviations, suggesting that there may have been countervailing factors. However, the reason greater integration had a positive impact was not that it allowed black children to attend wealthier schools. Rather, Hanushek and others have found that the test scores of African American students are higher in more-integrated classrooms. Reducing the number of black children in a classroom by 10 percent increases scores of the remaining African American students by 0.024 standard deviations per year. Unfortunately, space does not permit a full review here of the scholarly literature on peer effects.

DIMINISHING RETURNS

One possible reason for the apparent decline in school productivity is diminishing returns. Even before the 1953 Supreme Court decision on *Brown v. Board of Education*, American schools witnessed a dramatic closing of the gap in education resources between whites and African Americans. In 1920, the average length of the school year for Southern blacks was only 76 percent of that for Southern whites; by 1953, it had reached 96 percent. Average class sizes in black schools were 46 percent larger than in white schools in 1920; by 1953, they were nearly equal. Over the same time, teachers in black schools saw their salaries rise from 55 percent of that earned by teachers in white schools to 90 percent. This increase in inputs for education for African Americans was accompanied by a rise in achievement test scores for black males. Indeed, granted that the data are quite sparse, the increase in inputs between 1918 and the mid-1950s is much larger than in subsequent years (O'Neill 1990). For schools as starved of resources as black schools were, school inputs may matter, and this effect was captured by studies examining workers educated during those years. In subsequent years, however, the possible gains from additional resources are not as dramatic, and thus are much harder for researchers to find.

ALTERNATIVE PRIORITIES

The output measure used in education productivity studies is almost always student scores on standardized tests. One reason for the weak link between measured inputs and outputs may be that the those in control of public schools—parents, taxpayers, legislators, judges—want more from their school than maximization of NAEP scores per dollar.

Kenneth Sirotnik (1983) surveyed parents, teachers, and students to find out what each group felt was the most important function of a high-school education. The choices were (1) intellectual development, acquiring knowledge and basic skills; (2) social development, acquiring the virtues to participate fully in society; (3) personal development, acquiring traits such as self-confidence, discipline, and creativity; and (4) vocational training, learning the skills to get a job. In addition, he asked members of each group to identify the actual emphasis at their school. Although each group gave more votes to intellectual development as the main goal of a high-school education, in no group did intellectual development receive a majority of the votes. The rank ordering among groups is interesting. Social development came in last in all groups. Personal development placed second among teachers, while vocational training was second among students and parents. It is also worth noting that the preferences of parents are aligned most closely with the perceptions of actual emphasis. The results are similar for lower grades, except that vocational education is considered less important than social and personal development.

A survey of parents in New York City and its suburbs found that differences in what parents sought from schools were based on parental characteristics such as race and education (Schneider et al. 1998). African American parents considered high test scores and discipline important, but not diversity. Hispanic parents valued discipline, but not diversity. College-educated parents, on the other hand, placed less weight on test scores and discipline, but sought diversity and schools that teach values.

In addition to academic and personal development, stakeholders have other expectations—such as jobs, sports, or cultural activities—of their local public school. One of the rocks upon which the extravagant experiment in increasing school spending in Kansas City, Missouri, foundered was the fact that the school district was one of the two largest employers of middle-class African Americans in the city. School district workers were the backbone of the local churches. Consequently, African American ministers kept close watch on hiring and promotion in the district, which made it almost impossible for the district to fire mediocre teachers (Ciotti 1998).

Poor African American communities are not the only ones that want more than learning from their schools. According to the August 11, 2002, *Scottsdale Tribune,* a group of parents in the affluent, largely white community were upset over a proposal to redraw school boundaries. Although the proposed shift would put their children in an academically superior high school, they were worried about breaking up their children's circles of friends and involvement in sports. Residents in nearby Deer Valley School District wanted their school board to condemn and buy a piece of property for a warehouse so as to prevent an adult book store from opening on the site. This actually would have hurt them as taxpayers, since it would have been twice as expensive to condemn the site than to buy a larger parcel more suitable to the district's needs. The school board opted for the larger site (Mendoza 2002).

As communities have become more diverse, and as the voice of more and more stakeholders has become heard in school policy, the need to mollify assorted interests could be playing a role in the productivity decline.

CHANGES IN THE TEACHING FORCE

Economic and demographic trends that influence the teaching force are another possible reason for the productivity decline. An alignment of forces over the past several decades has encouraged smaller class sizes and a reduction in the skills of teachers—although the drop in teachers' skills is not as bad as some would portray it (Hanushek and Pace 1995). This has led to higher costs without a comparable increase in achievement.

The most important trend for the teaching profession has been, of course, the rapid expansion of job opportunities other than teaching for women since the 1960s. The growing attractiveness of nonteaching jobs for women can be seen in the reduction in the premium paid to female schoolteachers. In 1960, 53 percent of college-educated women and more than 87 percent of all working women earned less than the average woman teacher. By 1990, those numbers had fallen; 45 percent of female college graduates and 75 percent of all women in the labor force earned less than the average woman teacher (Hanushek and Rivkin 1997). Whereas educated women once had little choice but to become teachers, today schools have to draw teachers from farther down the ability ladder. The declining fertility rate among women has also made teaching less attractive. Fredrick Flyer and Sherwin Rosen found that, unlike women in other professions, teachers suffer no decline in wages from leaving the labor force temporarily to have children. As women have had fewer children, this flexibility has become less valuable (Flyer and Rosen 1997).

The increase in nonteaching staff and reduction in class sizes cannot be totally attributed to the demands of greater bureaucracy or union featherbedding. The increase in labor force participation by women increased the demand for teachers and other staff as more responsibility for caring for children was shifted from the home to the school. Parents expected their children to receive the same sort of individual attention at school that they would have received at home. This led to a demand for smaller class sizes and additional school personnel. Between 1960 and 1990, the growth in nonunionized auxiliary staff was 450 percent greater than the growth in teaching staff. Flyer and Rosen found that increased labor force participation by women accounted for nearly a third of the decrease in student-teacher ratios between 1975 and 1990. Increased teacher unionization accounted for less than 1 percent. Flyer and Rosen also speculate that, since smaller class sizes are an imperfect substitute for individual attention from parents, student achievement suffered due to the shift in responsibility from family to school.

Other trends reinforcing the movement toward less-skilled teachers and smaller class sizes are the stagnation in the productivity of teachers, the Baumol disease, and the decreasing value of the skills taught in grades K to 12 (Lakdawalla 2001). Most subjects taught in grade school have changed little over the past hundred years. The history books have added a few decades, and there are more poets in the anthologies, but algebra is still algebra, and grammar remains grammar. Contrast this with the fields of science and engineering, which have advanced rapidly over the century. Some of this has seeped down to the grade schools, but most advanced knowledge is imparted in college and graduate school. This advanced knowledge is also more valuable, so women and men with advanced skills have seen an increase in opportunities outside of the teaching profession. Schools have to hire less-skilled individuals. To compensate, schools substitute more individual time with students, leading them to reduce class sizes.

TEACHERS' UNIONS

The period after WWII saw an increase in the number and activity of institutions and interest groups involved in public education—judges and legislators, foundations, civil rights groups and parents' groups. Perhaps no interest group has incited as much controversy and study as teachers' unions. Teachers are the most visible and vital factor in education. Researchers in education and psychology have labored to find what makes a good teacher and have offered countless plans and techniques to make teachers more effective. Enthusiasts and administrators have sought to assist or replace teachers with the latest technology. Nevertheless, the pointed end of education policy remains the single adult in a room full of children.

The transfer of a significant measure of political power and operational authority to a collective organization can have two possible effects on the efficiency and quality of education. First, as front-line professionals, teachers might be expected to advocate for the means to be more effective, making schools more efficient and boosting student performance. On the other hand, as a group of self-interested individuals—as all human beings are—organized teachers might push for policies and resources that make their lives easier, regardless of the effects on students and taxpayers. This can lead to an increase in the cost of schooling with no change or even a decline in student performance. Of course, in the real world, the motivation of teachers' unions is a mixture of both effects, and the question is which has had the dominant effect on school policy.

The teaching profession has constantly been heaped with accolades; monarchs, ministers, and presidents have attested to its importance. Nevertheless, it is difficult to find times and places in Western history when the educators of young children and adolescents have received large amounts of deference, respect, and remuneration. In nineteenth-century Prussia, then the nation with the most organized and extensive school system, teachers were mostly from peasant and artisan backgrounds and had low social status. For support, a teacher relied on side jobs, usually as the church sexton, and the free board, free firewood, and the charity of the community. Throughout the nineteenth century, Prussian teachers were viewed with suspicion as dabblers in radical politics—another seemingly universal characteristic of the teaching profession (Schleunes 1989, 110–12, 129).

In one village in neighboring Bavaria during the early nineteenth century, the schoolmaster beat each pupil with a birch stick on Shrove Tuesday. The local peasants believed that this kept their animals from getting worms (Schleunes 1989, 84). In the United States, it is likely that few rural teachers were quite such servants of local superstition, but few were left in doubt about who was in charge. Teachers were hired directly by a board of trustees made up of parents and taxpayers. Teachers were the targets of the matrimonial wiles of the local maidens and the fists of the local swains. In the case of the latter, support from the community could not always be relied upon. After an Oregon principal came out the worse in a fight with a student, his board put him, not the student, on probation (Tyack 1974, 18–19).

Later historians called the nineteenth-century urban American school a "pedagogical harem." Women teachers were paid worse than men and faced barriers to promotion. Teachers were often hired directly by the school boards; they could be selected on the basis of an arbitrary test, political patronage, or bribery. Incompetent teachers were known to use political pull to keep their positions (Tyack 1974).

The earliest teachers' organization to gain a significant measure of influence was the Chicago Teachers' Federation (CTF) organized by Margaret Haley. In a 1904 address to the National Education Association, then a small professional organization, Haley complained that poorly paid teachers with little job security were working in overcrowded classrooms. Above all, she protested the weak voice teachers had in school policy. Schools were in danger of becoming factories, with teachers as white-collar proletarians mechanically following the instructions of their supervisors. Under Haley, the CTF fought for higher pay, pensions, tenure, and teachers' councils, and struggled against centralization of administrative power. It also extended itself into agitating for the larger reformist agenda of the day: women's suffrage, child labor laws, and higher taxes for corporations (Tyack 1974).

Despite the activity of Margaret Haley and others, teachers' unions remained a negligible force. By the early 1960s, the American Federation of Teachers (AFT), a traditional union associated with the AFL-CIO, represented only 50,000 teachers out of 1.5 million nationwide. Nearly half the teachers in the country were members of the National Education Organization (NEA), which considered itself a professional organization and opposed collective action. Its self-stated purpose was professional development. This state of affairs changed dramatically in 1961 when the AFT successfully organized the teachers in New York City. The NEA, sensing competition, reversed itself and began pushing for collective bargaining for its members as well. By 1997, 57 percent of teachers belonged to a union, up from around 27 percent in the early 1970s, and approximately 64 percent of teachers were covered by collective bargaining agreements, down from a high of nearly 70 percent in the early 1980s (Peltzman 1993; Goldin 1999, 69–70).

Determining working conditions through collective bargaining is paradoxical for members of an occupation that prides itself on being a profession. In professions like medicine and law, great weight is placed on individual skill and autonomy. Professionals provide what economists call credence goods. The key feature of a credence good is some uncertainty about the quality of service even after the good is provided. Has a doctor who lost a patient done his or her best, given the circumstances, or has he or she committed malpractice? Is a lawyer who loses a case unlucky or incompetent? Is the reason Johnny cannot read an incapable teacher or an impoverished home life? Aside from obvious cases of ineptness, it is impossible to say for certain. This is because the quality of the good—its success or failure—depends heavily upon factors outside the control of the professional: the nature of the disease, the facts of the case, the motivation of the child. Hence, we rely on the knowledge, experience, and judgment of the professional. Knowledge can be evaluated by a test, and experience can be measured by years, but scores and numbers give only an imperfect measure of individual ability. Ten years as a suburban pediatrician is different than 10 years in the emergency room of an urban hospital.

Like doctors' reactions to health maintenance organizations, teachers have resisted outsiders' trying to quantify, standardize, and second-guess their actions and decisions. This explains their opposition to policies such as merit pay. So it is ironic that working conditions for over 60 percent of teachers are determined by a method—collective bargaining on a labor contract—that stresses uniformity, standard procedures, and meticulous regulation. To cite what is probably an extreme example, the 204-page contract between the New York City Board of Education and the United Federation of Teachers covers teacher workloads, class size, pay and benefits, pensions and retirement, assignments, evaluation, promotion, dismissal, and many more issues of importance. Nationwide, teacher contracts cover programs offered by schools, teaching materials and methods, and the placement of students and teachers (Ballou 1999). The contract provisions are to ensure that teachers are paid decently, are treated fairly by administrators, and work under acceptable conditions. This is not only supposed to benefit teachers, but also to improve education by keeping morale high, allowing teachers to perform at their best, and attracting capable recruits into the profession.

Union contracts shield teachers from accountability to administrators. Whereas, 100 years ago, teachers served at the whim of school board members, principals, and functionaries of local political machines, today the pendulum has swung in the opposite direction. Contract rules require principals to justify assignments, discipline, and other personnel matters by means of thorough documentation and strict procedure. Again, this reduces the supposedly ineffable qualities of a good teacher into bullet points that can be digested by an arbitrator in a grievance hearing. Contract provisions can make it difficult to dismiss ineffective teachers.

Contract provisions hinder the professional discretion not only of administrators but also of teachers. The New York City contract, for example, specifies the teachers' workday at exactly six hours and 20 minutes. Since this is precisely the same length of time students are at school, teachers are under no obligation to talk with students before or after class, or meet with administrators outside of the allotted time. The contract specifies one 45-minute staff meeting per month. Victims of particularly grueling office meetings may consider this limit a blessing, but most would have to agree that 45 minutes can be an absurdly short time to conduct ordinary business, let alone settle serious workplace matters. The union has at times actively discouraged teachers from attending voluntary meetings with principals or parents. Restrictions on time also hinder faculty development. One principal wanted to increase instructional time by less than 5 minutes per day to free up one afternoon a month for professional development. The idea was aborted because the union would not permit a vote. Because of time restrictions, one principal believed, "We have less staff development than a worker in an auto plant" (Ballou 1999). In a perverse way, such time restrictions can preserve teacher autonomy by enabling teachers to avoid their supervisors. On the other hand, they are corrosive in that they hinder staff collaboration, administrative support, and professional development. Time restrictions also preserve union power by encouraging administrator-teacher interaction through formal, union-mediated procedures laid down in the contract.

Another feature of contracts that is contrary to the spirit of professionalism is the salary schedule. Professions, since they encompass the work of skilled individuals working alone or as part of small teams, are meritocracies. The most able are paid like rock stars; those in the middle earn a living that can range from the barely adequate to the quite comfortable; and the worst earn their living in some other occupation. The majority of teachers in public schools are paid according to a salary schedule. For the reader who may not have seen one, a salary schedule for teachers typically resembles a grid that matches years of experience with educational attainment. Where a teacher falls on the grid determines how much she or he will be paid, with additional bonuses for other credentials, such as bilingual or special education. While doctors chafe under the strict reimbursement schedules of medical insurers and government agencies, teachers' unions fiercely defend using salary schedules to determine their members' pay.

The irony of salary schedules is that they reduce the qualities of a teacher into a handful of quantifiable dimensions. Teachers resist being paid according to the test scores of their students on the grounds that scores are a narrow measure of a student's educational attainment and can be influenced by myriad factors outside the teacher's control. However, they accept and defend being paid based primarily on characteristics —seniority and credits earned—that at best are only a part of what makes an effective teacher.

The salary schedule is defended as a safeguard to prevent arbitrary compensation decisions by administrators. The danger of administrators making arbitrary and unfair salary decisions arises because teachers, unlike other professionals, are not chosen or paid directly by their clients. Competent and effective doctors and lawyers have full waiting rooms. A public school teacher's classroom is always full, regardless of competence or effectiveness. This has not always been the case. In the past, parents hired their children's teachers directly. The insertion of a layer of administration between teaching professionals and their clients was due in part to the needs of organizing schools on a large scale. However, the result is teachers who are shielded from direct accountability to their clients.

The salary schedule is also justified on the grounds of preserving teacher morale. Education, according to this justification, is a team effort among teachers, aides, and other staff members. Also, since success depends upon factors outside of a teacher's control, some teachers can be lucky or unlucky with the students they get each year. Consequently, differential pay can breed resentment in the teacher's lounge. However, basing pay and assignments on endurance and credentials limits imagination and energy in young teachers, and thus makes it difficult to attract and retain effective teachers in the first place. Southwick and Gill (1997) found that unified salary schedules make teaching uncompetitive with alternative employment opportunities for individuals with high verbal and math skills. They found that this has an adverse effect on student achievement. Salary schedules may also neutralize efforts to improve schools by raising teacher pay. Salary schedules typically cause extra funding to be backloaded, with a large fraction going toward more senior staff members. This does little to help recruit and retain young teachers, and it may encourage some of the older deadwood to defer retirement. Thus, additional funding for teacher salaries may do little to raise the ability of the teaching staff, and possibly could lower it (Ballou and Podgursky 1995b; Lankford and Wyckoff 1997).

Another feature commonly found in contracts that is contrary to the attributes of a meritocratic profession is staff assignments and protection from layoffs based on seniority. Assignments based on seniority can hamper innovation. Dale Ballou (1999) found one principal in New York who held off on implementing smaller academies within a large high school because of the individuals who were favored by contract rules to attain the positions of deans of the academies.

One final irony is that teachers' unions have sought greater professional control by bypassing local school districts and lobbying the state legislature. Recently, unions have pushed for state laws mandating that academic matters such as discipline, curriculum, teacher development, and selection of textbooks be subject to collective bargaining (Blair 2002). It is hard not to be a little sympathetic with the unions' effort. While college instructors from professors to graduate teaching aides may select books for their classes, textbook selection in public school classrooms is subject to scrutiny by school boards, outside interest groups, state committees, and U.S. senators. Yet to make textbook selection and other matters topics of collective bargaining merely makes them subject to yet another remote political process. By undertaking political action at the state and federal levels, unions contribute to the centralization of control that undermines efficiency and leads to standardization.

The Effect of Unionization on Teacher Pay

One of the most expected outcomes of unionization is higher pay for workers. Consequently, researchers were surprised that early studies of the expansion of teachers' unions during the 1960s found little initial impact on wages. This led some to speculate that public-sector unions tended to be weakened by taxpayer resistance and antipathy to striking public servants. By the mid- to late 1970s, however, there was evidence of a substantial union influence on compensation. Estimates from research range from a modest 5 percent to a whopping 22 percent differential between union and nonunion teachers. As can be expected from the nature of salary schedules, unions have a greater impact on the salaries of senior staff than of more junior teachers (Baugh and Stone 1982; Duplantis, Chandler, and Geske 1995; Chambers 1977; Hall and Carroll 1973; Hoxby 1996b; Kasper 1970; Kleiner and Petree 1988; Zwerling and Thomason 1995).

One possible reason for the larger impact over time is an increase in prounion legislation passed by state legislators during the 1970s. More states permitted teachers to bargain collectively and gave them the right to strike. However, unions have an impact even in states without state-level legislation that shelters collective bargaining by teachers (Duplantis, Chandler, and Geske 1995). Another possible reason for the growing impact on wages is that school enrollments started to decline during the 1970s, at the same time the baby boomers hit the labor market. Thus, a chronic excess supply of teachers put downward pressure on wages. At times of excess supply, it is common to see an increase in the gap between union and nonunion wages due to union success in defending the pay of their members.

Unions can have an impact outside their specific districts. They affect the entire labor market for educators in a region, causing wages to rise for union and nonunion teachers alike (Chambers 1977; Zwerling and Thomason 1995). Unions can also influence the entire labor market for teachers in a state by lobbying for legislation. Laws that toughen credentials for teachers, for example, can reduce the supply of teachers and thereby put upward pressure on wages. While unions have been found to increase the likelihood of stronger statewide certification requirements, these barriers have been found to have little effect on wages (Kleiner and Petree 1988).

Resource Allocation, Teacher Productivity, and Spending

We can expect teachers' unions to push for lower class sizes for two reasons. First, smaller classes create a better working environment for members. Second, smaller classes create a greater demand for teachers, which increases the number of potential union members. Thus, it should come as no surprise that greater union influence is linked with smaller class sizes (Eberts 1984; Hoxby 1996b). Chambers (1977), on the other hand, found that, by raising the wages of teachers regionwide, unions reduce the demand for teachers in nonunion districts, causing an overall increase in class size.

In a closer look at the impact of unionization on teachers and schools, Eberts (1984) found that collective bargaining reduced the time spent on instruction, but increased the time spent on preparation. Collective bargaining also increased the experience and education level of teachers. Finally, collective bargaining increased the number of administrative personnel per student. Hoxby (1996b) found that the impact of unions was greater in regions with fewer school districts and that unionization possibly reduced the effectiveness of school inputs. So, for example, while she found that reducing the average class size by one student lowered the dropout rate by 0.16 to 0.19 percentage points, but a one-student average decrease in class size in a unionized district only lowered the dropout rate by 0.10 to 0.16 percentage points.

With the increase in salaries and reduction in class size, we can expect that unions increase per-pupil spending. Research has found that this is indeed the case, with an increase of spending per student of 3 to 15 percent (Eberts and Stone 1986; Duplantis, Chandler, and Geske 1995; Hoxby 1996b).

Student Achievement

Finally, we turn to the most important question: what effect do teachers' unions have on student achievement? Teacher's unions are associated with factors—such as smaller class sizes and more-experienced teachers—that at first glance might seem associated with higher student achievement. However, the impact of teacher characteristics and other inputs on student achievement is far from settled. Teacher experience tends to have a positive effect. Greater teacher education and certification in general has been found to have little or even a negative effect (Eberts 1984; Goldhaber and Brewer 1997). Mark Berger and Eugenia Toma (1994) found, for example, that SAT scores are lower in states that require a master's degree for certification. However, they also found a positive impact on student achievement if additional teacher education is in the subject matter being taught.

Several studies have looked at the effect of teacher unionization on student achievement as measured by scores on the Scholastic Assessment Test (SAT) and the American College Test (ACT). Fans and detractors of teachers' unions have plenty of results to support their point of view. While Peltzman (1993, 1996) and Kurth (1987) found that expansion of teachers' unions contributed to the decline in scores on these two tests during the 1960s and 1970s, Steelman and her coauthors (2000) and Kleiner and Petree (1988) found that unionization raises student performance on the same tests. Register and Grimes (1991) made a more nuanced finding. Teacher unionization lowers the probability that students will take the SAT or ACT, but has a positive effect on the scores of students who do take the tests. In a separate study, Grimes and Register (1990) found that teacher unionization increases students' understanding of economics as measured by the Test of Economic Literacy. This may be a somewhat surprising result to those who believe that teachers' unions tend to be hostile to the field of economics.

As for studies that use other measures of student performance, Chubb and Moe (1990) found a negative effect on scores on non-SAT tests administered to high-school students due to constraints on school effectiveness caused by unions. Hoxby (1996b) found that unionization has a negative impact on the high-school dropout rate. In a more detailed examination of students in lower grades, Eberts and Stone (1987) found that for average students, teachers' unions had a positive impact of 7 percent on achievement test scores. However, they found that unions had a negative effect on students who were above or below average. Across all students, unions boost test scores by 3 percent. Martin Milkman (1997) made a similar finding regarding minority students. Unions have a positive effect on nonwhite student achievement in schools with a student body made up of primarily nonwhite students. In schools in which nonwhite students are the minority, unions have a negative impact.

The results found by Milkman and by Eberts and Stone are the effect that should be anticipated from an organization designed to influence policy through voice. The policy agenda of a union is the compromise of the collective, and the union seeks to implement its will through collective bargaining and lobbying. Hence, like all political-voice decisions, union policies aim to satisfy the broad majority in the middle rather than diverse groups at the edges. Furthermore, union policies are implemented through rules and policies laid down in contracts and legislation. It is impossible for written rules to encompass the full range of human diversity and behavior, so the act of codifying policy tends to induce standardization. Consequently, any special methods and policies that might be needed for students who are above or below average, or who make up a minority in some other way, will be stifled by the uniformity of official written procedures.

Of the studies cited, the greatest weight should be given to that of Eberts and Stone (1987). Consequently, we can conclude that unions have a modest positive impact on student achievement, at least for students near the average. This, combined with the undisputed boost unionization gives to school spending, leads to the result that unions probably have had a negative effect on productivity.

The preamble to the contract between the teachers' union and the New York City school district is a ringing call for the utter reformation of the public school:

[W]e must reinvent schools so that decision making is shared by those closest to students, including parents, teachers, administrators and other stakeholders. Layers of bureaucratic impediments must be peeled away so that flexibility, creativity, entrepreneurship, trust and risk-taking become the new reality of our schools. Before the millennium, the factory model schools of the 1900s must make way for the child-centered schools of the next century. (Ballou 1999)

Nearly a century after Margaret Haley warned of the danger of the factory school, those carrying on her legacy are still calling for its abolition. The final irony is that the actions of unions have contributed to the centralization, inflexibility, and standardization that have helped perpetuate the factory school.

PRIVATE SCHOOLS

Private schools are frequently cited as efficient education institutions. The purpose of such school-choice programs as vouchers is to give middle- and low-income students access to private schools in which education is both less expensive and more effective. Before leaving the discussion of productivity in public schools, it is worth examining whether private schools are really better at teaching young Americans. In terms of achievement, research on private schools has not yielded results that dramatically tilt the balance in the school-choice debate to either side. Readers who have picked their way through the uncertainties plaguing the research on public school achievement should not be surprised to learn that evidence on the superiority of private schools is ambiguous as well.

This discussion of public and private schools is also intended to bludg-
eon the reader with the idea that there are dimensions of private and
public schools important to parents and students that social scientists can
only tenuously grasp. This not only complicates the life of the researcher,
but also poses a larger problem for the policymakers the researcher is
seeking to inform. School characteristics that cannot be reduced to standard statistical measures make it difficult for centralized, bureaucratic systems to measure school performance comprehensively enough to capture
all that a parent or student might find important in a school. Thus, policies
to hold schools accountable to ever higher levels of bureaucracy have the
inherent danger of diverging from the desires and needs of parents and
children.

Figure 2.2 shows NAEP scores for seniors in private high schools. The
scores are higher than the national averages, but private-school scores
have remained flat for the 20 years during which the NAEP tracked performance for them. In addition to higher test scores, private-school students are more likely than public-school students to graduate high school
and attend college. They are also more likely to attend elite colleges and
study math, science, or engineering (Figlio and Stone 1999).

Are private schools better schools, or do they have better students? This
debate has raged for 20 years, fed by the growing movement for school

Figure 2.2
NAEP Scores for Nonpublic Schools

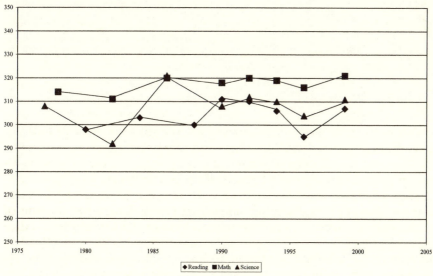

Source: Campbell, Hombo, and Mazzeo (2000).

choice. The commonly cited ignition point is a 1981 study comparing achievement in public and private schools by James Coleman, Sally Kilgore, and Thomas Hoffer, which concluded that Catholic and other private schools are more effective in educating students than their public counterparts.

This study has been repeatedly criticized for failing to adequately control for student characteristics. Consequently, it spawned an army of researchers who unsheathed sharper statistical techniques to determine whether private schools are superior educators, or if they are just selecting and being selected by brighter, wealthier, or more motivated students and parents. The research commonly focuses on Catholic schools because they account for the majority of private schools, and hence provide a database large enough for rigorous statistical analysis.

After employing various statistical methods to control for selection effect, researchers have found varied results for academic achievement in private schools. When achievement is measured by performance on standardized tests, some studies find that private school students outperform their peers in public schools. Performance differs by subject, with private school students doing better in mathematics, reading, writing, and vocabulary, but not in science or civics. The margin of superiority found by several studies was 0.1 standard deviations—equal to two extra grade levels over a four-year high-school career. Other studies that have examined the effect of private schools on test scores have found no difference between public and private schools. For other measures of academic achievement, however, research has consistently found that, even after controlling for selection effects, private-school students are more likely to graduate high school, attend college, attend a selective college, and graduate from college. Private high schools increase graduation rates from 10 to 26 percentage points—a huge difference (Altonji, Elder, and Taber 2002; Figlio and Stone 1999; Goldhaber 1996, 1999; Neal 1998).

Research consistently finds that the impact on graduation rates from attending private schools is greatest for African American and Hispanic students living in large cities, while the benefits tend to be smaller or vanish altogether for white students and for students who live in suburban and rural areas. For example, one study found no effect of private school attendance on graduation rates in rural areas (Sander 1997). Another estimated an 11 percentage point improvement for private schools over public schools in suburban areas, but a 17 percentage point margin in large cities (Evans and Schwab 1995). Neal found that attending private schools raised graduation rates 10 percentage points for urban whites and 26 percentage points for urban Hispanics and African Americans. For urban minorities, this increase in education attainment could lift their wages as adults by 8 percent (Neal 1998).

Neal argues that the impact of private schools was a result of the poor condition of public schools in large cities. These failed all children who attended them, and nonwhite students in particular. In the suburbs and rural areas, the graduation rates for white and nonwhite students were essentially the same once family background and community characteristics were taken into account. For large cities, however, graduation rates drop for all students, especially for nonwhite students, so that even after family background is taken into account, nonwhite students are less likely to graduate than their white counterparts (Neal 1998).

The narrow difference in academic quality of public and private schools, in the suburbs at least, is borne out by other measures. Although private school teachers were more likely to have graduated from more-selective colleges, public school teachers tended to have taken a greater number of courses in their fields of specialty. Students in private schools took fewer math and science classes, and the science classes were inferior to those in public schools in certain ways. Students in public schools spent more time in class and in the laboratory and conducted experiments more frequently. Private school teachers assigned less math and science homework than public school teachers, and were less likely to grade homework and return it to students (Figlio and Stone 1999).

Why do many parents go to extra expense to send their children to private schools? Several studies have looked at which sociodemographic populations were more likely to send their children to private schools (Betts and Fairlie 2001; Buddin, Cordes, and Kirby, 1998; Gemello and Osman 1984; Goldhaber 1996; Hamilton and MacCauley 1991; Lankford and Wyckoff 1992; Schmidt 1992; Wrinkle, Stewart, and Polinard, 1999). Wealthier and more educated parents have been found to be more likely to send their children to private schools, as have older and single parents. Despite the inconclusive evidence regarding the superiority of private schools, they still tend to be the choice of the elite. This cannot be dismissed as simple snobbery, since the elite are also likely to live in exclusive neighborhoods with public schools that are also filled with the offspring of the privileged.

Large Catholic and African American populations are almost universally found to have a positive effect on private school enrollment. The influence of the number of Catholics is due to the Catholic Church's long tradition of operating an independent school system. The increase in private school attendance caused by a large African American population raises the disturbing prospect of white flight and segregation academies. Goldhaber (1996) found that parents are sensitive to the racial composition of schools, with nonwhite as well as white parents preferring schools with a large percentage of white students. However, he also found that African American parents were more likely than whites to send their children to private schools. Similarly, Figlio and Stone (1999) detected no difference in the probability that white and nonwhite parents would send their children to private schools.

A different conclusion is that parents living in more diverse communities—either in income, race, or education level—are more likely to prefer private schools. White parents tend to send their children to private schools when the minority population is larger; college educated parents are more inclined to choose private schools when there are fewer college-educated adults in the community; and wealthy parents are more likely to choose private schools if their neighbors are less wealthy (Figlio and Stone 1999; Hamilton and MacCauley 1991; Schmidt 1999). This should not be dismissed as plain bigotry, racism, or snobbery. Public schools are the result of a compromise among diverse groups, and policies and procedures—from the school board to the classroom—reflect middle ground reached by a process of communal decision making. It is natural, then, that the odd family out will be more dissatisfied with the result. Race, income, and education are proxies for differences in values, priorities, and tastes that are inherent in human nature but cannot be captured by the social scientist's data set.

Parents may also select schools based on characteristics not measured by most studies, which typically focus on test scores. When asked, private school parents cite religion and other values, discipline, and academic rigor as the primary reasons for choosing to send their children to private schools (Crawford and Freeman 1996; Lankford and Wyckoff 1992). Private schools rate higher in instructional quality, discipline, safety, and peer relations. Public schools rate higher in academic freedom and job counseling. Private school students are 245 percent more likely to be expelled for possessing alcohol, 62 percent more likely to be expelled for possessing a weapon, and 170 percent more likely to be expelled for injuring another student. The extra emphasis religious schools might place on values and discipline does not necessarily lead to more upright behavior by students. Although children attending religious private schools are less likely to use cocaine, engage in sexual activity, or be arrested, they are just as likely as their public school peers to drink, smoke tobacco and marijuana, and be involved with a gang (Figlio and Stone 1999; Figlio and Ludwig 2000; Morgan 1983).

Parents are sensitive to school quality as measured by class size, spending, and test scores. Smaller classes and high test scores attract parents to private schools, while low levels of spending cause them to leave the public ones (Goldhaber 1996). There are also subtler differences between the two types of schools. Private schools tend to be more focused than public schools. Public schools offer students more academic and social variety—a feature that is appreciated by both students and public school officials. Powell and his coauthors quote a public-school student who prefers her public high school because there was nothing to do at the local parochial school "except go to classes all day." They also cite a PTA leadership that was proud of the "buffet" their public school offered compared to the "sit-down dinner" of the local private school. At their school, they boasted, "You can take as hard or as easy a program as you like" (Powell, Farrar, and Cohen 1985, 10, 41).

The reader should not draw conclusions about the academic quality of public and private schools from these statements. Powell and his coauthors found that the public schools they studied had academic and extracurricular programs equal or superior to those in private schools. What private schools did offer, they concluded, was focus, attention, prodding, direction, discipline, and cosseting. Some students needed this; others did not. They told the story of two brothers, one who thrived in the larger environment of the public school, the other who needed the attention and support of a private school. The brother attending private school found greater opportunity to participate in extracurricular activities (Powell, Farrar, and Cohen 1985, 195–196). This is true of private schools in general; private school students are 28 percent more likely than public school students to participate in extracurricular activities such as sports, cheerleading, drama, music, school government, yearbook, or the school newspaper (Figlio and Stone 1999).

Even more telling are the stories of Carlos and Glenn, who actually switched to each other's school. Carlos—self-directed, talented, and at the top of his class—took accelerated classes at his public high school that were as good, he felt, as those at the private school he left, and he was glad to be free of the rules and babying that constricted him at the private school. Glenn, on the other hand, left the public school Carlos attended to go to the private school that Carlos had abandoned. Describing himself as a "person in the middle," Glenn preferred the clear mission of the private school—to prepare students for college—to his old public school, a "big babysitting service" that allowed students to drift if they so chose (Powell, Farrar, and Cohen 1985, 198).

The experiences of students like Glenn and Carlos call into question the methodology of the research program that has compared public and private schools, and what that research program can say about school choice. While economic theory has been accused of trying to mimic theoretical physics, empirical economics, as applied to the question of private and public schools, has aspired to emulate medical research studies. The model framing the research is that there are two types of schools: public schools, which are centralized, bureaucratic, unionized, heavily regulated, and governed through politics; and private schools, which are selective, disciplined, and subject to market forces, and have nuns. To determine differences between the two, the researcher would ideally like to assign students randomly to the two schools, as in a drug test: Group A would take the experimental pill or go to a private school, Group B would receive a placebo or attend a public school. Indeed, some researchers have had the opportunity to do just that. Most, however, are not so fortunate. They must study situations in which the parents have done the choosing. In these cases, the researcher tries through statistical wizardry to manipulate the data as if students were randomly assigned. The assumption is that choice is a function of factors such as income, race, and religion that have no effect on school quality (Murnane 1984).

The result of this effort is supposed to be an answer to the question: Which institution is better, public or private? If the answer is private, then the commonly prescribed policies are that public schools should seek to emulate private schools, or barriers that prevent students from attending private schools should be lowered through some type of school choice program. However, the stories of Carlos and Glenn show that it is possible that no institution is uniformly better for all students. By neutralizing the effects of choice and solely examining differences in governance, the researcher is looking at the wrong question. It is the ability to choose, not the form of governance, that benefits students.

A confident analyst may counter that the studies finding no significant difference between the two types of schools demonstrate, in effect, that whatever Carlos and Glenn told their interlocutors, they would have done just as well by choosing a school with the flip of a coin. This assumes that the analysis is able to account for student characteristics such as a taste for independence and need for support—characteristics that we have seen may vary between brothers in the same family. This is a tall order for the typical research study. Moreover, the conclusion that there is no difference between the two types of schools flies in the face of the fact that many parents go to considerable expense to send children to private schools. Unless one is willing to dismiss them all as bigots and snobs, consumer sovereignty must be given its due: adults allowed to choose freely tend to make decisions that benefit them and their children—even if the researcher cannot detect the reasons behind their decisions. Thus, even though there is enough ambiguity in the evidence to provide ammunition to doubters, there is a compelling case for school choice to help other Glenns who are prevented by financial factors from attending schools more suitable to them.

Although school governance may not affect test scores, it can make a difference in cost. There is no doubt that private schools are less costly than public ones (Figure 2.3). The efficiency advantage of private schools has been estimated to be 30 percent (Cohen-Zada and Justman n.d.). Since private schools have an apparent advantage in productivity, and because parents do not have to pay additional tuition to send children to public schools, while private schools charge tuition, the present system has the perverse incentive of inducing parents to choose the more costly alter-

Figure 2.3
Private and Public Per-Pupil Spending

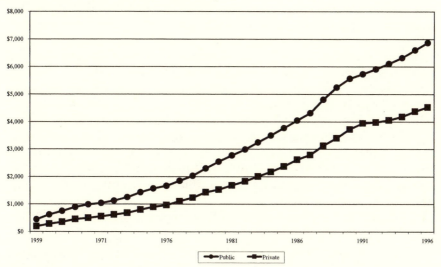

Source: U.S. Department of Education (1998a, 2002).

native. This can lead to a substantial waste of society's resources (Sonstelie 1982).

CONCLUSION

This chapter has reviewed six possible reasons why the productivity of schools may have declined over the past several decades. Of the six, only one, the changing demographics of the American population, can be dismissed due to lack of support. Of the remaining five, only two—teachers' unions and alternative priorities—have a relatively greater impact on public schools than on private ones. The remaining three—the Baumol disease, diminishing returns, and the changes in the teaching corps—have the potential to affect both public and private schools equally. Even though both private and public schools must cope with the Baumol disease and competition with other professions for prospective teachers, it is likely that private schools have a greater ability to adapt to these factors.

Given the importance of good teachers, the most productive schools are those that are best able to recruit and retain high-quality instructors. This is an area in which private schools have an apparent edge. In a pair of studies, Dale Ballou and Michael Podgursky (1995a; 1998) found that private school principals are more satisfied with their teachers than are their public school counterparts. They also found that private schools do a better job than public schools in retaining and developing their best new teachers. The researchers attribute this success to greater flexibility by private schools in personnel decisions, including pay and dismissal, and more mentoring and supervision of new teachers in private schools.

On the other hand, the standard policies in public schools—such as salary schedules—make it difficult to improve teacher quality. The typical policy initiative to improve teacher quality, an across-the-board pay raise may even reduce the quality of the teaching corps (Ballou and Podgursky 1995b). There is evidence that public-sector administrators can be indifferent to teacher quality. Dale Ballou (1996) found that a graduate with a high undergraduate grade-point average does have a better chance of finding a teaching job, other aspects of academic background—such as the quality of college attended and a degree or certification in math or science—do not. Ballou attributes this to lack of incentives for administrators to value these characteristics.

This is not to say public schools cannot obtain good teachers. The pay and benefits offered by public schools make them highly attractive. Private schools, however, are likely to be superior in quality of teacher per dollar of salary spent. An education system that persists in providing incentives for parents to use the less flexible, more costly alternative will continue to cost the nation a significant amount of resources.

NOTE

1. For those unfamiliar with statistical analysis, there is a difference between finding a positive effect and finding a statistically positive effect. Although a procedure to calculate and estimate may produce a positive value, variation in the data might make it impossible to state with a conventional level of confidence that the estimate is significantly different from zero.

CHAPTER 3

Creating the American High School

After the shootings at Columbine High School in Littleton, Colorado, Leon Botstein, the president of Bard College, called for the abolition of the traditional high school (Botstein 1999). Too many students, he felt, were marking time in a limbo that bore little resemblance to the real world. A national commission sponsored by the federal government and several foundations, including the Carnegie Corporation (like Harvard presidents, an eternal presence in education policy), fingered the high school as the weakest link in the chain of American education (National Commission on the High School Senior Year 2001). American students, who when young perform better than their peers in other nations on most international comparisons, fall behind by the time they reach high school.

One of the great achievements of twentieth-century American education was opening up secondary education to all the nation's youth. Yet the institution created by this achievement, the modern American high school, has continuously been at the eye of a storm of controversy over weak academic standards and performance. The political compromises that formed the high school made it egalitarian and forgiving, with a curriculum for students of every ability and aspiration. Furthermore, there are weak incentives for students to do well in high school. The nation's decentralized school system has hindered the creation of uniform standards and exams for high-school graduates on a national or even state level. In a nation with a highly mobile population, this has caused the depreciation of high school accomplishments by employers. Also, opening higher education to more students has similarly enabled students to enter college who have exerted minimal effort while in high school.

The modern American high school embodies the different trajectories of American education over the past century, both upward and downward. It is a model case study of how governance through voice has formed the nation's schools.

THE GREAT HIGH SCHOOL BOOM

The typical person who follows modern public policy discussions has likely gained the impression that the United States is a laggard compared to other advanced nations in the scope and generosity of its government programs to help children, the elderly, and the poor. The habitual consumer of newspaper editorials, academic tomes, and cable television roundtable discussions has no doubt heard much about labor benefits in Germany, early childhood education in France, health care in Canada, and elder care in Sweden. He or she has probably concluded—with either regret or satisfaction—that America's ethic of cowboy individualism has left it the odd nation out among its fellows across the globe.

Yet, as Theda Skocpol (1992) found, this perception is historically wrong. The United States government was one of the first modern nations to create a system to support the elderly. A wide-ranging and generous system to provide pensions for Civil War veterans and their survivors compared favorably to the nascent social security systems of other nations. Originating in federal legislation that was passed while battles between the Blue and the Gray still raged, the American old-age pension system predates that of Germany (1889), New Zealand (1898), and Great Britain (by 1908). By 1910, 28 percent of American men over 65, in addition to more than 300,000 widows and orphans of Civil War veterans, received pensions from the federal government that were substantially more generous than the those offered by governments of other nations. One observer commented: "Many of the old men and women who, in Europe, would be found in almshouses are found in the United States living upon pensions with their children or in homes to which paupers are not sent" (Skocpol 1992, xx).

The fate of the veterans' and survivors' pensions is one of those twists of irony that make history entertaining as well as instructive. The Grand Army of the Republic, after all, was a solid constituency of the Republican Party. Consequently, good-government advocates and progressive reformers, including Charles Eliot, the leading Mugwump and the president of Harvard University, denounced the veterans' pensions as blatant political patronage and profligate fiscal policy. Eliot was so disgusted by the abuse of the pension system by Republicans, in addition to Democrat Grover Cleveland's amenable stance on tariffs and civil service reform, that he announced he was switching to support the Democratic party (Skocpol 1992, 1). Advocates of responsible government got their wish.

Despite the desire and efforts of trade union officials and reformers to expand the veterans' and survivors' pension system into a universal support program, it was allowed to die with its beneficiaries.

Another social service in which the United States was among the world pioneers is public support for and access to education. The mid-nineteenth century saw the expansion of common or grammar schools, causing the U.S. school enrollment rate to be second in the world behind Germany. In 1850, 68 percent of American children between 5 and 14 were enrolled in school. By contrast, 73 percent of Prussian children, 52 percent of French children, and 50 percent of children in England and Wales were enrolled in primary school. At the beginning of the twentieth century, the United States led the world with a primary school enrollment rate of 94 percent. Britain's English-speaking colonies also ranked high: Canada at 90 percent, Australia at 87 percent, and New Zealand at 88 percent. By contrast, the enrollment rate in Germany was 73 percent (77 percent in Prussia alone), in France 86 percent, and in the United Kingdom 74 percent (Lindert 2001).

Figure 3.1, which shows the enrollment rates for primary and secondary schools in the United States between 1900 and 1993, displays another leap forward by the U.S. education system: the expansion of free public high schools. The proportion of young Americans between 14 and 17 years old

Figure 3.1
Enrollment Rates in Public and Private Schools

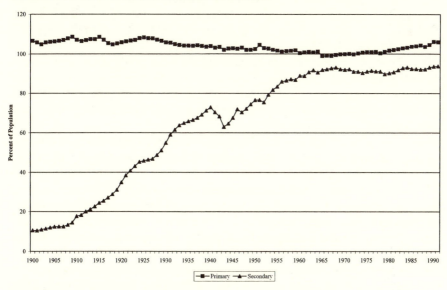

Source: U.S. Department of Education (2002).

attending high school doubled from 10.6 percent in 1900 to 20 percent before WWI. From 1910 to 1999, the high school graduation rate (the fraction of 17-year-olds that had a diploma) increased over six times. Even this statistic hides the rapidity of the increase: in 1910, only 8.8 percent of 17-year-olds graduated from high school; by 1938, 50 percent of 17-year-olds earned high school diplomas (Goldin and Katz 1997).

By the mid-1920s, the growth of high schools put the United States well ahead of other nations in schooling youth. The school enrollment rate of 5- to 19-year-olds was 90 percent in the United States, compared to 63 percent in France, 70 percent in Germany, and 69 percent in Great Britain. It would take other countries over 30 years to catch up. Great Britain did not guarantee a free secondary school education until the Labour Government passed the 1944 Education Act—the same year Franklin Roosevelt signed into law the GI Bill of Rights. By the mid-1950s, the full-time school enrollment for 15- to 19-year-olds was 80 percent in the United States, while in western Europe it was greater than 30 percent only among the Scandinavian nations. In no western European country were more than 50 percent of 15- to 19-year olds enrolled in school full time (Goldin 2001). Today, the United States has lost its lead in school enrollment. Indeed, for 15- to 19-year-olds, it is no longer above average among the developed nations (OECD 2000).

This boom was to profoundly transform the American high school. Once preparatory academies for a small group of students bound for college or certain white-collar jobs, high schools became educational bazaars that offered instructional alternatives that could lead to college, the factory, or the home. These changes were the result of a struggle among parents, taxpayers, business and labor leaders, and educators—both practicing and academic—over the purpose of education. What is the best way to turn children into productive workers and effective citizens? Is it by giving all students instruction in the fundamental academic subjects? Or is it by allowing students, based on their talents and ambitions, to choose from among several specialized scholarly and nonscholarly courses of study (or to choose for them)? Although the political compromise agreed upon 100 years ago was specialization, we still are debating whether this was a good decision. Critics contend that the diversity of classes has led to a decline in academic standards, while proponents argue for the multiple nonacademic purposes of education. Both sides are correct to some extent, but it is worth noting that the debate itself is fed by the fact that children are educated in institutions controlled by voice, which must be tailored to serve all interests. With a more flexible form of school governance such as school choice, parents could choose the form of education that best suited their children, and the debate would be literally and solely academic. With the barriers to choice in the present system, however, public schools become a brass ring to be captured by the latest movements in education reform that sweep the nation.

PUBLIC CHOICE AND PUBLIC EDUCATION

The reasons for the high-school boom and the expansion of public education in general range from the naïve and triumphal to the sophisticated and cynical. Almost invariably, the reasons offered by scholars imagine public education as something created by an elite group—motivated either by philanthropy or self-interest—and imposed on the masses. This chapter takes the opposite position. U.S. public schools were the creation of taxpayers and parents in local communities through a democratic process. The decisions made by voters in each community were influenced by economic and social factors such as immigration, emigration, increases in wealth, and technology that was transforming the workplace. Their decisions were also influenced by, or at least paid lip service to, the ideas emanating from colleges of education, universities, churches, business coalitions, and activists of every type. Ultimately, however, American schools were shaped by local compromises that absorbed and adjusted to various influences and movements.

Since before the days of Horace Mann, advocates of the expansion of public schooling have seen their mission as lighting a lamp against the darkness. They have tended to characterize their opponents as being too stingy and short-sighted to pay for the oil, as religious zealots unhappy with too much illumination shed on wicked and erroneous beliefs, and as general lovers of darkness. The sense of mission and triumphal pride in what public school advocates had accomplished suffused the histories in which they recorded their achievements.

These histories, churned out by scholars for the most part located in schools of education, were narratives describing the victory of the forces of progress, embodied in public education, over bigots, reactionaries, provincials, and skinflint businessmen. What was scripture for initiates in the public school crusade was seen as narrow, uncritical, moralistic, and generally uninfluential by scholars outside the band of believers (Ravitch 1978, ch. 2; Vinovskis 1985, 9). Historian Bernard Bailyn dismissed it as "the patristic literature of a powerful academic ecclesia," written by "educational missionaries" almost completely isolated from "the major influences and shaping minds of twentieth-century historiography" (Bailyn 1960, 8–9).

Harsh words, but one mustn't condemn the education historians too severely. Like many reformers, they believed that the institutions they created and served acted solely in the public's interest. Seminal histories of American education were written during the Progressive Era, when trustbusters and muckrakers thought that public institutions in the hands of well-intentioned experts could regulate industry and shape society in beneficial ways. This belief impelled the great waves of state action during the New Deal and the Great Society, and it is still commonly held by the public today. Discovering that government agencies and regulatory bodies are under the sway of special interests may not surprise modern social scientists, whose cynicism has been honed to a needle-sharp point, but the general public still expresses surprise and outrage at special interest influence.

The belief that public institutions are created and operated solely to promote the general welfare has come under attack from both the left and the right. Economists have reexamined a century of government regulation and found that much of it benefited certain groups at the expense of the general public. Theories were developed and statistical tests were done showing how legislators and regulators were "captured" in "iron triangles" by special interests (Viscusi, Vernon, and Harrington 1992, 308–25).

The canon of the Great School Legend was assailed by a cohort of historians who came to be known as revisionists. The revisionists were radical-left critics of the liberal, post-WWII status quo. Their work gave historical roots to the radical criticisms of the public schools that were widespread at the time: that public schools were unjust, coercive, moralistic, and racist. The debate launched by the revisionists was typical of many postwar historical controversies, pitting radical-left critics of the institutions created during the Progressive Era and New Deal against liberal-left defenders (Hamby 1992). Whatever one's thoughts about their politics and conclusions, it is widely acknowledged that the revisionists brought much-needed critical thinking and strong empirical methods to the study of education history (Vinovskis 1985, 9).

After over 40 years of scholarship, historians, economists, political scientists, and sociologists have unearthed numerous interest groups that are alleged to have tried to influence the growth of public education to their particular benefit in countries around the world. Following Peter Lindert (2001), they have been classified in the following bestiary.

Landed aristocrats. Also called "educational Tories" by Kaestle (1976), these are found mostly in Europe and in the American South. They are predominantly landowners and aristocrats ensconced in castles and manor houses who worry that educating the lower classes will upset the social order. Bernard Mandeville's 1723 criticism of charity schools and education of the poor articulates their objections:

The Welfare and Felicity therefore of every State and Kingdom, require that the Knowledge of the Working Poor should be confin'd within the Verge of their Occupations, and never extended (as to things visible) beyond what relates to their Calling. The more a Shepherd, a Plowman or any other Peasant knows of the

World, and the things that are Foreign to his Labour or Employment, the less fit he'll be to go through the Fatigues and Hardships of it with Chearfulness and Content. (Mandeville 1989 [1723], 294)

A hundred years later, the same arguments could still be read in Great Britain—albeit with more modern orthography—in newspapers, essays, sermons, and transcripts of parliamentary debates. Education, the educational Tories said, would make the lower classes discontented with their lot, insubordinate, and refractory, and leave their minds vulnerable to Jacobinism and religious dissent (Kaestle 1976).

Educational Tories were rare in the United States. Only when it came to educating slaves was there significant opposition to mass education on the grounds of the danger it posed to social stability. In response to slave rebellions and the dissemination of abolitionist tracts, slave codes prohibited educating slaves. An 1836 pamphlet entitled *The South Vindicated from the Treason and Fanaticism of the Northern Abolitionists* (published in Philadelphia!) asserted that educating slaves would leave them unfit for their station in life and foster insurrection. Besides, education would only burden the slaves with cares and anxieties; they naturally prefer their "rustic pleasures" (Kaestle 1976).

Capitalists. The modern bourgeois capitalist, unlike the rustic aristocrat, prefers to bolster education to preserve social stability. The typical narrative of education as capitalist social control starts with the decline of independent artisans, yeomen farmers, and small shopkeepers into an urban proletariat. Added into the mix in the United States are immigrants—Irish, German, Italian, and Jewish—whose different manners, religions, and languages threaten the WASP elite. Ever present, and even more outcast, are the nation's African Americans. In these scenarios, the conditions faced by the working class are always precarious and increasingly dire, despite decades of technological progress and economic growth. Naturally, this leads to unrest and the risk of society exploding. Formal schooling in bourgeois-controlled schools is the prescription to convert the dangerous proletariat into a docile and productive workforce.

Government. Rulers who are more enlightened than the landed gentry realize that an educated workforce is a productive workforce; and a more productive workforce means the government—be it controlled by nineteenth-century autocrats, twentieth-century dictators, or welfare-state bureaucracies—has more to appropriate and redistribute (McGuire and Olson 1996). In addition to enhancing productivity, indoctrination through public education may also make the tasks of ruling and redistribution easier. John Lott (n.d.) has found that societies that are totalitarian, or in which there are high levels of government wealth transfers, tend to have government-controlled media (television) and spend more on public education. Lindert (2001), to the contrary, finds that more democratic nations have historically been more supportive of education.

In addition to ensuring domestic tranquility, education can also reinforce the national defense. Napoleon is credited with spurring Prussian support of education by trouncing Prussia's army on the battlefield at Jena-Auerstadt in 1806 and imposing the humiliating Treaty of Tilsit. From the ashes of defeat, Prussia launched the "good revolution from above." It dismantled the remaining vestiges of the old feudal order by fully emancipating peasants, allowing burghers to own land, and permitting nobles to engage in commerce; it created a conscript army, allowed municipal self-government, and promised full civil equality for Jews. Finally, it established modern government ministries including a Ministry of the Interior, within which was a Section for Worship and Public Instruction. The section's first head was the scholar and statesman Wilhelm von Humboldt (Schleunes 1989, 3, 50, 66–68).

Sixty-four years later, Prussia in turn annihilated the French army at Sedan, a victory that some Frenchmen attributed in part to Prussia's schoolmasters. The shock of defeat demolished political barriers to the centralization of education in France. In 1881, tuition and fees for public elementary schools were abolished, and teachers were put on the national government's payroll (Lindert 2001). Similarly, the Soviet victory in the first leg of the space race with the launch of *Sputnik* helped smash resistance to a greater federal role in education in the United States, leading to passage of the National Defense Education Act in 1958 (Ravitch 1983, 229).

The education establishment. Finally, as an organized body of self-interested individuals, educators can seek not only to do good, but also to do well. Three main characteristics of American public schools established in the nineteenth century—tax financing, exclusive attendance boundaries, and compulsory attendance—can not only be attributed to philanthropic or paternalistic motives, but also to the creation and protection of an education monopoly (West 1967).

Early in the nineteenth century, it was common for a child's education to be financed through a combination of tax monies and rates paid by parents. This meant that if a dissatisfied parent left, he would take his rate payment with him. Consequently, abolishing rates and supporting schools wholly through taxes diminishes the ability of individual parents to select schools. When tax money is divided among schools based on the number of students attending, mandatory attendance boundaries and compulsory education laws ensure market share for inferior schools. Boundaries force parents to send their children to the school mandated by the state, even if they would prefer the children to travel to more desirable options. Truly dissatisfied parents may take their children out of school to teach them at home or—a more viable option 200 years ago—to put them to work. Compulsory education permits the government school to close off these options if it so chooses.

Eugenia Toma (1983) has found modern evidence of self-interested action by the education establishment. Toma hypothesized that state education boards whose members are appointed would be more easily influenced by such special interests as teachers, school administrators, and local boards than state boards whose members were elected and hence more accountable to the public. As the chief state regulators of education, boards under the influence of the education establishment could enact policies that the establishment prefers. Toma found that in states with appointed state board members, per-pupil spending, teacher salaries, and the number of administrative staff per pupil were higher than in states with elected state board members. Class sizes were smaller. Using enrollment in private schools as a proxy measure of school quality, Toma found that enrollment in private schools was lower in states with elected state boards of education. This indicates that the public was more satisfied with schools in states with elected boards.

The net effect of self-interested action by the education establishment on the overall level of schooling is unclear. The steady flow of tax dollars would seem to ensure the expansion of education. However, taxpayers can occasionally be reluctant, and tax financing may cause some children to receive less education than if their parents wholly paid the cost of schooling. Furthermore, opening up education to the masses in the nineteenth century meant making the curriculum more practical and less difficult. Thus, instructors of Greek and Latin and other masters of the traditional curriculum may resist mass education (Lindert 2001; West 1967).

All the specimens in this bestiary—whether squires, bishops, government ministers, or industrial tycoons—represent some facet of the elite establishment. They are not mutually exclusive, and many can be found in the same country, at the same time, and even in the same person. The predecessor agency of Prussia's Section for Worship and Instruction was called the Department for Schools and Poor Relief. Poor Horace Mann has been the target of darts from both the left and the right as a capitalist ally, a promoter of a self-aggrandizing education establishment, an advocate of social control, and an intellectual cousin of the Ku Klux Klan (Rothbard 1974). The idea that public education originated as an instrument of the elite suits scholars of both the left and the right. For both libertarians and radical-leftists, it confirms the notion of schools as soul-destroying conformity factories, the only difference being the particular values to which students are being conformed. Relatively neglected has been the role that parents and taxpayers themselves have played in shaping public education (Laqueur 1976).

THE HIGH SCHOOL BOOM AS CAPITALIST CONTROL

Capitalists, collaborators in the Progressive Movement, and the new social scientists are the forces usually placed behind the expansion of high school enrollment in the United States at the beginning of the twentieth century. Like American elites during the previous hundred years, the American establishment at the end of the nineteenth century had to cope with social strains caused by technological change and waves of immigration. The Industrial Revolution undoubtedly was changing the nature of work in America. According to several modern histories of education, this change almost invariably caused a decline in the skills needed by workers (Edson 1982; Nasaw 1979). Mechanization and the division of labor turned artisans and craftsmen responsible for fashioning entire products into machine tenders with ever more specific and repetitive duties. Making a pair of men's pants, for example, once had been the job of a single tailor, but by 1859 it had been split (no pun intended) in some factories into 17 different tasks (Edson 1982). Added to this was the new "scientific management" personified by Frederick W. Taylor. Men, these histories contend, became mere extensions of machines.

According to the typical account, the new nature of the American workplace had several consequences for the American laborer—all of them bad. First to go was worker control over the workplace. An independent artisan in his own shop could set his own hours, opening and closing when he chose—perhaps taking a break to enjoy cider and a political discussion with a visiting neighbor. The modern worker had no power over his or her workplace. The time and pace of the job was set by the time clock and the assembly line, with constant monitoring by the growing ranks of technical and supervisory personnel with their Taylorist ideas and time-and-motion studies. Factory work also destroyed pride in work, identity, creativity, and self-worth.

In traditional American republicanism, independent artisans took their place beside yeomen farmers as free labor. Unlike wage laborers, free laborers were independent, not beholden to squire or boss. More than putting food on the table, free labor instilled the virtues needed by citizens in a democracy: industriousness, temperance, individual initiative, and social harmony. Americans of all classes were worried that importing the factory system from Europe would degrade the worker. Being a wage earner, journeyman, or apprentice was a temporary condition during which the individual could acquire a skill and save seed capital, with the ultimate goal of becoming an independent proprietor (Sandel 1996).

In the story of the origins of public schooling told by modern revisionist historians, the republican ideal of work as a school for citizenship and the hope of upward mobility was crushed by the factory system. Falling real wages and repeated economic downturns made it difficult for would-be entrepreneurs in the working class to accumulate the capital to strike out on their own. By the end of the nineteenth century, middle-class moralists—who had believed that economic success was a matter of ambition, good morals, a modest education, and pluck—realized that the traditional ladder of success had rotted away (Nasaw 1979).

The new industrial order led to worker unrest. Discipline fell; workers kept irregular hours, took part in slowdowns and work restrictions, constantly switched jobs, went on strike, and voted for socialist candidates. Studies in the first decades of the twentieth century found that the average worker moved to a new job every three years. In 1913, the Ford Motor Company suffered a turnover rate of 370 percent; in 1914, the Armour meat packing plant experienced a 100 percent turnover of its workforce (Edson 1982). The Knights of Labor—whose membership was over 700,000 in 1886—called for abolishing the wage system; government control of railways, telephones, and the telegraph network; and a mandatory eight-hour day. In 1892, Pinkerton agents and striking steelworkers fought it out in Homestead, Pennsylvania, using rifles, dynamite, flaming oil, and artillery. Eventually, the National Guard was called in to settle the strike. Two years later, nearly to the day, President Cleveland used federal troops to end the Pullman strike.

At the same time industrialists were combating worker agitation, their associates among the intellectuals, humanitarians, and moralists in the elite classes were worried about unrest among America's youth. Social workers, educators, writers, ministers, university professors, and other members of the establishment intelligentsia had discovered a stage in human development between the child and the adult: the adolescent. Credit for the discovery of the adolescent is commonly given to psychologist G. Stanley Hall—the flamboyant president of Clark University, student of William James, and teacher of John Dewey, who was the first person in the United States to earn a doctorate in psychology. Hall's views are described as being imbued with both Social Darwinism and the romanticism of Jean-Jacques Rousseau. Somewhat of a Progressive Era Dr. Spock, Hall filled the pages of the academic and popular press with his theories on child rearing. The establishment saw the adolescent as a dangerous brew of antisocial, criminal, and sexual urges. The cities of America were teeming with these dangerous individuals, who had no money, no entertainment, and no way to occupy themselves constructively (Ravitch 2000, 69–72; Nasaw 1979, 88–99). This problem was exacerbated by technological improvements that were eliminating jobs typically filled by adolescents.

In histories that see public education as an instrument of capitalist social control, both capitalists and moralizing child-savers found a common tool to deal with the social and economic problems of industrializing America: the public high school. The idea that a high school education would benefit large numbers of American youth was novel. In nineteenth-century America, a grammar school education was all that was commonly believed necessary to succeed in life. The youth who with hard work and little education rose from humble origins to the top had been an American archetype since Ben Franklin. Henry Ford went to school in a one-room schoolhouse and left home at 16 to become an apprentice machinist. The railroad mogul James J. Hill had only 9 years of formal education, although 4 of these were spent in a private high school run by a Quaker minister. Hill began his first job as the clerk in a general store when he was 15. His adversary E. H. Harriman created the modern American railroad and rose to head the Union Pacific despite leaving school at the age of 14. He started as a "pad shover" on Wall Street—one of the myriad messenger boys whose place has been taken by silicon chips and fiber optic wire. Andrew Carnegie, whose fortune in the following century was a large influence on education policy, came to the United States as a poor youth and embarked on his career at the tender age of 13 as a bobbin boy in a textile mill. His big break came when he was 18 and the personal telegrapher and assistant to Thomas Scott, the chief of the Pennsylvania Railroad's western division. Edward Bok, who was to make a fortune in publishing, began as a poor immigrant child from the Netherlands. He began work in a bakery for 50 cents per week, but soon supplemented his income by delivering papers and selling ice water to passengers on streetcars. When he was 13, he left school to become an office boy for Western Union. His autobiography, *The Americanization of Edward Bok*, was a motivational bestseller. Like Carnegie, Bok was to have a significant influence on education both while he was alive and after his death. Unlike Carnegie, his legacy came through his descendants rather than through treasure: his grandson, Derek Bok, was president of Harvard (Lehmann 1999, 50).

In school, the child was to be trained in the basics—reading, writing, and arithmetic—and to internalize the moral character, discipline, and self-reliance needed to continue on the path of self-improvement. High school at the time was an institution for an elite few, and was seen as unnecessary for the vast majority. "[A] child who has a good English education, if he has any snap about him, will succeed better than the average graduate of the high school who knows a little of everything," pontificated one Gilded Age businessman (Edson 1982, 153). Even at the end of the century, the National Education Association's Committee of Ten, whose mandate was to chart the future course of the American high school, stated that the purpose of the high school was "to prepare for the duties of life that small proportion of all children in the country . . . who show themselves able to profit by an education prolonged to the eighteenth year, and whose parents are able to support them while they remain so long in school" (Edson 1982, 152).

With the Horatio Alger story gone in a puff of smoke from the factory chimney, a new type of education was needed. Industrialists wanted vocational education modeled after the German system and an easy-to-manage workforce. Progressive education reformers were allegedly happy to oblige: "For the child-saving reformers as for their colleagues in the larger progressive movement, the route to social amelioration lay in adjusting the people to fit the new productive order, not the reverse. They would 'school to order' future generations of American workers and citizens, preparing them for adult life in the new industrial society" (Nasaw 1979, 100). If bad work habits were a problem, schools would train children through regular attendance, punctuality and classroom order. If workers were bored and alienated, schools would teach future workers about the interdependency and intricacy of modern life, and how every job, no matter how small, was important. If workers lacked a long-term commitment to their jobs, schools would inculcate into students a "life career motive," job loyalty, and an individualistic and antiunion work ethic. The values of discipline, punctuality, obedience, and teamwork needed to be instilled, and this was to be done by giving American adolescents high school diplomas (Edson 1982, 146–47).

The story is compelling and even dramatic—conjuring images of stark class differences, crowded ethnic slums, dark and noisy factories, and workers defying the boss and his hired goons. However, as Paul Peterson states:

If nineteenth-century school officials conceived their primary missions to be training a docile work force, they could hardly have pursued their objective more haphazardly. Instead of concentrating their limited fiscal resources on the most deprived segments of the community, they ignored them until adequate facilities had been extended to the more favored. Instead of insisting on attendance in publicly controlled institutions, they allowed foreigners to go to their own schools. Instead of keeping potential troublemakers under their watchful eyes, the poorest, most outcast segments of the community went uneducated altogether. (Peterson 1985, 12)

As Peterson notes, although the bourgeoisie may build a conformity factory, it is difficult to force proletarian parents to have their children attend it. Even in more hierarchical and authoritarian societies, parents have successfully defied those in control by not sending their children to schools they felt were hostile to their values. In England, where the predominant myth in the history of the rise of public education has also been an anxious middle class using schools to control a passive working class, nineteenth-century working-class parents chose to have their children attend fee-charging private schools despite the bounties paid by public schools, the repeated claims by public school advocates that private schools were inferior, and the occasional bibulous schoolmaster. During an 1837 Parliamentary inquiry, it was noted that 4,000 boys in Manchester attended private day schools, while only 1,001 attended free, publicly supported schools (Laqueur 1976). In imperial Germany, the Kaiser's Polish subjects went on strike against schools they felt were hostile to their language and religion (Schleunes 1989, 224).

In the United States, by 1900, compulsory attendance laws had been in existence in many states for at least 25 years. Massachusetts passed the first such law in 1852, and by 1918 all states had them. The typical law in 1890 required students aged 8 to 14 to attend school for 12 to 20 weeks each year. The seat time required by these laws was hardly sufficient for a social dragnet to keep young ruffians off the streets, even if attendance requirements were binding. However, as Landes and Solmon (1972) found, even though attendance was higher in states with compulsory attendance legislation on their books, the laws were more often a codification of already existing facts. That is, enacted laws frequently required no more time in school than the amount most children were already spending.

Furthermore, compulsory education and child labor laws were often toothless and weakly enforced. Parents resisted interference in what they felt were their rights. Children, or their parents, could easily claim exemption due to poverty or literacy. In Pennsylvania, 13- to 16-year-olds could work if they had certificates assuring that they could read and write at a third-grade level. Obtaining certification was absurdly easy; indeed, a certificate could be purchased for 25 cents. Truants were punished with minimal fines, and authorities had to prove that the infraction was "willingly and knowingly committed." Forty-three years after Massachusetts became the first state to enact a compulsory attendance law, an investigative task force found that Massachusetts parents still considered their children's education as their personal affair and flouted the law without fear. New York's superintendent of public instruction judged the 1874 revision of that state's 1853 law as having "failed to accomplish anything except to subject itself to ridicule." In the 1890s, Massachusetts had 33 inspectors to uphold the state's workplace laws, and New York had 44. Illinois had 12 to cover about 6,700 companies and 200,000 workers (Troen 1976).

In the late nineteenth and early twentieth centuries, compulsory attendance laws were often flouted by the tacit mutual consent of both children and public-school officials. To begin with, schools often did not have enough places for all the children required to attend. In 1881, New York had to turn away 9,189 students; in 1886, Chicago had space for only one-third of children eligible to attend; Philadelphia did not have room for 20,000 pupils; and parents in San Francisco had to beg the school board to allow their children into already packed classrooms (Tyack 1974, 71).

Teachers and administrators were reluctant to admit some students even if they did have desks for them. Students forced to attend school were unruly and disruptive. They "cause[d] sufficient disturbance to have their absence heartily desired by the teacher and principal," reported a committee of Chicago's school board (Tyack 1974, 70). Many children, on the other hand, found school to be undesirable. Helen Todd, a factory inspector in turn-of-the-century Chicago, found that 412 of the 500 children she asked in one survey preferred working in a factory to attending school. Some chose the factory because of the money they earned, or because they felt school offered nothing useful. For most of the child workers Todd spoke with, however, school was harsher than the sweatshop. In the factory, they weren't taunted by their coworkers or struck by their supervisors (Tyack 1974, 177).

Ironically, stifling uniformity and military-like discipline in American schools were under attack in the last decades of the nineteenth century. American schools were not famous for a liberal attitude toward spontaneity and freedom in child behavior. Students in one New York school marched from room to room—sometimes in double-quick time military style (Tyack 1974, 51). An 1874 pamphlet endorsed by 77 college presidents and city and state superintendents of education instructed that classes should be regulated with "military precision." Teachers, it said, should stress punctuality, regularity, attention, and silence. These habits, it informed the reader, are what the child would need to successfully fit into the working world as an adult (Tycak 1974, 49–50).

Toward the end of the nineteenth century, progressive educators like John Dewey and G. Stanley Hall were pushing to ameliorate the harsh conditions of education (Ravitch 2000; Tyack 1974, 82–83). Hall thought the best education freed a child from stress and strain and provided lots of opportunity to play. Also worried about overstressed children, Edward Bok, as editor of *The Ladies Home Journal*, called homework "A National Crime at the Feet of Parents." Bok felt that no child under 15 should be given homework or should spend more than four hours a day in school. Children under 7 should not have to go to school at all. Too much book learning, Bok believed, left children "permanently crippled" (Ravitch 2000, 90). This hardly has the appearance of a blueprint to control dangerous urban adolescents.

Finally, one has to wonder why the European elite did not use this instrument like their American counterparts. Surely if an upper stratum were in need of an effective means of quelling social strife, it would have been the leaders of the fragile democracies and tottering monarchies that dotted Europe at the beginning of the twentieth century. Europe had a more centralized education system than the United States, theoretically making it easier to implement changes. At the turn of the century, primary education in the more developed European nations was universal, but only the select few could obtain a secondary education. In Germany, students were separated into different educational tracks depending on whether they were headed for manual labor, commercial pursuits, or the university. In France, the purpose of the secondary school was to train a small corps of civil servants, scientists, and technicians. In Great Britain, the secondary school taught Homer, Virgil, and other ancient classics to the few who continued schooling past the years the law required (Goldin 2001).

REASONS FOR THE GREAT HIGH SCHOOL BOOM

The boom in high school enrollment at the end of the nineteenth century was ignited by technological change that both eliminated the unskilled jobs held by adolescent workers and increased the skill required for other positions. At the end of the nineteenth century, most child workers performed menial functions that basic office equipment like telephones and computer networks perform today. They held jobs as messengers of various sorts: delivering telegrams or parcels, or working as cash boys and girls in department stores. An occupation that is extinct in the developed world, cash boys and girls carried parcels and change between sales clerks, cashiers, and inspectors. It was easy work, relatively safe and clean, and highly valued because it provided experience for more advanced careers in business. Department stores were among the largest employers of youths between 12 and 16. In the 1870s, cash girls represented one-third of Macy's labor force (Troen 1976).

In 1902, Macy's started to replace the cash boys and girls with the mechanical antecedents of today's electronic networks. Pneumatic tubes and conveyor belts carried parcels and messages from office to office. Other modern office equipment—the telephone, the typewriter, the adding machine, the Dictaphone, the mimeograph, the cash register—started to thin out the ranks of unskilled office workers. In the first decades of the twentieth century, companies like Curtis Publishing and Montgomery Ward cut their staffs in half; Western Union's workforce in downtown Chicago fell from 375 to 267—with the number of 14- to 16-year-old boys plunging from 189 to 64. The office jobs that remained required greater skill and familiarity with the new technologies (Troen 1976).

The restructuring of the American office sparked by new technology led to a boom in the demand for workers in management and information services. The proportion of clerical workers as a share of the nonfarm labor force increased from 4.8 percent in 1900 to 7.7 percent in 1910, reaching 11 percent by 1920. The entire white-collar workforce—clerks, managers, professionals, sales workers—increased from 28.2 to 34.2 percent of the nonfarm workforce (Goldin and Katz 1995). Manufacturing industries started hiring high-school graduates for production-line jobs. Surveying the job descriptions posted by companies in the first decades of the twentieth century, Claudia Goldin (2001) found that businesses wanted workers with such skills as knowledge of algebra; ability to read blueprints; freehand drawing; familiarity with chemical formulas; knowledge of electricity; knowledge of the properties of glass; general knowledge of photography; knowledge of grammar, spelling, and punctuation; and knowledge of Latin and Greek (desired by printing firms). Even farming required greater skill. The farmer needed to be familiar with new crops, techniques in animal husbandry, modern machinery, and management innovations that were inundating the twentieth-century farm.

The change in the nature of work finally made child labor laws relevant. Such laws became more widespread due in part to the declining demand for child workers. Growing, capital-intensive industries were finding child labor wasteful and inefficient, and labor needs were met through natural population growth and immigration (Peterson 1985, 15).

The need for skilled production workers is evident in their rising wages and in the narrowing wage gap between blue-collar and white-collar workers. Real earnings for production workers steadily increased. In 1902, a male worker earned $626 per year; by 1929, this had increased 66 percent to $1,043. In 1909, the average male worker in a clerical or supervisory job earned 2.3 times the amount a production worker earned. Twenty years later, this ratio had fallen to 1.6. Interestingly, the earnings premium of 1.2 for public school teachers in the late 1920s was the same as it had been in 1909, helped no doubt by the demand for teachers caused by the school expansion (Goldin and Katz 1995).

The financial rewards for staying in school were phenomenal. An additional year of high school increased the earnings of the average 18- to 34-year-old man in a white-collar position by 8 percent, and of a blue-collar worker by 9 percent. For farmers it was equally high. These figures are for Iowa residents in 1914—the earliest such estimates available for a population this large and diverse. They are double that for Iowa residents in 1960. They are also probably lower than the returns obtained by those educated in Iowa who moved to other states. So technological and managerial innovation at the beginning of the twentieth century did not create a need for easily managed drudges, but rather created a need for a labor force with even more skills—skills that Americans chose to obtain through a high school education (Goldin 2001).

For much of the nineteenth century, advocates of public education had been urging local communities to build high schools. This historical debate may be disconcerting to those familiar with the modern party lines on school policy, since the policies advocated by the political factions in the last century tended to be the exact opposite of those pushed by their successors in recent decades. Supporting the expansion of public schooling were Whig-Republicans, who believed that public schools were a key to national improvement. They were also amenable to authorities at the state level nudging local communities in the right direction. Generally opposing the expansion of public high schools were Democrats, who, true to their Jacksonian heritage, resisted centralized control over schools just as they resisted centralized control over banks. Democrats in the nineteenth century also opposed high schools because they were elitist. Building high schools, they believed—and at the time this belief was also generally correct—would not allow the masses to grasp the privileges held by the few, but instead would tax the many to enable a select few to rise above the common citizens. Horace Greeley wanted to transfer tax dollars from the high schools to public charities because he felt it was not right to use public funds to benefit the advantaged while the needy went wanting (Reese 1995, 65.)

The boom in high schools started in New England, America's traditional leader in education. High schools appeared rapidly through what Goldin and Katz call the "education belt": states in the Midwest, West, and Plains such as California, Oregon, Washington, Nebraska, Kansas, Iowa, and Indiana. Contrary to the capitalist control theory, the industrial states—New York, New Jersey, Pennsylvania, Michigan, and Wisconsin lagged behind. Lagging even farther behind was the South. Expansion was greatest in the sparsely populated states in the Great Plains (Goldin and Katz 1997). In the first decades of the twentieth century, high school attendance was greater in rural areas and small towns than in cities. In 1910, the attendance rate for 16- and 17-year-olds in towns with less than 10,000 people was 48 percent; in cities with more than half a million population, it was 21 percent (Goldin and Katz 1998).

The decentralized nature of American education allowed for a more rapid expansion of high schools than would have been possible with more central control. Local control allowed regions more inclined to expand their education systems to do so without being held back by sections of the country more reluctant to increase funding for schools. Expansion of high school education was also helped by improving technology. Better rural transportation, brought by the automobile, made it easier for children to attend schools and allowed high schools to draw from larger areas. Before it became an extension of the modern suburbanite, the automobile was a blessing for the isolated farm family. In 1930, the states with the highest auto registration per capita were California, Nevada, Kansas, Nebraska, and Iowa (Goldin and Katz 1998).

Looking at the expansion of high schools nationwide and in the state of Iowa, Claudia Goldin and Lawrence Katz found several other factors that influenced the growth of high schools at the beginning of the twentieth century. High school graduation rates were positively affected by a community's per-capita wealth and the proportion of its population older than 65 (Goldin and Katz 1997, 1998). The beneficial effect of wealth is obvious: richer communities are more able to afford the investment in building and operating a high school. Goldin and Katz believe that a more elderly population indicates a more stable community, making it easier to reach a political consensus on education policy. Another reason that the elderly supported the expansion of education, Goldin and Katz believe, was an implicit social compact like the one outlined by Gary Becker and Kevin Murphy: the older generation agrees to pay taxes to educate the young; the young in return work to support the elder generation in their dotage (Becker and Murphy 1988). The social compact theory would not work as well in rural communities, where the skills and ambition that education encourages would make it hard to keep young workers down on the farm. For the social compact to function, a national system of social security would have to be in place to ensure that workers support the elderly no matter where they are located. Of course, several decades later this is precisely what happened.

One factor that negatively affected high school graduation rates in a local community during the first decades of the twentieth century was the fraction of workers with jobs in the manufacturing sector—again a con-tradiction with the capitalist control theory (Goldin and Katz 1997). Plenty of manufacturing jobs meant lucrative opportunities other than high school for young people, so there was less of an incentive to stay in school. Also, due to the seasonal nature of agricultural work, students in rural areas sacrificed less income by attending school.

Another factor that impeded the growth of public high schools was a large Catholic population (Goldin and Katz 1998). In the United States, Catholic dissatisfaction with the dominant Protestant culture that suffused public schools through the nineteenth century led to the establishment of parochial schools. Catholics resented having to pay double for education: through taxes to support the public schools, and through tuition to send their own children to parochial schools. Attempts to obtain, or in some cases restore, public support for parochial schools has been a source of constant controversy in American education, involving public figures as diverse as President Ulysses S. Grant and First Lady Eleanor Roosevelt. The dispute over the support of religious schools was a major impediment to increased federal involvement in education. So in terms of community consensus on support for the local high school, the more Catholics, the more difficult for agreement to be reached.

The social characteristics of a community can endure for decades, if not centuries. Support for education is seemingly one of these traits. Com-munities on the front end of the Great High School Boom could apparently call upon a stock of social capital that still exists today. States that led the wave of school expansion still score high in social capital measures such as the number of nonprofit organizations, newspaper circulation, voter turnout, and the level of social trust expressed in surveys. The present level of social capital in these states is highly correlated with their 1928 high school graduation rate and with their level of wealth in 1912 (Goldin and Katz 1998).

The spread of high schools first through the small, homogenous communities of the Plains—rather than in the cities full of disgruntled workers, unruly adolescents, and scary immigrants—underscores the proposition that the education boom was primarily a grass-roots movement and not imposed on an unwilling population by an elite. However, high schools do not spontaneously generate. Organizing a community to build a school requires leaders, like the black pastors who built schools for their congregations in the South, and leaders are almost universally drawn from the financial, intellectual, religious, and social elite. Economist, education reformer, and U.S. senator Paul Douglas thought that the high school boom happened because "business interests of the country were willing to have so much of the resources of the country, and incidentally of their own, devoted to furthering secondary education" (Goldin and Katz 1995, 19).

This elite could and did give to other elites, their communities, and themselves many reasons why local high schools should be built: untrained workers, unwashed youth, un-American immigrants. Middle-class and upper-class citizens may well have concurred with the reformers as they voted to impose taxes on themselves to pay for expanding the high schools. But in the end, the high school boom could not have happened without the agreement of ordinary parents and taxpayers that it was a worthwhile enterprise.

THE TRANSFORMATION OF THE AMERICAN HIGH SCHOOL

In 1992, the *Wall Street Journal* reproduced an entrance examination given in 1885 by the Jersey City High School. The following were some of the questions:

- Find the product of $3 + 4x + 5x^2 - 6x^3$ and $4 - 5x - 6x^2$.
- Write a sentence containing a noun used as an attribute, a verb in the perfect tense potential mood, and a proper adjective.
- Name three events of 1777. Which was the most important and why? (*Wall Street Journal* 1992)

Offered as evidence of a decline in public education, the questions actually demonstrate how American high schools were transformed by the boom in attendance at the beginning of the twentieth century. High schools were originally preparatory schools for the college bound or for certain white-collar professions. They were exclusive institutions that selected students using tests like the one above. In Atlanta, only 638 students attended the public high schools in 1890; in Chicago that same decade, 6 percent of youths between 14 and 17 went to the public high schools (Peterson 1985, 61).

In the decades following 1885, American public high schools opened up to all American youths regardless of their future career plans. In 1910, 49 percent of high school graduates intended to continue on to higher education, by 1937, only 29 percent of graduates planned to do so (Goldin 1998). The conversion of the American public high school into a vehicle for mass education brought great innovations and changes. Exclusivity and admission tests disappeared. Vocational education and other elective classes—along with other now-standard features such as tracking, 45-minute periods, and Carnegie units—appeared (Goldin and Katz 1997).

High schools expanded their curricula in response to demand from parents and in order to attract students. One of the first additions to the curriculum was the teaching of modern languages. The large blocs of ethnic immigrants were a potential market or constituency—depending on whether one wishes to use an economic or political metaphor. Like any organization seeking to grow and prosper, public schools began offering bilingual programs to reach out to this untapped market. The reaching out was especially urgent because the immigrant groups were more than willing to found schools of their own to teach their children in their native tongues. In the second half of the nineteenth century, private schools in the United States taught in Polish, French, Czech, Norwegian, Dutch, Lithuanian, Japanese, Korean, Chinese, Spanish, and especially German. Cincinnati had a bilingual German program from 1840 until the United States entered World War I. Baltimore, Indianapolis, and Chicago also had bilingual German public schools. In 1865, the last year of the Civil War, San Francisco opened schools that taught in French and German, with English as a secondary language. The superintendent of schools in the city defended these Cosmopolitan Schools both as a compromise with the city's "foreign elements" and as a way to draw immigrant children away from their private ethnic schools into the public system, where they could be Americanized. Public school officials in Chicago defended teaching German in the same terms (Ravitch 1978, 59–60; Peterson 1985, 53–55).

Vocational education was another addition to the curriculum of the American public school. In the final decades of the 1800s, many wealthy philanthropists and businessmen, impatient with what they felt was the impractical nature of the traditional nineteenth-century high school, became a chorus advocating manual training and vocational education. Surpassing mere public advocacy, they founded private trade schools and commercial high schools; supported vocational counselors in urban settlement houses; created "parental schools" and institutions for delinquents; and even helped pay for education research bureaus. J. P. Morgan gave $500,000 to the New York trade schools. In 1882, George Pullman, Marshall Field, and several other prominent Chicago businessmen launched plans for a private manual school in the city, and two years later the Chicago Manual Training School opened its doors. In San Francisco, the business community supported two private manual training schools: the Lick school, which taught the machine trades, and the Wilmerding school, which primarily focused on the building trades. Neither charged tuition (Tyack 1974, 186, 189; Peterson 1985, 66–67).

At the time, these trade schools were opposed by educators who still believed in the traditional scholarly education and were worried about losing students to the competition. Labor unions were also suspicious of schools controlled directly by business. Labor leaders were concerned that trade schools were a way of bypassing the traditional apprenticeship system and that they would flood the market with cheap labor. Existing public high schools felt threatened enough that they started offering vocational classes. Although business fought for a separate vocational system, the public schools teamed up with labor to incorporate vocational training into the existing public system. Public schools gained access to a new market and an important justification in the face of a frequently hostile business community. Labor expected to have more control over vocational education in the public schools than in a separate system that was more closely supervised by business. In another contradiction to the capitalist control theory, the vocational curriculum in public schools was often more in line with what labor desired than with what industrialists wanted. Although the factory owners may have wanted semiskilled workers suited for the assembly line, the schools taught highly skilled crafts like plumbing, bricklaying, carpentry, and electrical work. In addition to satisfying their allies in labor, schools that taught the craft trades were more appealing to their customers—students and parents—and teachers. So strong was the labor-public education alliance that it was successful in obtaining federal government support for vocational education with the passage of the Smith-Hughes Act in 1917 (Nasaw 1979, 116–17; Peterson 1985, 16–17; Powell, Farrar, and Cohen 1985, 240).

The new shape of the high school dovetailed smoothly with the new theories of psychology, sociology, child development, and pedagogy that were fermenting. Applied to education, these new ideas have been woven together into a tapestry that has been labeled "progressive" or "new" education. According to critics like Diane Ravitch, E. D. Hirsch, Arthur Powell and his coauthors, and Andrew Coulson, these new pedagogical fads led to the abandonment of essential studies, academic rigor, and effective teaching methods in favor of watered-down, often silly curricula that denied students necessary skills for upward mobility and left them without an understanding of the common cultural heritage of the nation. The first strand of the new education was an attempt to reform classroom teaching. Credit and blame for the new "child-centered" education are given to the American philosopher John Dewey. To Dewey, G. Stanley Hall, and other advocates of child-centered education, America's youth were not wild and profane proto-delinquents who, according to some historians, worried the WASP establishment. Child-centered education was based on a concept of the child taken straight from European Romantics like Rosseau and Wordsworth. Children, according to the Romantics, were born with the instinct to develop into well-adjusted adults. Left unconstrained by textbooks and lessons, children would naturally seek to educate themselves through experience with the skills and habits they would need to succeed as adults (Hirsch 1987, 118–19). Not for the child-centered educator were the methods of the traditional school, where discipline and learning were imposed on the child by the teacher. Instead of passive learning by rote and drill, children were to learn actively in ways that mirrored their everyday activities. For John Dewey, learning in the modern American school should be patterned after how children used to learn in farm, workshop, and home: assisting their parents with cooking, cleaning, tending livestock, spinning, forging tools, and making furniture (Ravitch 2000, 58).

Child-centered education provided a theoretical foundation for the adaptations high schools made for their new students. If many of the new students entering high school could not cope with the traditional curriculum, the child-centered advocates said there was no need to worry. Carpentry, writing and publishing a school newspaper, and beekeeping offered better ways for students to learn about geometry and biology than did the traditional courses. Indeed, the more courses added to the high school curriculum the better. Electives offered adolescents the chance to explore and expand their interests. Whether students actually learned the same amount of math, English, and science is unknown, but the new types of classes became places to shunt students without the talent or ambition to pursue the traditional college-preparatory curriculum (Powell, Farrar, and Cohen 1985, 250–52, 262).

A second strand of the new education that offered direct advice on what to do with the new students entering the high schools was the social efficiency movement. To the social efficiency advocate, the role of education was solely utilitarian: to shape students to fill the particular roles society needed filling at the moment. Foreign languages, higher mathematics, history, classic literature, and advanced science were all useless to the modern citizen, according to the two leading prophets of socially efficient education, David Snedden, a commissioner of education in Massachusetts and professor at Columbia's Teachers College, and Ellwood Cubberly, a teacher, superintendent, and professor at Stanford. Instead, students should be prepared to fill jobs as clerks, factory workers, salesmen, bookkeepers, farmers, and housewives. The social efficiency and child-centered movements differed in the reasons why high schools should add sewing and surveying classes. For the child-centered movement, these new classes were better avenues to learn through exploration and activity. For the social-efficiency movement, however, the classes were ends in themselves to mold the child to fit in his or her vocational niche. Snedden advocated separate schools for each vocation, which put him beyond the pale of many reform advocates. Dewey thought that separate vocational and academic schools were undemocratic and would narrow what was supposed to be the education of the whole child (Powell, Farrar, and Cohen 1985, 247; Ravitch 2000, 81–86).

The social efficiency movement gave public schools new prestige and justification. It is hard to find a time in the United States when the teaching profession and public schools have been widely esteemed, but the first decades of the twentieth century were a particularly perilous time for educators. Budgets were tight; salaries were low; and city schools were victims like other municipal departments to politics, patronage, and corruption. "[T]eachers were an embarrassment—poorly educated, mostly female, and drawn heavily from the lower orders of society." Schools were subject to constant critiques as unbusinesslike and inefficient, and at times struggles with business and political leaders put their very existence in danger. The new science of education gave educators control of a sharp, new instrument of social progress and economic prosperity. It made them gatekeepers to economic success for the new mass of students enrolling in school and important lieutenants to the captains of industry (Powell, Farrar, and Cohen 1985, 248, 255).

Although competition and demands from parents and others had been pushing high schools to expand their curricula since the last decades of the nineteenth century, the serpent that most critics say introduced progressive education into the garden of America's schools nationwide was *Cardinal Principles of Secondary Education*, published in 1918. According to its critics, it had the same effect on the quality of education in the United States that the Versailles Treaty, drafted the following year, had on lasting peace in Europe. The *Cardinal Principles* were composed by the National Education Association's Commission on the Reorganization of Secondary Education, made up of high-school principals, current and former professors of education, and education bureaucrats. Tens of thousands of copies were sold, and the U.S. Bureau of Education distributed it widely (Ravitch 1983, 48).

The principles of secondary education set forth by the commission were: "1. Health. 2. Command of fundamental processes. 3. Worthy home-membership. 4. Vocation. 5. Citizenship. 6. Worthy use of leisure. 7. Ethical character." "Command of fundamental processes," the one nod by the commission in the direction of schools actually teaching children reading, writing, and arithmetic, was not included in the original draft. A utilitarian document, the *Cardinal Principles,* stressed that schools should impart practical skills that would be directly useful to society and to the children when they became adults. For example, the report stated that, given the likely future responsibilities of most girls, college preparatory courses were inappropriate. They urged that homemaking be given equal status with other subjects. The report also cited modern psychology to justify tossing aside a core curriculum for all students, and instead recommended that schools introduce a wide variety of classes to meet students' individual needs (Ravitch 1983, 48; Hirsch 1987, 118, 120).

Cardinal Principles is often contrasted with a report published 25 years earlier and also issued by the National Education Association: the *Report of the Committee of Ten on Secondary School Studies.* The Committee of Ten was more oriented toward the traditional college preparatory role of the high school; 5 of the 10 members were college presidents, and the chairman was the omnipresent Charles Eliot, the president of Harvard University. Still, the committee recommended giving all high-school students, college-bound or not, the same education. It advocated the traditional curriculum with a new emphasis on the natural sciences: Latin, Greek, English, foreign languages, mathematics, physics, chemistry, astronomy, botany, zoology, physiology, history, civics, economics, and geography (Hirsch 1987, 117).

The Committee of Ten's report and the *Cardinal Principles* contrast two differing philosophies of how the American education system should cope with diversity—two philosophies that are still fighting for the curricula of American public schools. The *Report of the Committee of Ten* was not a wholly egalitarian document. However, it was egalitarian in believing that every child who attended high school should be given the same education. The Committee of Ten's philosophy is echoed by modern advocates like Hirsch and Ravitch, who believe that schools should weld a diverse society together by giving all children the same basic education. On the other hand, the authors of the *Cardinal Principles,* while believing that all children should be able to attend high school, did not believe that all children would be able to learn the traditional academic curriculum. Like many today, they believed that a diverse population should be fed an equally diverse curriculum.

By the first decades of the twentieth century, most American public high schools that were large enough had implemented a system of internal choice, or, to use the phrase later coined by Powell and his coauthors, they had built the shopping mall high school. Students attending the shopping mall high school could study the traditional college preparatory curriculum. Some highs schools had split it into two: the traditional classical course of study and a second emphasizing math and science. Or students could choose to pursue a vocational or general education path. In keeping with the California tradition of being ahead of the nation, Los Angeles expanded its curricula from 4 in 1906 to 48 by 1914. One study found that, in 1906–11, one school in six had a general education curriculum, one in six had an industrial arts curriculum, and half the schools surveyed had commercial curricula. By 1930, five out of six schools surveyed had a general education curriculum, the same fraction had an industrial arts curriculum, and all had some commercial course of study. The relative importance of commercial versus industrial curricula is another piece of contrary evidence—if more is needed—that the training of factory operatives was not the paramount reason behind the expansion of the high school. Commercial courses such as bookkeeping offered a way off of the factory floor and into white-collar work (Powell Farrar, and Cohen 1985, 246; Ravitch 2000, 101).

In their study of "Middletown," Robert and Helen Lynd found that the local high school offered 102 different classes and 12 separate courses of study, including college preparatory, music, shorthand, applied electricity, machine shop, home economics, and general education. This was in sharp contrast to 1889. Then, the 170 students attending Middletown's high school—like students in the three decades before them—could choose from one of two courses of study: the English and the Latin. The only difference between the two was whether one took "the language" (Lynd and Lynd 1956, 192).

The Lynds found a proliferation of vocational courses. In classes patterned after the city's factories, the boys repaired items brought from home, worked on an old car, and designed and built a house. In the home economics courses, the girls learned skills more appropriate to the pioneer wife: canning, baking, and sewing. The future homemakers of Middletown did receive some training in modern consumer skills, including field trips to the local stores to examine household items. However, not all changes were at the expense of the academic curriculum. Students in Middletown in the 1920s learned more civics, history, and social sciences than had their predecessors a generation earlier. Previously, a student who completed his studies through high school would have taken one course in American history, one course in general history "covering everything from the Creation to the present in one little book of a hundred or so pages," and a civics class. At the time of the Lynds's study, students took history and civics straight through elementary school, American history in their third year of high school, and civics and sociology as seniors (Lynd and Lynd 1956, 195–97).

The Lynds found even more profound changes outside the classroom. In the nineteenth century, the school board directed that, once the daily studies were completed, students were to be shooed away from school and sent home to help their parents as soon as possible. Fifty years later, school had become the eye of a hurricane of social and extracurricular activities, including clubs, dances, music, drama, and sports. This being the Midwest, basketball had supplanted God as the chief topic of chapel, and the Mothers' Council was successful in getting the first period set aside for club and committee meetings. Said one senior:

Oh, in civics I know more or less about politics, so it's easy to talk and I don't have to study that. In English we're reading plays and I can just look at the end of the play and know about that. Typewriting and chemistry I don't have to study outside anyway . . . I've stuck out Latin for four years for the Virgil banquet: I just sit next to —— and get it from her. Mother jumps on me for never studying, but I get A's all the time, so she can't say anything. (Lynd and Lynd 1956, 215)

Those looking for a Golden Age when public high schools were serious academic institutions focused on scholarly subjects and filled with diligent pupils will have to leave 1920s Middletown and continue looking.

In Middletown, some teachers and "parents of the business class" worried that vocational education would lower academic standards and distract college-bound students from their academic studies—and with good reason. The Middletown students tracked down in college by the Lynds were on the whole making a poor showing. However, the new classes received widespread support from the Rotary and Kiwanis clubs and the students themselves. Rather than being a grind, as it was for Middletown's adults at the end of the nineteenth century, high school was something students actually enjoyed. For the expansion in the high school curriculum to spread as it did through America's decentralized school system, it must have had equal acceptance in Middletowns across the country (Lynd and Lynd 1956, 195, 218).

Figure 3.2 shows the percentage of high-school students enrolled in selected classes for nearly 100 years—from before the boom in enrollment to the year of the release of *A Nation at Risk*. The data are for percentage of students enrolled in a given year, so the precise numbers underestimate the fraction of graduates who ever took a particular course. However, they still provide a good indicator of emphasis on and exposure to certain subjects. For example, the fact that over 90 percent of high-school students are enrolled in English classes implies that the vast majority of students are taking English all four years they are in school. Similarly, the downward trends in physics and algebra enrollment indicate that a smaller portion of students has been exposed to those subjects over time.

The beginning of the high school enrollment boom saw increases in enrollment in algebra, English, history, German, and Latin. Since these are percentages, this can indicate a strengthening of the curriculum. The fraction of students enrolled can increase if more classes are being offered or required in a subject. This strengthening perhaps reflects the influence of the Committee of Ten's report released in 1893. Enrollment in physics and chemistry did not increase, however, and in fact declined through most

Figure 3.2
Subject Enrollment Rates by Subject

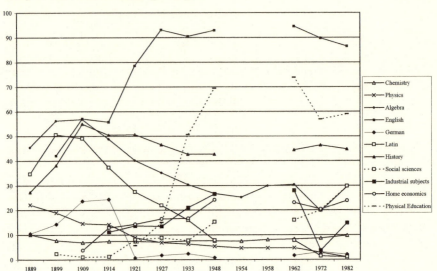

Source: Goldin (1999).

of the century. This decline was soon followed by a decline in enrollment in algebra. Enrollment in biology, earth science, and geometry also fell (not shown). At the same time, more students were taking general science and general math classes. The decline in the teaching of math and science is ironic, coming during a century when science and technology issues were increasingly dominating politics, warfare, society, and the economy. Interestingly, although there is a temporary, post-*Sputnik* blip in algebra enrollment, enrollment in the other sciences was barely affected by launch of the Soviet satellite and the ensuing wave of criticism, reform, and federal intervention.

Enrollment in English continued to increase, reaching over 90 percent. Unfortunately, even the enticement of Virgil banquets could not save Latin, and German enrollment was shattered by the wave of patriotism accompanying WWI. Although Spanish and French picked up the slack somewhat, they could not replace the special status of German, promoted as it was by large immigrant communities. By the middle of the 1950s, 54.6 percent of high schools in the United States offered no courses in a modern foreign language (Ravitch 2000, 69). Although the decline in the study of foreign languages has been considered a symptom of the overall decline of public schools, the data show that, aside from immigrants like the Germans who sought to preserve the culture of the homeland, Americans by-and-large have not been interested in learning foreign languages.

Although critics have lamented the replacement of history by classes in the nebulous and academically watery subject of social studies, history, after a small drop, has held its own against the encroachment of these alternative classes—a durability that was confirmed by a report at mid-century (Wesley 1944).

Figure 3.2 shows the increase in the importance of nonacademic subjects such as industrial arts and home economics. However, it also suggests that critics' attention has been focused in the wrong direction. The most significant development has been the mass movement of students out of the classroom onto the playing field and into the gym; the enrollment of students in physical education classes exploded during the past century.

The United States is likely one of the few countries that began a scathing self-examination and raucous debate over its education system after a military victory. After WWII, public schools found themselves the targets of increasingly vehement attacks. Despite widespread consensus during the first half of the twentieth century, there were always critics, like the small group of businessmen in Middletown, who complained that the new methods weren't teaching the basics; that traditional Western culture was being abandoned; and that schools were wasting money on ineffective frills. In the early 1950s, the balloon of education crisis was sent up again, and the volume of criticism redoubled. An avalanche of books and articles accused American schools of being anti-intellectual, undemocratic, out of step with the needs of a modern technological society, and slave to the official dogma of an "educationist" monopoly. That debate over the new shape of America's schools has continued to rage to the present day.

This debate has been fueled by a growing demand for academic skills caused by an increase in the returns to cognitive skills and growing benefits from a college degree. More high-school graduates are completing academic courses of study like the ones recommended in *A Nation at Risk* (U.S. Department of Education 1998b). Since 1982, the number of units of physics, chemistry, foreign languages, and math at a level of algebra or higher taken by the average high-school graduate has grown (U.S. Department of Education 2002, table 140). The greater demand for academic subjects has caused the multiple curricula and internal choice of the shopping mall high school to become increasingly obsolete.

The quality of the tracks offered by the typical high school can be quite diverse. Within-school differences in achievement among students on different curriculum tracks are greater than between-school differences. Indeed, the achievement difference between high-track and low-track students is greater than the difference between low-track students and dropouts (Gamoran 1987). Internal choice between tracks has been left largely to students (Powell, Farrar, and Cohen 1985). This has worked to the disadvantage of students of low socioeconomic status, who frequently lack the information to choose wisely between tracks. Researchers have found that, although students on lower tracks have aspirations for college, the courses they have chosen to take leave them woefully unprepared to continue their education (Rosenbaum 1978). Wealthier, better-educated parents are also better able to influence principals and counselors to place their children in the higher tracks. This wide divergence between tracks is not found in Catholic schools, where more children are pushed into the college preparatory curriculum (Gamoran 1992; Lee and Bryk 1988, 1989). This helps account for the advantage these schools have, especially in poor, nonwhite communities. Apparently, parents find greater professional assistance and responsibility for their children's education in Catholic schools than in public schools. This has led some to comment that the vision of the common school has become a greater reality in Catholic schools than in public schools.

INCENTIVES FOR MEDIOCRITY

Herrnstein and Murray (1996) observe that few middle school students today could pass the 1885 entrance examination for the Jersey City High School cited at the beginning of the previous section. This inability should not be attributed to vague symptoms of decay in public education or society as a whole. The fact that many middle-school students cannot answer the questions is a rational response to the incentives in the education system. Students do not know the answers because they do not need to know the answers, as they did over 100 years ago. If, once again, high schools were made exclusive academies where obtaining admission depended upon passing an exam, we can be almost sure that middle school students would begin to acquire the skills needed to pass any test that was necessary.

Just as the American high school was formed as a political compromise to attract and accommodate an influx of new students from the bottom, it was also a response to the incentives that came into being at the top: a rational reaction to the education and labor markets that high-school students would face after graduation. One reason American schools appear to perform poorly is that there is not incentive for students, particularly in high school, to do better.

Doing well in high school pays off, but only after several years. For students still in high school, good grades or performance on achievement tests has no effect on the probability of finding a part-time job while in high school or on how well they are paid. For those who go to work right out of high school, students who are a full standard deviation above average in test scores or grade-point average see only a 1 to 4.7 percent increase in pay. After 4 or 5 years, this increases to 4.3 to 6 percent. During the first 10 years after graduation, young men receive no boost in earnings from skills in science, language arts, and mathematical reasoning. Only quickness in simple computations and technical knowledge of things such as electronics, automobiles, and shop tools pay off (Bishop 1990).

Potential employers display little interest in how graduates did in high school. In one survey, employers listed the following as the top five attributes they look for in potential hires (Berliner and Biddle 1995, 89):

1. No substance abuse

2. Honesty

3. Follows directions

4. Respects others

5. Punctuality

The five least important attributes were proficiency or knowledge in

1. Mathematics

2. Social sciences

3. Natural sciences

4. Computer programming

5. Foreign languages

A 1987 survey of small and medium-sized businesses found that they had obtained high school transcripts for only 14.2 percent of those they had hired; 15 percent of the businesses had asked for an applicant's grade-point average; 5.2 percent of hires had been recommended by vocational teachers; and 2.7 percent of hires had been recommended by another school employee. In a large country with a mobile population, those in charge of hiring often are unacquainted with the quality of the many schools from which applicants come. Collecting and verifying information about an applicant's academic performance is time-consuming, and requesting it may risk trouble with antidiscrimination laws (Bishop 1990). With little interest from potential employers and any payoff far in the future, the incentives for the typical 14- to 18-year old to do well in high school are weak.

There is also a weak incentive for those students who are bound for college to do well. The years after WWII saw yet another boom in educational attainment. This time, more and more Americans started going to college. From 1939 to 1960, college enrollment in the United States more than doubled from 1.5 million to 3.2 million students; in another decade, enrollment had redoubled to 7.1 million students. Most of the new students attended less-selective public universities, where admission was often based on being a resident and taking some required courses. Unless a student was aiming for a selective school, he or she had little motive to work hard in high school. The high school studied by Powell and his coauthors offered enough different classes for students to meet the course requirements for the state's public university in several ways. Since entrance depended on taking the class rather than on the grade received, students had the incentive to take the easier classes. If a student still ran into difficulty or was just lazy, poor grades could be negated by good SAT scores, or by going to an even less selective college. Finally, the fact that most scholarships are awarded based on need rather than on merit further shrinks the incentive to do well in high school (Powell, Farrar, and Cohen 1985, 43, 289; Bishop 1990; Herrnstein and Murray 1996, 426).

Harbaugh (2002) attributed slack college admission standards to competition for students among colleges and universities. Schools competing for students select the best applicants by emphasizing scores on aptitude tests such as the SAT, rather than knowledge achieved as measured by grades or performance on achievement tests. Bright students prefer to be chosen by performance on aptitude tests because it allows them to do less work in high school. In effect, competing colleges are lowering the price of admission in terms of effort expended while in high school. Admittedly, how hard students work can also affect SAT scores, but Harbaugh's model holds as long as not studying for the SATs causes a smaller drop in scores than not studying for an achievement-based test.

All this is in contrast to other advanced nations, where achievement in high school is much more crucial to a student's future. In other nations, as in nineteenth-century New Jersey, the quality of the high school a child is able to attend depends upon how well he or she does in middle school. In Germany, school grades have significant influence on whether a child gets one of the more coveted apprenticeships; at the best firms in Japan, clerical, service, or blue-collar positions are open only to applicants with recommendations from their high schools. School systems in Europe, Japan, Canada, and Australia administer achievement exams. These exams provide a common standard that employers can use when selecting applicants, and that parents can use when judging their child's school. A student's test scores also are the primary factor in determining whether he or she is admitted to college (Bishop 1990).

The effort put in by high school and college students in other countries is often the opposite of what is found in the United States. In other nations, students work hard to be admitted to the university, but once admitted, a student is on track for a privileged job in business or government. Hence, once admitted to a university, a student tends to slow down. In the United States, on the other hand, getting into the university is easy, but students must work much harder than they did in high school to graduate. Employers in the United States also pay close attention to college grades and professors' recommendations (Bishop 1990).

High barriers to being admitted to college, theorize Simon and Woo (1995), will cause students wishing to continue on to college to work harder in high school. High barriers will also cause students not planning on pursuing a college education to work hard; for them, high school is one of their last chances to acquire human capital through formal schooling. Consequently, we can expect high-school students in countries with more-exclusive university systems to perform better on achievement tests. This is consistent with what Simon and Woo found. In countries in which a large number of students continue on to college, high-school seniors do worse on the international comparison tests of academic achievement. Which system is better is unclear. Making universities very exclusive lowers the overall education level of a nation, even one with superior high schools. Having moderately exclusive universities increases the quality of high schools and possibly raises net education levels overall. In addition, it is unclear whether allowing students to remedy the deficiencies in their high school education and acquire more human capital by lingering for another four years in a university is cost-effective.

CONCLUSION

For most of the nineteenth century, reformers in cities and towns across America pushed for their local communities to build high schools. They were impeded by the perception that high schools were for the elite few. By the end of the nineteenth century, they had hit upon the alternative of making high schools less elite. They found a ready market due to technological change that caused the disappearance of low-skilled work typically filled by adolescents and increased the need for high-skilled workers.

Thus, Americans created a public high school system true to their democratic and egalitarian heritage. Students following academic or vocational careers were not shunted off to separate schools, as in other countries. The teenager aspiring to college sat next to the teenager training for the factory—or at least in a nearby room in the same building. A system of internal school choice was created. The high school building contained an educational bazaar of academic, general, and vocational study tracks, elective courses, and extracurricular activities. Although serious social engineers tried to guide students by means of IQ tests and counseling, the path of least resistance was to let students and parents decide. This bypassed the difficulty of a diverse community having to reach a consensus about the shape and purpose of their school. Questions about classes to be taken and standards to be met could be left to parents and students (Powell, Farrar, and Cohen 1985).

The high school was open to all and forgiving of performance. Social promotion—promoting students to higher grades based on age and attendance rather than academic achievement—became widespread, de-spite the new, less-rigorous curricula that students could choose to follow. A 1933 survey found that more than 50 percent of schools promoted students who had failed to meet even the watered-down performance standards (Powell, Farrar, and Cohen 1985, 267).

In 1959, a half-century after the Great High School Boom began, James B. Conant, a former ambassador and president of Harvard, defended and endorsed what the American high school had become in *The American High School*, a book sponsored by the Carnegie Corporation. A supporter of ample choice among curricula and high schools open to all, Conant pushed for the creation of the education "big box." He called for closing all high schools that had graduating classes of fewer than 100 (Ravitch 2000, 362–64), and he got his wish. In 1959, there were 8.5 million students in 25,784 secondary schools; by 1996, there were 13 million students in 23,793 schools. There were slightly fewer high schools in 1996 than in 1929, when only 4.4 million students attended high school (U.S. Department of Education 2000, tables 38, 89).

Despite the changes in the American high school due to the influx of new students, the expansion of American education in the twentieth century was a significant investment in human capital, which in turn led to a significant improvement in the nation's economic prosperity. From 1913 to 1996, the productivity of American workers increased at an average rate of 1.62 percent per year. Goldin and Katz (2001) credit the increase in skills for 0.37 percentage points, or 23 percent, of this yearly productivity growth. Maddison (1987) credits 13 percent of the average yearly growth in the U.S. economy between 1913 and 1950 to improvements in labor quality, including education.

Studies like these, however, typically measure human capital investment in terms of additional years of schooling. The quality of those extra years is left unexamined. To critics, the expansion of the American high school was a story of opportunity denied. Instead of being challenged and pushed to master a rigorous academic curriculum that would build skills and instill a common culture, the new mass of students entering America's high schools were diverted—or allowed to divert themselves—into weak nonacademic courses. How the nation might have benefited had the quality of schooling been different is unknown. The new curriculum, however, was the result of a political consensus among parents, taxpayers, the education establishment, business, and labor facing individual and community values, opportunities, and constraints, of which critics can only be partially aware.

A new political consensus may be forming that will again transform the education system. The labor market is increasing the rewards to cognitive skills. Not only is the premium for the college educated increasing, rewards for doing well in high school are appearing earlier in the working career (Murnane, Willett, and Levy 1995; Murnane et al. 2000). College is an aspiration of more and more students who are dissatisfied with being pushed into vocational classes like cosmetology, auto shop, and bank-telling. The implementation of graduation tests may also change the incentives faced by high-school students. After a half-century of stress and storm about the state of American education, the stars may have lined up to produce the incentives that will bring about another fundamental change in the American high school.

CHAPTER 4

No Choice and No Voice: The Erosion of Local Control

In his 1919 history of American education, Stanford professor Ellwood Cubberly observed that the history of growth of American education was "completely local." "Everywhere," he wrote, "development has been from the community outward and upward not from the State downward" (Cubberly 1919, 155). Cubberly did not believe that this circumstance should or would continue. He saw education as becoming more paternalistic, even socialistic, and children increasingly belonging more to the state than to their parents. A new time called for national initiatives to "Americanize the foreign-born"; eliminate illiteracy; institute health, physical, and vocational education programs; improve rural schools; and improve teacher pay and teacher training (Cubberly 1919, 481; Ravitch 2000, 97).

Like the vast majority of reformers, Cubberly looked toward central power to undertake actions he felt were desirable. The central authority has the resources and the scope to ensure that every corner of the nation implements reforms. Whether the programs are suitable or desired in every corner is another question. Education reform has consistently been accompanied by a relentless centripetal force, as each new plan places greater power in higher authority levels: from district to town, town to state, and state to the federal government. This chapter reviews the 200-year assault on local control of schools. Although I acknowledge that this movement has had legitimate and beneficial aspects, this chapter emphasizes the damage that increasing centralization may and actually has caused. It does so to provide balance to the vast output of reformers and their chroniclers, past and present, who tout only the benefits of universal adaptation of their agendas.

THE BENEFITS OF LOCAL CONTROL

This chapter focuses primarily on the tangible effects of allowing small, local communities to have primary authority over education. The normative or value-based arguments for local control focus on the right of parents to raise their children as they wish, free from the meddling of distant bureaucrats; and the individualism, self-reliance, and diversity fostered by governing through small communities. Individualism and diversity can also be called parochialism and inequality, and those wishing for schools to promote a national culture or values or to spend an equal amount of money on all students may desire a stronger role by a central authority. Reasonable people may disagree on the relative importance of values such as individualism and equality, and the desirability of specific governance policies lies in the eye of the beholder. In contrast to these subjective values, I wish to make the distinction of objective results of school governance policies. Research has found substantial effects between school governance and support for public education and the efficiency of schools. One may argue the importance or magnitude of these effects, but in devising education policy one cannot wish them away.

Local Control, Voice, and the Expansion of Education

The first objective result of local control of education I examine is the apparent link between it and greater public support for public education. Decentralized control promotes the two fundamental methods, following Albert Hirschman (1970), of influencing an organization: voice and exit. Small, decentralized organizations make control through voice easier. One's voice has more weight when it is one of a hundred or a thousand instead of one of ten thousand or a million. Members of small groups can more easily communicate with one another; face-to-face contact is common; and expensive, impersonal means of communication can be avoided. Smaller communities also tend to be more homogeneous. Reaching a political consensus is easier when voters have much in common—income, religion, race, and language. When voters are surrounded by people like themselves, they feel more assured that their tax money is going for a good purpose—not to help the wealthy, the undeserving poor, unbelievers, or outsiders. Private schools are more common in countries that are diverse in terms of language and especially religion, because large segments of the population are dissatisfied with the political consensus regarding the shape and nature of the public education system (James 1993).

The ability of small communities to reach political agreement with relatively greater ease has allowed nations with more decentralized education systems to be much more fertile ground for the expansion of education (Lindert 2001). Large countries have diverse geographic populations and develop unevenly, with rich regions and poor ones, which is important given that the demand for education is strongly correlated to income. Thus, every country will have regions, typically the poorer ones, with less demand for education: the United States had the South; Prussia had the Junker-controlled east; and France had a poorer, patois-speaking south and west. With centralized control, political compromise with the representatives of areas reluctant to expand education leads to less public funding allocated to schools. Decentralized control allows regions in which residents want to expand education to move forward without having to sacrifice to political give and take in the national capital.

In 1870, 779 out of every 1,000 American children between 5 and 14 was enrolled in primary school. The figures for France, England and Wales, and Prussia were 737, 732, and 609. In 1880, the United States spent approximately 1 percent of its national product on education at all levels. At the same time, France devoted 0.87 percent of national product to schooling, the United Kingdom 0.9 percent, and Germany 1.6 percent. The rank order of these nations is roughly equivalent to the level of local control as measured by source of funding. In reputedly autocratic Prussia, we find school funding left largely in local hands and higher enrollment. Meanwhile, the sources of education funding in England, populated by a race jealous of its rights and liberties, resembled that in France. Although, as might be expected in England, the vast majority of support came from private sources, the central government played a larger role than in the United States or Prussia. The fraction of funding for schools originating from the national government during the 1870s and 1880s was 35 to 42 percent for the United Kingdom, 8 to 10 percent for Prussia, 13 percent for France, and 0 for the United States (Lindert 2001). Private funding of education tended to be highest in countries with more-central control, indicating a large demand for education unmet by public schools—as can be found in developing nations today.

While the story of decentralization and the growth of education seems to fit the United States perfectly, its apparently paradoxical application to Prussia and England is surprising. Prussia's leadership in education in the nineteenth century is and was well known. The nation was one of the world leaders in school enrollment, spending, the education of girls, and the mixing of social classes within its schools (Lindert 2001). Throughout the nineteenth century, the kingdom was a model for education reformers in other nations and a magnetic pole for fact-finding missions. In 1836, Calvin E. Stowe—education reformer, seminary professor, and husband of Harriet Beecher Stowe—embarked on an investigative trip to Europe on behalf of the Ohio General Assembly. He found a ferment of interest in education reform from Spain to the Sublime Porte. His highest praise was reserved for the king of Prussia, an autocrat whose manner and appearance was "as simple and unostentatious as an Ohio farmer" (Stowe 1930 [1837], 255). The Prussian monarch, Stowe enthused, was "pursuing a course of instruction for his whole people, more complete, better adapted to develope [sic] every faculty of the soul, and to bring into action every capability of every kind that may exist, even in the poorest cottage of the most obscure corner of his kingdom, than has ever been imagined" (Stowe 1930 [1837], 251). Stowe's report, although not the bestseller that his wife's *Uncle Tom's Cabin* was, did receive a significant amount of circulation. The Ohio legislature had 10,000 copies printed and given to every school district in the state. The legislatures of Massachusetts, Michigan, North Carolina, Pennsylvania, and Virginia also had it reprinted (Cubberly 1919, 276–77).

Widespread perceptions of Prussian autocracy influenced nineteenth-century debates about adopting the methods and organization of the Prussian system. Opponents saw the reforms as carrying the dangerous seeds of centralization and despotism. In the United States, Democratic members of the Massachusetts legislature countered Horace Mann's commendation of Prussian education with the observation that "In France or Prussia, the smallest bridge cannot be built, or any village road repaired, until a central Board has been consulted" (Fraser 1999, 29). This kind of government interference was not wanted in Massachusetts. In 1840, New York's Catholic bishop, John Hughes, fighting against Protestant-dominated, state-supported schools, stated ominously that the idea of common schools had come from "the dark regions of Prussia" (Kaestle 1983, 168). An English opponent of state education, Edward Baines, replied to advocates of the Prussian model in his country: "Nearly all the Continental Governments which pay and direct the school, pay and direct also the pulpit and the press" (Smith 1982, 123). Even an advocate of state provision, the English radical William Lovett, despised the Prussian system, "where the lynx-eyed satellites of power . . . crush in embryo the buddings of freedom" (Smith 1982, 126). Lovett originally held out hope that it was possible for state funding to come without state control. While he continued to uphold the idea in theory, he had such strong doubts and suspicions about the actual policies of the English government that he urged workers to set up their own schools, free from government control.

Nineteenth-century investigators, however, were taken not only with what one might expect to find in a Prussian system—thoroughness, order, and state-run teaching academies—but also with features decidedly contrary to what might be expected from a despotic government. Stowe praised Prussian schools for their thorough and practical curricula, comfortable facilities, and progressive teaching methods. Seminary professor that he was, he particularly admired the emphasis on moral and religious instruction—which, he claimed, was free from sectarian bias (Stowe 1930 [1837], 260). He was also quite interested in the "excellent order and rigid economy" of Prussian schools. Sounding like a proto-environmentalist, he considered his fellow Americans too wasteful, and believed that frugality would be beneficial in a future of increasing scarcity (Stowe 1930 [1837], 257–58). Finally, Stowe noted the flexibility of Prussian-controlled schools in teaching in the native languages of the king's non-German subjects (Stowe 1930 [1837], 257–58). A Frenchman sent to investigate the Prussian system found "no injudicious spirit of centralization or of official despotism (*bureaucratie ministérielle*); almost everything is left to the parochial, departmental, or provincial authorities; little more than the general supervision and direction are reserved to the minister" (Cousin 1930 [1836], 205–6).

As these nineteenth-century observers discovered, Prussia and the German Empire were not entirely autocratic monoliths. In the nineteenth century, Prussia faced a situation similar to that of the United States: it was a nation with growing boundaries encompassing a diverse population. Territorial expansion after the Napoleonic wars and the wars of 1866 and 1871 left Prussian leaders with the task of governing what had once been a patchwork of kingdoms, principalities, bishoprics, and assorted dominions. Its various inhabitants did not make this task easier—in the west were Catholic Germans with a different religion than the Protestant king of Prussia, and in the east were Catholic Poles with both a different language and a different religion than their rulers.

Efforts to expand central control could meet with vehement resistance. Six different bills to expand the state's power at the expense of the Church failed, and nonconfessional schools were as scarce by the end of the nineteenth century as at the beginning. When Bismarck's education minister introduced a bill that removed the clergy's exclusive right to serve as local school inspectors and transferred the power of appointment to the state, over 300,000 citizens signed petitions opposing the measure. Poles continually resisted government efforts to Germanize them through the education system. In 1842, after 12 years of effort by the governor of Posen to Germanize the province by, among other things, replacing Polish with German in the schools, Frederick William IV appeased his Polish subjects by restoring Polish as the official language of instruction in their local schools. The previous year, he had created a separate section for Catholic instruction in the education ministry. In the first decade of the twentieth century, another effort to remove the Polish language from schools met with mass protests and school boycotts. In October 1906, 75,000 schoolchildren in Posen participated in a general strike of their schools; another 70,000 children stayed home in Silesia and West Prussia (Schleunes 1989).

While Prussia and Germany had a decentralized education system wrapped in an orderly and efficient autocratic cape, schooling in England was a combination of a public system under the stultifying control of the central government and a wide-open private system controlled by the invisible hand of the market. At the beginning of the nineteenth century, the country had two competing systems of charity schools. The earliest, founded in 1808 by Dissenters, was the British and Foreign School Society, which operated schools in the Lancastrian method. Three years later, in response, High Church Tories founded the National Society for Promoting the Education of the Poor in the Principle of the Established Church, called the National Society for short. Both societies operated schools supported by private donations until 1833, when the government began to grant the organizations funding on a matching basis. The National Society, with a larger base of private donors, soon far outstripped their rivals in receiving government aid (Laqueur 1976; Smith 1982).

Meanwhile, the working-class objects of all this charity frequently eschewed sending their children to local charity schools in favor of local private schools. The publicly supported schools were paternalistic institutions imposed on communities by outsiders. Parents did not like their curricula; their inflexible schedules and procedures; their uniforms, which carried the stigma of charity; and the cost and inconvenience of rules about cleanliness and grooming. The private schools, on the other hand, were often run by friends and neighbors. They were accommodating to the special needs of working-class parents, structuring the curriculum around the sporadic attendance of students, taking a liberal attitude on dress and appearance, and even accepting payment in vegetables when parents were short of cash (Laqueur, 1976).

Parliament put up obstacles to local initiatives by local communities to establish their own tax-supported schools. A local community had to approve an initiative via a property-weighted voting procedure. The plan then had to be approved by Parliament. Furthermore, many in the lower classes were unable to vote. The Second Reform Act of 1867 extended the franchise to only 31 percent of males. The Third Reform Act, passed in 1884, gave only 63 percent of men the vote (Lindert 2001). Workers were naturally suspicious and hostile toward a government in which they had little say. State-supported education would only mean more taxes to be "wrung from the working man" (Laqueur 1976, 200).

The British experience is a cautionary tale all around. For advocates of a minimal state role in education, despite the thirst for education among the public and heroic efforts by parents to obtain education for their children, educational attainment in the United Kingdom still fell short of the publicly financed local systems of Prussia and the United States, and even that of France. Those who believe public education is a vital underpinning of society should also be cautioned. Despite being behind in conventional measures of support and scope of education, Great Britain had a level of education sufficient to make it a world power and leader in the arts and sciences during the nineteenth century.

Local Control, Exit, and the Efficiency of Schools

Small, decentralized organizations also make control through exit easier, for exit requires choices. Although individual action through exit may seem relatively weak next to the collective action of voice, there is ample evidence that numerous individuals acting through markets can spell success or failure for organizations ranging from symphony orchestras to dry cleaners. The market application of this principle is clear: a firm is more disciplined facing competitors than if it had a monopoly. Similarly, the government of a region is more efficient if its residents can vote with their feet and move elsewhere. Just as businesses that produce goods for the market compete for customers, political jurisdictions from national governments down to local school districts compete for residents in the quality of the public goods they provide. Citizens migrate from poorly managed school districts, cities, and states to those that are well managed. Ever since the first white settlers rowed ashore in the New World nearly 400 years ago, colonies, local communities, and states have competed for residents. Heavily male Western states gave women the vote and enacted community property laws to attract female migrants. One delegate to the California constitutional convention called a community property law "[T]he very best provision to get us wives" (Brinig and Buckley 1996). This form of competition among governmental jurisdictions is called Tiebout competition, after the economist Charles Tiebout who first described it formally (Tiebout 1956).

Tiebout competition can lead to more-efficient schools, using two senses of the word *efficiency*. The first meaning is the common meaning of producing an output with minimal cost, what economists call productive efficiency. The second meaning is what economists call allocative or Pareto efficiency. Everyone lives in a community with a school that most closely fits their income and taste. Tiebout competition promotes efficiency in both senses. Everyone moves to the jurisdiction of a government that provides public goods closest to his or her own taste, and governments have an incentive to provide goods at the lowest cost to taxpayers.

The property tax combined with Tiebout competition creates an even more powerful inducement for local government officials. Migration to a more effectively managed region drives up the prices of houses located within it. Poor government managers, however, see residents leave, causing housing prices within the community to fall. Thus, housing prices incorporate to some extent the quality of local government services. As economists would put it, the quality of local services is capitalized into housing prices. Competent public officials who raise the value of homes in their jurisdiction consequently see greater property tax collections. This pleases them, since it gives them larger budgets to spend on the items that they prefer: more services, larger staffs, higher salaries, bigger offices, or newer cars for the motor pool. Local officials who do a poor job of running the town or school district see tax collections dwindle. In addition, since property values reflect expectations of future value, public officials have an incentive to be more forward looking than they might otherwise be (Glaeser 1995).

Tiebout competition and its effect on property values result in two corollaries with respect to school districts. First, homeowners, even those without children, care about the quality of local schools since it affects the value of their houses. Second, high housing prices can act as a barrier to good public schools just as tuition is a barrier to private schools. Following pioneering research by Wallace Oates (1969), statistical analysis has sought to estimate the exact magnitude of these prices, and consequently what value homeowners place on their neighborhood school (Black 1999; Weimer and Wolkoff 2001; Haurin and Brasington 1996). This value can be substantial. One study of the Cleveland area found differences in home values from $4,600 to $18,000 due to differences in school quality (Bogart and Cromwell 1997). Researchers have also used housing prices to find the implicit value that parents put on various aspects of school quality. It is no surprise that schools with high test scores have a positive impact on the price of nearby houses (Brasington 1999; Downes and Zabel 1997; Haurin and Brasington 1996). By one estimate, a 5 percent increase in test scores can lead to a 2.5 percent increase in home prices (Black 1999). Housing prices indicate that parents pay attention to "school report cards" and other administrative rankings (Figlio and Lucas 2002). They also indicate that parents value local control. Home values fall when school districts are consolidated and parents' voice is diluted in a larger district (Brasington 1998). Paradoxically, despite the fact that academic research is mixed regarding the impact of per-pupil spending and class size, housing prices indicate that parents place a value on small class sizes and greater per-student spending (Brasington 1999, Downes and Zabel 1997; Oates 1969).

Any realtor can testify to the existence of Tiebout competition. Homebuyers are acutely interested in the quality of local schools, parks, neighborhood appearance, crime, and other factors that might affect property values. Once situated, homeowners can be fiercely territorial, as the member of any school board that has attempted to close a school or alter attendance boundaries can attest. One mother in the affluent Phoenix suburb of Scottsdale complained in the November 24, 2001, *Arizona Republic* that the local school board's proposal to alter school attendance boundaries was "terrorism on a local level," akin to the September 11 terrorist attacks. "We purchased our homes predicated on the neighborhood schools," she continued. "We spend extra money on tutors and trainers. . . . We join the parent-teacher organizations and volunteer our time. . . . " Clearly, she made a large investment in the education of her children in terms of time, money, and the choice of where to live:

A potential problem that looms large over the threatened boundary changes is the devastating effect on property values. No family moves into a neighborhood without inquiring about the schools. Our school board threatens to make part of Phoenix, all of Paradise Valley, and all of Scottsdale family unfriendly: virtually unlivable.

Research has linked Tiebout competition and the efficiency of local schools. Schools in areas in which parents have a greater choice among local districts typically are more efficient. The standard study attempts to determine the relationship between the number of school districts in a "market"—usually a county or metropolitan area—and educational outcomes: spending, achievement, the number of children attending private schools. The more school districts serving a region, the easier it is for families to choose among them, and hence the greater the discipline of Tiebout competition.

Researchers have found that student achievement is higher in regions with more school districts (Blair and Staley 1995; Borland and Howsen 1992; Zanzig 1997). Greater satisfaction with public schools means less demand for alternatives. Private school attendance is lower the greater the choices available in the public sector (Martinez-Vazquez and Seaman 1985).

Caroline Hoxby (2000a) found that regions with greater competition have lower per-pupil costs; despite this, class sizes are smaller as well. Student performance—as measured by educational attainment, wages, and test scores—was higher in schools in more competitive areas. Tiebout competition did not have an adverse impact on minorities or the poor. Finally, Hoxby found that Tiebout competition did not affect the diversity of schools' student bodies. This is unexpected, since the heart of Tiebout competition is sorting families into areas where the neighbors are like them. While it may be heartwarming to conclude that, when it comes to sorting, families do not care about income or race, Hoxby does not do so. Instead, she believes that families sort themselves by school regardless of the number of districts in the area. Thus, sorting by race and income takes place, Tiebout competition or not.

The impact of Tiebout competition on the overall size of the public sector is uncertain. As Lott (1997) points out, making government agencies like school districts more efficient can either lower their overall spending, or, since competition lowers the effective price of public goods, it can raise public demand for them, leading to a net increase in spending. Research on government spending in general has found evidence for both: greater decentralization can decrease net government spending or can have no effect (Nellor 1984; Oates 1985; Eberts and Gronberg 1990). The same has been found for school districts in particular. While Hoxby (2000a) found that Tiebout competition lowers spending, Urquiola (1999) found the opposite.

Aside from the benefit of a number of separate school districts due to Tiebout competition, research has found that the sizes of schools and school districts matter as well. Although financial economies of scale argue for large districts, aspects of bigness adversely affect both fiscal efficiency and student achievement. Large organizations become difficult for managers at the top to supervise. With less monitoring from above, individual departments grow more self-interested instead of focusing on serving clients. Studies find that student performance is better in small schools and districts (Fowler and Walberg 1991). Friedkin and Necochea (1988) found a difference in the effects of size between rich and poor districts. In rich districts, size generates the resources to hire well-qualified teachers, buy better equipment and facilities, and provide more programs and extracurricular activities. Poor parents, however, are less able to negotiate the maze of bureaucracy of a large district.

Local Control, Grassroots Tyranny, and Segregation

There are aspects of local control and Tiebout competition that many find unsettling or objectionable. I have used the neutral term *sorting* to describe the movement of individuals into more homogeneous communities. Individuals have different tastes, and they voluntarily choose their communities and schools like they choose their cars. Within the assumptions of the model, the fact that some choose differently is no reason for concern. It allows local governments to closely match the public goods they provide with public preferences. This point of view is probably very difficult for many to understand or accept—especially in the case of education. For many, sorting means inequality, and sorting means tribalism. Others, when describing sorting into different school districts, use the more loaded term *stratification*, as in an upper stratum and a lower stratum. Finally, sorting may be viewed as *segregation*, a word with even more sinister connotations. While Tiebout competition may enable the like-minded to send their children to a school that best meets their preferences, one of those preferences may be, in the blandest economic terms, a "taste for disassociation," or the desire to be apart from people of a different race. There is evidence that this is in fact the case: states with more racially diverse populations tend to have more school districts, implying that people are more resistant to school consolidation if it means sharing control with people of a different race. Individuals are apparently especially sensitive to race when it comes to education; the racial diversity of a region has no effect on the number of other types of local governments (Martinez-Vazquez, Rider, and Walker 1997).

As Shain (1994) tells us, in the American tradition, local control has frequently meant the freedom of local communities to harass dissenters and burn witches without meddling by higher authorities. Some American political thinkers, including Madison, saw the danger this majoritarian rule posed to individual liberty:

Wherever the real power in a Government lies, there is the danger of oppression. In our Governments the real power lies in the majority of the Community, and the invasion of private rights is chiefly to be apprehended, not from acts of Government contrary to the sense of constituents, but from acts in which the Government is the mere instrument of the major number of Constituents. (quoted in Bolick 1993, 39)

Madison and others saw a national government as a counter to the possible tyranny of local majorities. The efforts of the state and national governments to protect minority groups and individuals against what Clint Bolick calls "grassroots tyranny" has been a fundamental source of tension and conflict in American history and in education policy.

THE PUSH FOR CENTRALIZATION IN THE UNITED STATES: THE FIRST HUNDRED YEARS

Thomas Jefferson, along with George Washington, Benjamin Rush, John Jay, and James Madison, believed that an educated public was vital to the preservation of liberty and the survival of the new nation. Proud to be the founder of the University of Virginia—he placed it after the Declaration of Independence and the Statute for Religious Freedom as his most significant achievement—Jefferson created a plan to educate all citizens and support the education through college of those who lacked the means to support themselves. He balked at compulsory education, feeling that free education and disenfranchisement of the uneducated would provide sufficient incentive for parents to send their children to school (Jefferson 1817). However, he did favor taxation to support public education, seeing it as insurance against the tribute that otherwise would have been paid to "kings, priest and nobles" (Jefferson 1786). Jefferson was also an advocate of local control of education: "There are two subjects, indeed, which I shall claim a right to further as long as I breathe: the public education and the sub-division of counties into wards. I consider the continuance of republican government as absolutely hanging on these two hooks" (Jefferson 1814).

Even so, the idea of free, tax-supported education for all children, with a small but significant supervisory role for state government, was still too much government for Americans at the time. Jefferson's several attempts over nearly 40 years all failed. After the final defeat, Jefferson also set a precedent in rhetoric for future supporters of public schools by attributing resistance to his plan to "ignorance, malice, egoism, fanaticism, religious, political and local perversities" (Kaestle 1983, 9). Virginia did not have free, statewide public schools until 1870.

For the first 50 years after the creation of the new Republic, despite the urging and plans of Jefferson and others, little government action was taken to inculcate the necessary republican virtues into citizens. The matter was not mentioned in the Constitution. State governments also did little. New York, for example, passed a law in 1795 appropriating $50,000 per year over five years to support local schools. After five years, the money had run out, and the legislature was faced with enacting a property tax for state support to continue. Lawmakers demurred, and the law was allowed to die without being renewed. Four years later, the state created a school fund from the proceeds of the sale of state-owned land. The interest, once it had reached the amount of $50,000 per year, was to be distributed to schools; the first distribution was made in 1815. Connecticut also provided aid to local schools from interest on a school fund constituted by the receipts from land sales. Massachusetts enacted a law in 1789 requiring each town of over 50 families to provide an elementary school, and a town with more than 200 families to build a grammar school; no state aid was provided, however (Kaestle 1983; West 1967).

These first five decades were known as the "sleepy" period by subsequent advocates, such as Horace Mann, and their chroniclers, like Ellwood Cubberly. For them, the period was a kind of educational Dark Age—one of stagnation and even decline in the school system—between the ancient virtue of the Puritan founders, who required each town in the colony to have a school, and the common school reforms of the mid-nineteenth century (Kaestle and Vinovskis, 1980, 10–11).

Children in the early Republic were served by a motley system of schools—public, private, and those that do not conveniently fit the modern labels. In small towns and rural areas, children were educated by local ward schools, known as district schools, similar to those envisioned by Jefferson. The ward schools received financial support from local taxes, some state aid, and rates and fuel contributions paid by parents. In one New York town during the 1830s, parents paid one to three times as much as aid received from the state. The state superintendents of education in New York were staunch advocates of having parents pay substantial fees to keep them interested and active in their children's education. They believed that local energies rather than state money were essential for good schools. For support, they cited neighboring Connecticut, where schools received per-pupil state aid four times the amount given to New York schools: "But even there, with an ample fund, there is much complaint in regard to the low state of common school education" (West 1967). In Massachusetts, parents did not have to pay to have their children attend during the regular school session. However, communities typically assessed parents a fee to extend the school year, and only children whose parents paid the fee were allowed to attend (Kaestle and Vinovskis 1980, 16).

In the cities, children had an educational buffet of charity schools operated by churches, towns, or private organizations; academies; dame schools; and other private, entrepreneurial schools. Schools were supported by philanthropic donations, tuition payments from parents, and government funds. In New York City, this diversity was supported through government policy. The city's common council in charge of distributing state funds from the 1795 act decided not to establish state-operated schools but rather to give money to the 10 religious charity schools and the African Free School (Ravitch 1974, 7).

Even though schooling was noncompulsory and free only to the very poor, the fraction of children attending school during the sleepy period grew and reached levels comparable to the enrollment rates experienced after the common school advocates awakened the nation. In 1825 in New York State, 64 percent of youths younger than 19 were enrolled in school, as compared to 60 percent enrolled in 1850, 10 years after the free-school movement had been launched. The enrollment rate in New York City in 1850, 26.3 percent, was barely greater than in 1796 (25 percent). The fraction of children attending school in Salem, Massachusetts, in 1875 was only marginally greater than in 1820 (Kaestle and Vinovskis 1980). In 1787, at the beginning of the sleepy period, 65 percent of free males were literate; in New England, the literacy rate may have been over 80 percent. In 1850, 90 percent of whites, male and female, were literate (Coulson 1999, 84; Kaestle 1991a).

Education in the United States was officially awakened from its sleepy period on April 20, 1837, when Massachusetts created a state board of education. The board itself had very little power; its charge was to collect data on schools in the state and submit its findings in yearly reports to the legislature. Its most important function was to serve as the pulpit for its first secretary, Horace Mann. Mann's appointment as secretary was actually a surprise; the favorite was James G. Carter, who had been working for years to reform schools in Massachusetts. Upon accepting the position, Mann swore to himself that "Henceforth, as long as I hold this office, I dedicate my-self to the supremest welfare of mankind upon earth" (Kaestle and Vinovskis 1980, 209).

By the time he was appointed secretary, Horace Mann already had a prominent career as a Whig legislator and a social reformer. He played an important role in the establishment of a state mental hospital and of regulations covering liquor retailers. He was a member of a society to prevent pauperism and of the Prison Discipline Society. Mann served with the board until 1848, when he took John Quincy Adams's seat in the U.S. House of Representatives, where he became an active opponent of slavery (Brown University 2002; Nasaw 1979, 32). In 1900, 41 years after Mann's death, William Torrey Harris acclaimed Mann's appointment as the beginning of the modern urban school system with its larger size, centralized control, staff of education professionals, and broader and more comprehensive educational offerings (Kaestle and Vinovskis 1980, 101).

In his 12 reports as secretary and by stumping the countryside lecturing at county meetings and teacher institutes, Mann campaigned for such educational reforms as increased teacher training and pay and the abolition of corporal punishment, and against the locally controlled district schools. His reports to the legislature painted a picture of crowded, woefully maintained schoolhouses and poorly trained teachers. The answer, he felt, was to overcome the parochial, short-sighted resistance to paying more for schools by consolidating control at the town level. Another of Mann's objectives was to drive out private schools. In his first report, Mann used arguments against private schools that are still heard to this day: private schools damage the public school system by creaming off the best students. Along with the students go their wealthy and influential parents, undermining support for public education in an important stratum of society. Religious private schools, Mann believed, divided society along sectarian lines (Kaestle and Vinovskis 1980, 33–34, 100).

Mann was not the first state officer responsible for education, but he and the others were the standard bearers of the common school movement, a reform effort to create modern public schools. The six key features fought for by reformers, as outlined by Cubberly, were

1. The battle for tax support
2. The battle to eliminate the pauper-school idea
3. The battle to make the schools entirely free
4. The battle to establish state supervision
5. The battle to eliminate sectarianism
6. The battle to extend the system upward [to establish public high schools] (Cubberly 1919, 128–129)

The objective was to create a school system for children of all social classes (hence common) wholly supported by taxes, forbidding rate payments by parents (hence free). The stigma of charity needed to be erased for free schools to attract children of all classes, hence the battle against the idea of pauper schools. Reformers waged these battles against local communities that perceived them as an attack on parents' control of their children's education.

An example of what so vexed the common school movement can be found in the excellent sketch drawn by Martha Coons, John Jenkins and Carl Kaestle (1980) of the school system in the small rural community of Boxford, Massachusetts. In response to the 1789 Massachusetts law requiring towns to create districts and furnish a school in each, Boxford divided itself into six districts. Although there were committees at the town and district level to supervise the schools, much power and responsibility rested at a level below that of the districts. Parents were held to be most responsible for their children's training and socialization. Schools placed third in influence—behind the church. "God places children upon their entrance into life, not in schools, but in families; he has imposed the responsibility in regards to the training they may receive, not upon teachers, but upon parents," intoned the Boxford school committee in its 1857 annual report (Coons, Jenkins, and Kaestle 1980, 151). Consequently, school officials in Boxford complied half-heartedly with state mandates regarding compulsory education.

Parents also jealously guarded their right to select their children's textbooks. As early as 1796, the town's school committee recommended that the town furnish uniform texts for all children. However, teachers frequently had books they preferred to use, and Boxford parents—thrifty Yankee farmers that they were—found it cheaper and more convenient to hand down used textbooks to younger children. Thus, children in the same classroom often studied out of a hodgepodge of books in various editions, with some students not even having a book for some subjects. The school committee was still fretting about the variety of books used at the end of the nineteenth century.

Local residents also kept a tight grip on school facilities, despite the town committee's repeated complaints about the dilapidated condition of the buildings. Another matter of perpetual concern to the Boxford school committee was the quality of the teaching staff. Parents stoutly resisted measures by schools officials at both the town and state level aimed at improving teacher quality—such as uniform certification requirements—that infringed on their selecting teachers. Parents viewed the selection of teachers as an important part of their traditional authority over the upbringing of their children.

Throughout the nineteenth century, the members of Boxford's school committee believed that the ills of the town's schools could be cured by centralization of control and consolidation. Consolidation would have allowed more equal funding among the different schools and would have saved money. In 1843, it would have allowed the town to hire three teachers to teach in schools of 40 students each instead of having to hire six teachers to staff schools of 20 students. Larger schools would have allowed students to be placed into grades, enabling teachers to be more effective. Yet until 1869, the citizens of Boxford voted down every attempt to centralize control by abolishing the power of the local districts and consolidating schools. In that year, a new state law required towns to abolish their district committees or lose state funding. Faced with the loss of $75 in state money, citizens voted to do away with their district committees.

The town of Boxford offers an interesting test of the modern reader's philosophy of school governance. One may, like the common school advocates, be appalled at backward and tight-fisted rustics shortchanging their children's future. On the other hand, one may admire the fierce independence of Boxford residents who took responsibility for and maintained a vigorous interest in their children's education. These Massachusetts farmers were putting into practice the vision of Virginia aristocrat Thomas Jefferson. Coons, Jenkins, and Kaestle provide no indication of the "educational outcomes" in Boxford other than their fictitious example Sarah, who after 10 years of school could read, write, and do arithmetic, and knew something of geography and history. Instilling these skills along with discipline, proper behavior, and moral education was what the Boxford school committee reiterated as the goals of their town's schools. Schools were "accountable" directly to parents and local taxpayers. Parents had the opportunity to see their children's progress in evening programs that served as town social events, and at the public examinations at the end of the term, when children demonstrated their skills in spelling, reading, and arithmetic for their parents and other interested citizens.

The efforts of Mann and his fellow reformers met with considerably stronger resistance than the rustic indifference of towns like Boxford. Many leaders in the Massachusetts Democratic party—or "political madmen," as Mann referred to them (Kaestle and Vinovskis 1980, 214)—hewed to the principles they inherited from Jefferson and Jackson and viewed increasing central control as an assault on the rights of parents and local communities. One of Mann's most outspoken critics, Orestes A. Brownson, declared himself to be an unequivocal supporter of universal education and of the obligation of local communities to provide the best education within their resources. The real difference, Brownson asserted, was whether the power to determine the purpose, means, and methods of education should reside with parents in local districts or with some state agency. With district control, parents managed the schools to which they sent their own children. With state control, commissioners, secretaries, superintendents, and other political creatures managed schools that their children did not attend. Brownson singled out Mann's high regard for the Prussian system as a dangerous symptom of latent autocracy:

A government system of education in Prussia is not inconsistent with the theory of Prussian society, for there all wisdom is supposed to be lodged in the government. But the thing is wholly inadmissible here ... because, according to our theory, the people are supposed to be wiser than the government. (Nasaw 1979, 64)

On January 1, 1840, the newly elected Democratic governor of Massachusetts put forward his agenda in an address to the state legislature. It was the standard Democratic program (for the time): no special legislative favors for corporations, no state aid for railroads, and a reduction in the size of government. He also put in a general good word for local control of schools. The "little pure democracies" found in town and district meetings were the best trustees of the schools in the state. As part of a general effort to reduce state salaries and eliminate government offices, the Massachusetts Board of Education was put on the chopping block by a special House committee. State regulation of schools, the committee held in its report, was unnecessary. Instead of centralizing control in one "grand central head," the government, the committee believed that it was better to heed the "good old principles of our ancestors" and diffuse the power and responsibility for educating the young "not only into the towns and districts, but even into families and individuals" (Kaestle and Vinovskis 1980, 214–16).

The first swipe of the budget cutter's axe narrowly missed the Board of Education, but the issue was referred to the Committee on Education. The committee issued another report blasting the Board of Education. Like true Jacksonians, committee members worried that the board was the beginning of a "monopoly of power." Packed with Unitarians, it threatened religious freedom in the state:

Schools may be used as a potent means of engrafting into the minds of children, political, religious, and moral opinions;—but, in a country like this, where such diversity of sentiments exists . . . the difficulty and danger of attempting to introduce these subjects into our schools, according to one fixed and settled plan, to be devised by a central Board, must be obvious.

The committee went on to affirm that the right to shape the political, moral, and religious beliefs of children rested exclusively with parents (Fraser 1999, 30).

The committee also worried about Unitarian influence in the board's push to create libraries in all state schools. Libraries in themselves were fine; what the committee objected to was the board's compiling a list of recommended books. The committee saw an officially approved list of books as posing one of two dangers. The first was an intentional or unintentional imposition of certain values and beliefs. The second was the possibility that the board, in a sincere attempt to promote only unbiased texts, would recommend dull, insubstantial books (Fraser 1999, 30).

In the end, the board easily survived the threat; the bill to abolish it was defeated 245 to 182. However advances elsewhere were not so permanent. What reformers viewed as progress came in fits and starts. Next door to Massachusetts, in Connecticut, Henry Barnard was left without a job when the board of education was abolished four years after its creation (Nasaw 1979, 59). Massachusetts passed and soon repealed a law that required towns to abolish their district committees in 1859; in 1869, legislation again ordered abolishing districts, but in 1870 the legislature reversed itself again and gave local communities the option of reestablishing districts with a two-thirds vote. Districts were finally permanently done away with in 1883 (Kaestle 1983, 152).

Similar backtracking came in the fight for schools wholly supported by taxes. In the perpetual bureaucratic quest for the grail of a dedicated funding stream, school reformers advocated that states require districts to support their schools through property taxes. Once again, we turn to Horace Mann:

> . . . If education, then, be the most important interest of society, it must be placed upon the most permanent and immovable basis that society can supply. It should not be found upon the shifting sands of popular caprice or passion or upon individual benevolence: but if there be a rock anywhere, it should be founded upon that rock. (West 1967, 110)

Mann literally meant rock, or "PROPERTY," as the transcription of his speech has it. Property was the mother of all tax bases. As Mann put it, property was the distillation of eternal natural forces: the fertility of the soil, the bounty of the sea, the sun's heat and light, the wind, and so on. Property taxes were just because property owners had the most to gain from educating the masses. Reformers urged landowners, merchants, and manufacturers to look upon paying school taxes as a particularly economical form of insurance against social unrest, pauperism, vice, and crime. The good Whig Mann wobbled into social democracy in his tenth report, asserting that in the end property owners were "merely the 'trustees' of the community's wealth." Property was the gift of past generations, nature, and God, so owners had an obligation to give back to the community by supporting the upbringing of its children (Nasaw 1979, 52–54).

To individuals in local communities, however, state-mandated property taxes were an attack on fundamental rights, not only as property owners, but also as parents. Under the traditional system, schools were supported by a combination of taxes and payments by parents known as rates. Rates gave parents immediate leverage over their schools. Dissatisfied parents could easily remove their children and their money. Rates make it easier for parents to send their children to private schools, since they would not be burdened with paying tuition and taxes for public schools at the same time. Indeed, one motivation for the free school movement—the push for rate-free, taxpayer-supported common schools—was to foreclose the private school option. Finally, rates left decisions regarding charity in local hands. Poor families were often exempted from paying, but at the discretion of the community, so citizens could decide which of their neighbors merited support.

In the West and South, local districts were unable to tax themselves unless enabled by state law. In Illinois, a "permissive" law allowing districts to tax themselves to support public schools was passed in 1825. Two years later, it was amended to require that citizens give written permission before they could be taxed for schools. An 1824 "permissive" law in Indiana was repealed in 1837. After New York abolished rates in 1849, a flood of petitions caused a repeal in 1851. In some districts, abolishing rates actually backfired. Rates paid by parents had allowed schools to stay open for up to eight months. Once the burden was shifted to taxpayers, many poorer districts voted to keep their schools open only for the required four months. Rates in the Empire State were not successfully ended until 1867 (Nasaw 1979, 52, 55; West 1967).

When, in 1834, Pennsylvania enacted a law that permitted districts to tax themselves to support common schools—and used the leverage of state aid to encourage them to do so—the legislature was beset with petitions asking for repeal of the law. Local communities, many made up of German immigrants, had already established their own schools. These schools were often affiliated with religious sects—Mennonites, Quakers, Lutherans, or German Reformed—but were open to those who were not church members or were unable to pay. These communities were unable to support both the church schools and a nonsectarian, tax-supported system. The Pennsylvania law was pushing them to abandon schools that taught the religion, language, and customs of community residents. The law was never repealed, but over half of the districts in the state forfeited state aid rather than give up their schools (Nasaw 1979, 55).

States resisted other Yankee innovations. New York created the first state superintendent of education in 1812. The first holder of the office, Gideon Hawley, so upset things that the legislature abolished his position in 1821. New York recreated the office in 1854. Maryland established a superintendent of education in 1826, eliminated it in 1828, and reestablished it in 1864. Ohio created a state position for education in 1837, abolished it three years later, and finally reestablished it in 1853. Illinois and Indiana did not have state boards or superintendents until 1854 (Cubberly 1919, 158; Nasaw 1979, 59).

Nineteenth-century reformers tried to extend state power and influence local decisions through means that would be familiar to their twentieth-century counterparts. Horace Mann exercised moral suasion by releasing an annual list that ranked all the towns in Massachusetts by spending per student (Kaestle 1983, 122). State aid was made conditional on conforming to state requirements regarding taxes, curriculum, teacher certification, filing reports, and other mandates (Cubberly 1919, 157). As we have seen, state aid in Pennsylvania was used as leverage to prod local districts to tax themselves for common schools. Although some districts refused, by 1847 only 158 out of 1,225 districts still chose to forswear state funds in order to maintain local independence (Kaestle 1983, 149).

What all this bureaucracy and imported Prussian organization did for educational outcomes is not clear. In Massachusetts, despite the push to consolidate, average school size fell slightly from 32 students in 1840 to 29 in 1875. Average class size fell from 31 to 19 over those same years. Per-pupil spending and teachers salaries increased after accounting for inflation, but more than 80 percent of funds still came from local taxes. The percentage of children 19 or younger who were enrolled in school actually fell from 67 percent in 1840 to 49 percent in 1880. Reformers did succeed in decreasing the market share of private schools. The fraction of students enrolled in private schools fell from 14 percent in 1840 to 8 percent in 1880 (Kaestle and Vinovskis 1980). Other states saw more substantial jumps in attendance, but nationwide the proportion of 5- to 19-year-olds in school rose only slightly from 47 percent in 1850 to 51 percent in 1900. Those who did attend spent more time in school: 71 days in 1880 compared to 61 days 40 years earlier (Goldin 1999; Kaestle, 1983, 106).

The end of the nineteenth century saw another wave of centralization batter against public schools. It was stirred by the agitation of progressive reformers, education professionals, muckrakers, and business leaders. Many urban schools were governed by a ward system that closely guarded local control over schools, as did the district system in rural areas. Pittsburgh was governed by 39 subdistrict boards that individually levied local taxes; were responsible for hiring teachers and building and maintaining schools; and that selected the superintendent in a tri-annual convention. In Buffalo, school taxes were assessed by district rather than citywide. When the boroughs of New York were unified, the new charter explicitly prohibited the superintendent from interfering with the way any school in the city was actually operated (Tyack 1974, 88–91).

School boards were large: one survey of 28 cities found an average size of 21.5 members, Typically, members were elected by ward instead of citywide. Philadelphia had 42 members sitting on its central board and 504 members on the local boards for its 42 wards. Ward representatives, or trustees, reflected the ethnic makeup of the Irish, German, Jewish, and other minority neighborhoods that elected them. In response to the movement to abolish the ward boards, New York teachers praised the trustees' hard work and active interest in students' welfare. The ward committees were sensitive to the religion and customs of their immigrant constituencies. They permitted instruction in the immigrants' native tongues, removed textbooks with offensive passages, and allowed teachers to ignore Protestant indoctrination when teaching their Catholic pupils. This was part of a larger menu of services—job placement, charity, help negotiating municipal red tape—provided by the urban machines. This is not to say that Gilded Age cities were a sort of people's democracy run by colorful but sensitive figures in spats and bowler hats. There was plenty of corruption in the urban machines. Teachers were expected to provide kickbacks and help get out the vote on election day. Graft siphoned off money meant to be used for buildings and supplies. Publishers used money, jobs, and sex as bribes to get their textbooks chosen (Tyack 1974, 94–95, 100–103, 127).

To the reformers, the ward committee members were not only corrupt, but also overtly political and amateurs in the management of schools. The solution was small boards with nonpartisan members elected at-large from the city. Once the schools were out from under the control of political hacks and ward heelers, professional experts in education could manage them. Characterized by their opponents as "pink-tea ladies," aristocrats, "old-maids in the Civic Club," and the "University clique" wanting to gain control of the school system, the reformers followed the same line of attack in all cities: an opening barrage of newspaper stories exposing corruption in the existing system, followed by a flank attack around the local power structure into the state legislature, where the enabling law was passed. One by one, the citadels of the old system fell: New York in 1896, St. Louis in 1897, Philadelphia in 1905, and Chicago in 1917. By 1913, the average number of school board members in cities of 100,000 or more was 10.2—mostly elected at large; ward trustees were virtually extinct. By 1923, the median board size was 7 (Tyack 1974, 127, 155; Nasaw 1979, 109–13).

The Forces behind the Nineteenth-Century Centralization Movement

Ellwood Cubberly lined up the interest groups for and against the public school movement of the nineteenth century thus:

For

"Citizens of the Republic"

Philanthropists and humanitarians

Public men of large vision

City residents

The intelligent workingmen of the cities

Non-taxpayers

Calvinists

"New-England men"

Against

Belonging to the old aristocratic class

The conservatives of society

Politicians of small vision

Residents of rural districts

The ignorant, narrow-minded, and penurious

Taxpayers

Lutherans, Reformed-Church, Mennonites, and Quakers

Southern men

Proprietors of private schools

The non-English-speaking classes (Cubberly 1919, 120)

Many modern historians would add industrialists or capitalists to Cubberly's "for" list. Wealthy textile mill owner Edmund Dwight nominated Mann for secretary of the school board, urged him to accept the position, and personally augmented his annual salary by $500. What the common schools offered manufacturers was a trained, docile workforce and social order (Nasaw 1979, 44–47). The difficulty with the model of education as training for the proletariat is that the mills themselves offered a lucrative alternative to school—even for children under 12 years old. As we saw in the case of high schools at the beginning of the twentieth century, school attendance was higher in rural than in urban areas. In 1860 Boston, 31.5 percent of children younger than 19 went to school, compared to a state average of 35.5 percent and a 38.4 percent average for towns of less than 1,250 inhabitants. For older children, it was even worse. The attendance rate for 16- to-19-year-olds in Boston in 1860 was 7.7 percent, compared to 28.7 percent statewide (Kaestle and Vinovskis 1980). Compulsory education and child labor laws had no teeth, and rather than pressing the issue, reformers were content to urge mill owners, parents, and local communities to comply with existing laws (Kaestle 1983, 107–9).

The Progressive Era attack on the urban ward system is portrayed as pitting WASP businessmen and middle-class professionals against ethnic, working-class leadership (Tyack 1974, 126–28). However, as Paul Peterson (1985) found, Progressive Era attacks on the ward system were internecine conflicts among the local elite. In Atlanta, for example, control of the public school board before reform was firmly in the hands of the local establishment. Twenty percent of those who had served on the board the 15 years before reforms were enacted in 1897 were the heads of banks or corporations; 29 percent were lawyers; and 27 percent were professionals and other minor corporate officials. The public was increasingly frustrated with the board's torpor in the face of demands for reforms in such matters as choosing textbooks and expanding the curriculum to include vocational training. Above all, the public was incensed with the board's position on corporal punishment. Modern sensibilities were leading to a growing dissatisfaction with continued use of the hickory switch—to the point where the mayor publicly announced that he put his children in private schools so they would not be in danger of being beaten. The board, however, maintained its support of the district's teachers, who felt corporal punishment was necessary to maintain order. After the smoke had cleared, the board had been reduced from 17 to 7 members with shorter terms, and a significant amount of power had been transferred from the board to the administrative staff. The board was no longer in control of ordering supplies or judging disputes between teachers and parents. Gone were the corporate chieftains, mostly replaced by lawyers, minor businessmen such as realtors and insurance agents, politicians, and labor union officials. In Chicago, middle-class reformers sided with the Chicago Teachers' Federation against antiunion measures pushed by business and Mayor Thompson's machine. The resulting compromise passed by the state legislature gave the school superintendent more power, the school board increased autonomy from the city council, and teachers greater job security, but the mayor still had the power to appoint board members.

The simple theory of education for state control is also more complex and has a distinctive American twist. American citizens obviously did not have to learn to love the Kaiser, but it was widely believed that republican virtue needed to be instilled for the new nation to survive. To modern sensibility, to live in a free nation means having a large degree of liberty of thought and action, with a wide variety of beliefs and manners being tolerated. However, in America's infancy, to be a citizen of a nation conceived in liberty required rigorous adherence to a specific set of virtues (Sandel 1996). Benjamin Rush, who introduced a plan for public education in Pennsylvania similar to Jefferson's, thought it was possible and essential to turn men into "republican machines" if they were to take their places in the "great machine of state." A pupil should "be taught that he does not belong to himself, but that he is public property" (Rush 2002 [1786]). Noah Webster wanted to begin attaching individuals to the nation while they were still in the cradle; he wanted an infant's first word to be *Washington*; even the way children spelled words was to make them distinctively American (Kaestle 1983, 6–7).

Benjamin Rush and Noah Webster are singular examples of one school of thought on the most effective way to infuse republican virtue. Training by formal institutions was to instill into children, immigrants, freed slaves, and the poor the temperance, discipline, industriousness, and self-reliance that they would need if not to be full participants in society, then to be less of a burden on it. Presently, the chief mission of education is thought to be development of a child's cognitive skills in order to enable him or her to follow a successful and prosperous career. However, for the Whig reformers in the previous century, the goal was precisely the reverse. Intellectual development was a secondary consideration, while education's public benefits were viewed as paramount. The emphasis was on moral education: teaching children good habits over and above the three Rs. The purpose of public education, and other benevolent institutions as well, was chiefly to benefit society, not the individual. It did not matter that graduates of African American schools found their intellectual accomplishments useless because careers were closed to them; what was important to the whites who supported the African free schools was the moral instruction that was supposed to help African American children avoid falling into an immoral life. The Whig view was vigorously paternalistic. Charity, infant, and Sunday schools were intentionally designed to take the place of parents viewed as unfit (Kaestle 1983, Nasaw 1979, Miller 1940).

Whigs favored an active government role in education for the same reason they pushed for an active government role in economic development. Just as education was to foster public morality and a national consciousness, a network of government-promoted roads, canals, and railroads was to link the Union. The steam engine and the telegraph would bring civilization, refinement, and morality to wild and remote Western hamlets. An active and munificent federal government would earn gratitude and prestige from the public, replacing provincial state loyalties (Sandel 1996, 162–63).

While the pronouncements of nineteenth-century advocates of public education in the United States have been used to portray them as protototalitarians, it is important to emphasize that the common schools were not imposed on the lower classes by a WASP elite, or exclusively by the members of the Whig party. Many Democrats supported common schools and helped fight for Whig reforms. John Pierce and Isaac Crary, who were responsible for the authorization of an office of state superintendent of education by the Michigan constitution, were Democrats. A Democrat was the loudest advocate for a state school superintendent during the Illinois constitutional convention of 1847 (Kaestle 1983, 154–56; Sandel 1996, 156–67).

Schools were part of an effort by all political parties and social classes to build the social capital needed to cope with a society being rapidly transformed by industrialization and immigration. People of every social level recognized the need to bind society together, and they proceeded to bind it through grass-roots organizations. In the young United States, as the eighteenth century turned into the nineteenth, Americans of all social classes were forming voluntary associations for education, mutual aid, and charity. Benevolent societies built schools for poor children; Quakers established schools for the newly manumitted slaves in the Northern states; workers sharing the same occupation formed mutual aid associations (Kaestle 1983, 37).

In subsequent decades, Whig reformers, along with pushing for common schools, constructed an entire apparatus of social uplift to care for the infirm, give moral instruction to the dissolute, and assimilate the alien. They took action to muster both public and private resources. Benevolent societies built and supported asylums for the mentally ill, Sunday and charity schools, juvenile reformatories, and penitentiaries. Horace Mann was active in private charities and as a legislator worked for the establishment of state-supported institutions for the amelioration of social ills. In cities like Philadelphia and New York, most of the charity schools were consolidated under the umbrella of a charity or free school society that obtained and distributed subsidies from the state and city.

Workers' associations funded reading rooms and libraries for their members; encouraged education through their own lyceums, mechanics' institutes, and lecture series; and promoted the idea of personal advancement through self-education. Advocates claimed that one of the benefits of the 10-hour day was to give workers the time to educate themselves. Workers' groups were also early supporters of free schools. Unlike their counterparts in England, who were openly hostile to public schools as a middle-class conspiracy, American workers supported public schools as an alternative to the private, philanthropic schools, which carried the stigma of charity and were not under parental control (Kaestle 1983, 138–41; Nasaw. 1979, 26–27, 49–50).

As the nineteenth century wore on, immigration and technological change accelerated. The Whig party disappeared, but the cause of middle-class reform, centralization, and management by professionals was taken up by the Progressives. The Progressives had lost the religious sentimentality of a Calvin Stowe, but the void was filled with faith in science. As with the common school movement in the first half of the century, the Progressive reforms in education were preceded and accompanied by a grass-roots boom in social activity. Seeing a society in need of being knitted together, Americans once again took the task on themselves and became a nation of joiners—forming unions, fraternal organizations, benevolent societies, professional associations, hobbyist clubs, and numerous other types of organizations. In the four years between 1864 and 1868, the Knights of Pythias, the Grange, the Benevolent and Protective Order of the Elks, and the Grand Army of the Republic came into existence. The 1870s saw the creation of the National Rifle Association, the Shriners, and the American Bar Association; the 1880s the Red Cross, the Knights of Columbus, and the Loyal Order of the Moose (Putnam 2000). Just as at the century's beginning, private philanthropists founded educational institutions to meet newly perceived needs. Like the charity schools, the new vocational schools were subsumed in the public school system. Reform leaders at the beginning of the twentieth century could indulge in scary, seemingly totalitarian rhetoric and claim state ownership of the child. Nevertheless, the latter movement, like the former, demonstrates that social cohesion is built from the bottom up in institutions Americans create for themselves, not imposed from the top down.

Finally, the causes of centralization and professionalization were pushed forward by changes in transportation and communication technology, demographics, and new theories of organization and management. Although the word *town* invokes the image of a small community close both physically and socially, American towns were historically large jurisdictions of 20 to 40 square miles. In Boxford, it was said that some citizens lived their entire lives without seeing the other side of town (Kaestle 1983, 151). In colonial New England, residents were required to live within a half-mile of the meeting house. However, as the population grew and dispersed, the available transportation and communication technologies made central control by the town administration difficult. Towns were divided into wards and parishes for the purposes of tax collection, road maintenance, and mustering the militia (Cubberly 1919, 41–44). Since the town school was too far away to be convenient, parents sent their children to local dame schools or private academies. One public alternative was the traveling school, in which a schoolmaster rode the circuit through the separate wards, staying in each ward in proportion to its tax contribution supporting education. Eventually, however, wards assumed responsibility for funding and control of permanent ward or district schools. The decentralization of the district system is credited with fostering the spread of education through the states where it was adopted (Kaestle and Vinovskis 1980, 26).

However, as the nation grew, one-room schoolhouses found it hard to accommodate the children in rapidly growing districts—class sizes sometimes reached 80 or even 100 pupils. Towns responded by building in more populous wards schools that attempted to divide children by age and achievement level. They also built centrally controlled and located grammar schools to relieve the local schools of the burden of the older students. The lay members of the school boards became overwhelmed with their supervisory duties. A school board member at the time was typically responsible for visiting the schools in the ward he represented, monitoring teachers, and carrying out other administrative duties. School boards sought to ease this burden both by delegating duties to local principals and by hiring professional administrators, including superintendents (Coons, Jenkins, and Kaestle 1980).

Through the Gilded Age, the supposed high noon of laissez-faire capitalism in the United States, public services were professionalized and taken over by city governments (Tyack 1974, 30–33). Private volunteer

municipal fire departments—which seemed to spend as much time ca-
rousing and brawling with rival departments as putting out fires—were
fully absorbed into the public sector and staffed with professionals. Sanitation, road repair, transportation, light, and water were all made municipal departments in many American cities. Many of these had been
quasi-private, ward-based services like education. New York policemen
originally received no formal training and had to reside in the ward they
served. Untrained part-timers, however, were unable to cope with the
needs of growing cities and the new technologies that their functions required. To man an old-fashioned, hand-operated fire pump required only
a strong back; to operate the new steam pumps required more training.
Kicking out the amateurs did not necessarily imply public provision. Private corporations at the time were structured using the principles of modern management and staffed by skilled professionals. Indeed, some
municipal services were provided by corporations. However, voters evidently preferred the inefficiencies and padded payrolls of government
agencies to the corruption that seemed to plague the private operation
(Glaeser 2001).

By the end of the nineteenth century, schools had been public for some
time and, according to the muckrakers, had long been suffering from corruption. Restructuring was impelled by the new duties the schools were
assuming. Education leaders, the faculty of the new colleges of education,
and the public all expected more from schools: vocational education, expanded high schools, extracurricular activities, and nursing and counseling services. To cope with these new duties, a new organizational form
was needed. The revolution in management that had made the United
States a global industrial giant offered a successful model. Progressive Era
management principles called for control centralized in a hierarchy of
professionals. Instead of a large board of ward representatives with administrative duties, the school board was to be the counterpart of the
corporate board of directors: small and distant from everyday operation.
Day-to-day administration was to be left to the professionals. Looking
upon the mess that the modern education bureaucracy has become, one
may dismiss the reformers as placing a naïve faith in the power of bureaucracy and regret the passing of a seemingly more accountable ward
system. However, the management structure chosen by an organization
is a function of its mission, the norms and skills of the personnel staffing
it, and the technology it has to work with. Given the technology, resources,
social norms, and workforce available at the time, the private sector was
wildly successful using the hierarchical model. It was probably the most
reasonable solution to the problems facing education leaders of the time
(Peterson 1985, 205; Tyack 1974, 143–45).

LOSING CONTROL: THE MOVEMENT TOWARD
CENTRALIZATION FROM THE 1950s

In the middle of the twentieth century, the balance in the tug-of-war between central and local control in education was altered decisively. The Great Depression, World War II, the Cold War, and the *Brown* desegregation decision gave the federal government—and central authority in general—the purpose and moral authority allowing it to steamroll over the traditional bastions of local control (Shain 1994). The judicial, legislative, and executive branches of government at every level, from municipal through state on up to federal, became more involved in school oversight.

This wave of centralization carried its own concepts and methods of social science to measure its effects. As legislators, judges, and agency officials became more involved in school policy, they needed ways to measure the impact of their actions. Obviously, it was impossible to easily and cheaply monitor the many facets of individual schools from a perch at the metropolitan, state, or even national level. What was needed was numbers—easy to collect, compile, compare, and evaluate.

Educational measurement came in with the scientific education movement at the beginning of the twentieth century. For half a century, education administrators and scholars had been giving IQ and other tests and collecting data on enrollment and dropouts. In the 1960s, however, the growing education bureaucracies began collecting and digesting numbers with the gusto of Pentagon analysts reviewing Viet Cong body counts. A national achievement test to monitor student progress, the NAEP, was created in 1969. The mother of all modern educational studies, *Equality of Educational Opportunity* Report—commonly known as the Coleman Report—set the terms of education policy research and debate that have been dominant until the present. Written to fulfill a legislative mandate included in the 1964 Civil Rights Act, the Coleman Report was the first great effort to link education inputs to outputs. For the next three decades, education research and policy would revolve around how effective public schools were in converting resources into student achievement. Since the method of analysis was statistical, inputs and outputs had to be in numerical form: money and test scores. While the results of the nineteenth-century battles over local control have been described in terms of institutions created or shifts in power between various groups, a phalanx of researchers were ready to gauge the impact of twentieth-century centralization with a host of measures, including school funding, the integration of schools and neighborhoods, and, of course, student achievement (Wise 1979).

As in the nineteenth century, the centralizing juggernaut was assisted by improvements in technology for communications and the gathering, storage, and handling of large amounts of data. Note cards and file drawers were replaced by computers and magnetic storage. Computers complemented advances in statistical methods, and soon the halls of government agencies and universities were filled with social scientists doing regression analysis, cross-tabulation, analysis of variance, and other wizardry to inform and influence policymakers building the perfect school system. The science of organizing and managing the modern government bureau had been maturing for several decades. However, one of the most significant organizational developments in the postwar period took place outside of the formal bureaucracy. It was the technique of creating and managing nationwide, grass-roots movements pioneered by the civil rights movement. These methods were adopted by other groups with a grievance that looked to state and federal governments for assistance (Ravitch 1983).

Centralization at the Federal Level

These forces of centralization were aimed directly at public schools. In addition to the cancer of racial segregation, the method of local financing led to wide disparities among schools. Seeking to remedy these two problems would radically transform public schools over the last five decades of the twentieth century. Immediately after WWII, the National Education Association, allied with labor and civil rights groups, began a push for federal aid to local schools. The standard techniques—congressional hearings and articles in the *New York Times* decrying the abysmal state of the existing system—were employed. Leaders from President Truman to "Mr. Conservative," Ohio senator Robert Taft, were on board. The venture broke up, however, on the timeworn rocks of aid to religious schools. Taft's bill left the matter to the states, but Protestants, anti-Catholics, advocates for church-state separation, and others objected. The controversy stirred passions at the highest level: Cardinal Spellman and Eleanor Roosevelt exchanged missives in the press. Meanwhile, the Supreme Court muddied the waters with conflicting decisions: one, *Everson,* saying that auxiliary aid such as transportation to parochial schools was constitutional; and another, *McCollum,* holding that release-time during school hours was not (Ravitch 1983).

Of course, the Supreme Court had a tremendously greater impact on public education than just deciding whether parochial school children could ride school buses at taxpayer expense. In 1954, it handed down its landmark decision in *Brown v. Board of Education,* ruling that officially segregated public schools were unconstitutional. The impact of *Brown* and the subsequent struggle for racial equality in public education deserve a book of their own.

Wise (1979) points to *Brown* as the genesis of the modern education accountability movement, with its emphasis on quantitative measurement of school characteristics and outcomes—or as Wise puts it: the hyperrationalization of modern education. In its opinion to *Brown*, the court attempted to demonstrate why segregation was not merely immoral, socially corrosive, and unconstitutional but harmful in precisely measurable ways as well. It touched on topics that would continue to be the focus of future debates in education policy: inequality of resources and the obligation of the state to make sure that all students had equal educational opportunities. *Brown* set the tone for later efforts by all levels of government to regulate public schools: lofty expectations for schools that are assumed to be measurable, debates about the definitions of concepts such as "opportunity," and plenty of work for social scientists.

Sputnik brought the first break in the legislative logjam at the federal level with the passage of the National Defense Education Act in 1958. Resistance was swept away seven years later, when the Elementary and Secondary Education Act (ESEA) was made law. Upon signing it, President Lyndon Johnson declared: "No law I have signed or will ever sign means more to the future of America." Subsequent amendments and reauthorizations were hailed with equal hyperbole (Kafer 2002).

Originally intended to help poor children, the ESEA was expanded to help other children at a disadvantage in the existing system. The method of expansion generally followed the same pattern for each additional legislative action: mobilization of an afflicted group, a congressional champion, hearings and publicity, another addition to federal education law, and the establishment of an executive branch agency to ensure a lobbying base for the interest group regardless of the occupant of the White House (Ravitch 1983).

In 1968, the Bilingual Education Act, sponsored by Senator Ralph Yarborough of Texas, created Title VII of the ESEA in order to address the problems of Hispanic and other children who had limited English. In 1972, Congress passed the Higher Education Act, whose Title IX prohibited discrimination on the basis of sex in education programs receiving federal support. This was followed two years later by the Women's Educational Equity Act. In 1975, Congress passed the Education for All Handicapped Children Act, which lay down detailed administrative procedures for districts to follow for handicapped children.

The result was an explosion of federal bureaucracy and regulations. From 1964 to 1976, the number of pages of federal education legislation increased from 80 to 360; the number of pages of federal regulations multiplied over 10 times, from 92 in 1965 to nearly 1,000 in 1977. In the last 4 years of the 1960s, there were over 1,200 decisions by federal courts affecting education—more decisions on schools than had been handed down in the previous 20 years (Wise 1979). The interests of minorities and women in schools were looked after by the Commission on Civil Rights; the Office of Civil Rights in the old Department of Health, Education, and Welfare; and the Equal Employment Opportunity Commission. Women alone had the National Advisory Council on Women's Educational Programs. The Office of Bilingual Education represented non-English speakers. For the handicapped, Congress created the Bureau of Education of the Handicapped and a National Advisory Committee on Education and Training of the Handicapped (Ravitch 1983).

The new laws and regulations led to increasing involvement by the federal government in local education issues. In the name of sexual and racial equality, the Office of Civil Rights became involved in writing textbooks (Ravitch 1983). Washington imposed performance requirements and administrative procedures on local schools. In the case of handicapped children, federal law went as far as to require districts to produce a five-part individualized education program for each student.

Centralization at the State Level

State legislatures were also active during this time. In the name of furthering the education of all students, state laws began mandating that districts adopt the latest methods in management science. Between 1963 and 1974, states passed at least 73 laws requiring state education agencies and districts to adopt systems such as management by objectives; cost-benefit analysis; zero-based budgeting; program, planning, and budgeting systems; and performance contracting. Further organizational mandates were aimed at measuring the output of schools: competency-based education, performance-based education, competency-based teacher education, learner verification, mastery learning, and criterion-referenced testing (Wise 1979).

The purpose of all this jargon was the grail of accountability. Each year between 1969 and 1976, the Florida state government enacted an educational accountability law. Among the stated goals of the 1976 version were to "provide a system of accountability" to guarantee all students "similar" educational opportunities and guarantee that all students receive "meaningful and relevant educational experiences designed to give students at least the minimum skills necessary to function and survive in today's society." The law also declared its intent to provide information to the public and to decision makers at all levels on the cost and effectiveness of educational programs and the progress of local school districts in meeting the goals set by the State Board of Education. Laws in the other states were similarly peppered with calls for accountability, efficiency, equity, and adequacy (Wise 1979).

Of course, this was not the first time public schools were urged to implement the latest in management science mumbo-jumbo in the name of efficiency—and not the last time either. The difference between the movement that began in the 1960s and the reforms 60 to 70 years earlier was that, at the turn of the century, the push for change was initiated at the local level. To be sure, as in Chicago, the state legislature was brought in if the local school board proved recalcitrant. The more recent reforms, however, came down from the state capitols. Like amoebae, schools have been able to ingest organizational reforms and assimilate them without a trace, leaving reformers to trumpet similar accountability measures today as if newly hatched (Tyack and Cuban 1995).

More recently, state officials and mayors have completely muscled elected school boards aside, and have taken over districts. As of 2001, 24 states had given state officials the power to take over local school districts that were performing poorly. Between 1988 and 2000, 40 school districts had been taken over, including districts in Chicago, Boston, Baltimore, and Washington, D.C. (Wong and Shen 2001).

Courts and School Finance Reform

When the legislative branch proved reluctant, an alternative path for reformers was through the courts. In the first decades of the twentieth century, there were approximately 2,010 cases regarding education each year per thousand population in state appellate courts, and 23 cases each year per thousand population in federal courts. By the mid-1970s, this had ballooned to 3,150 state appellate cases and 1,936 federal cases annually per thousand population—a doubling of the litigation rate and a profound shift to the federal courts (Tyack, James, and Benavot 1987, table A-3).

The late 1960s saw the beginning of a state-level movement that was to strike at the heart of local control: a court-driven reform of school funding. The American tradition of local control of school funding has historically meant widespread and persistent disparities in spending across school districts. In Massachusetts, for example, despite the state's traditional role as a leader in educational progress, spending inequality among school districts actually increased during the nineteenth century (Kaestle and Vinovskis 1980, 198–99). Disparities in funding between urban and rural schools was one of the rationales put forward by the movement for federal legislation that immediately followed WWII. By the late 1960s, attempts to equalize funding made up another front in the campaign against perceived injustices in the education system.

The fight to equalize school spending primarily took place in the courts. As with most recent developments in education, school finance litigation had occurred before in the 200-year history of American education. In the 1819 case *Commonwealth v. Dedham* (16 Mass. 141), the Supreme Judicial Court of Massachusetts ruled that schools must "be maintained for the benefit of the whole town, as it is the wise policy of the law to give all the inhabitants equal privileges, for the education of their children in the public schools. Nor is it in the power of the majority to deprive the minority of this privilege."

In the 1970s, advocates tried but failed to win a national mandate for school finance reform in *San Antonio v. Rodriguez* (411 U.S. 1973). Plaintiffs hoped to have the Texas school finance system declared unconstitutional on the grounds of equal protection under the Fourteenth Amendment. However, in 1973, the Supreme Court overturned a victory by the plaintiffs in a lower court, ruling that education was not an explicit or implicit right so protected by the Constitution that it warranted court intrusion into an area where it had traditionally deferred to the states. The equalization movement had more success in state courts. Two years before *Rodriguez*, in the landmark *Serrano v. Priest* (487 P.2d 1241, Cal. 1971), the California Supreme Court ruled its state's method of financing schools unconstitutional. In *Serrano*, the court ruled that the difference in per-pupil spending among districts should be no more than $100 in 1971 dollars. Ironically, after his victory, the plaintiff who gave his name to the case, John Serrano, chose to improve his son's education through Tiebout choice and moved to a better school district (Fischel 1998).

By 2002, lawsuits had challenged the school finance systems in 43 states. Eighteen states had successfully defended their systems; in others, the threat of litigation had motivated legislators to act (Access Education Finance Litigation 2002). Victory, however, did not always usher in happier days. Advocates frequently returned to court to fine-tune legislative attempts to meet the courts' decisions. *Serrano* was followed by *Serrano II*. In New Jersey, the original 1973 *Robinson v. Cahill* case was followed by five subsequent versions, then by a new string of cases, *Abbott v. Burke* and its sequels. In 2002, the education system in New Jersey was still being challenged under *Abbott v. Burke VIII*. The *Abbott* lawsuits spawned an industry featuring *Abbott* K–12 programs and a watchdog nonprofit with its own annual benefit concert (Education Law Center 2002).

The finance equalization movement found it easier going at the state level due to more agreeable language found in state constitutions. Unlike the silence regarding education in the U.S. Constitution, state constitutions frequently contained vague declarations of principles and goals, and exhortations regarding their state's schools. Arizona's constitution, for example, calls for a "general and uniform" system (Article 11, section 1). New Jersey's requires its schools to be "thorough and efficient" (Article VIII, section IV, paragraph 2). The Massachusetts constitution—in Chapter V, section II, *The Encouragement of Literature etc.*—declares that it is the duty of the state legislature and magistrates to "cherish the interests of literature and the sciences, and all seminaries of them; especially the university at Cambridge, public schools and grammar schools in the towns." Lawsuits demanded that courts translate these general principles into concrete, operational terms. Court interpretations, however, could lead to a proliferation of standards and goals almost equally ill-defined.

So, for example, when declaring the entire education system of Kentucky unconstitutional, the Kentucky Supreme Court stated that an efficient school system was one that had nine essential characteristics. The first was that "establishment, maintenance and funding" of Kentucky schools be the sole responsibility of the state's General Assembly. The second was that schools should be free for all children. Starting with the third characteristic, the court's essential features started becoming vague. The court declared that Kentucky schools should be "available" and "substantially uniform," and "provide equal educational opportunities." In its sixth stated essential characteristic, the court asked that schools be placed above the realm of ordinary human behavior. The General Assembly should monitor schools, the court held, so that schools are operated "with no waste, no duplication, no mismanagement, and with no political influence." Finally, the court wound up its list by mandating that the General Assembly allocate sufficient funding to schools to enable them to provide an "adequate education." An "adequate education," the court went on to define, is one that gives children at least seven capacities:

1. sufficient oral and written communications skills to enable students to function in a complex and rapidly changing civilization;

2. sufficient knowledge of economic, social, and political systems to enable the student to make informed choices;

3. sufficient understanding of governmental systems to enable the student to understand the issues that affect his or her community, state, and nation;

4. sufficient self-knowledge and knowledge of his or her mental and physical wellness;

5. sufficient grounding in the arts to enable each student to appreciate his or her cultural and historical heritage;

6. sufficient training or preparation for advanced training in either academic or vocational fields so as to enable each child to choose and pursue life work intelligently;

7. sufficient levels of academic or vocational skills to enable public school students to compete favorably with their counterparts in surrounding states, in academics or in the job market. (*Rose v. Council for Better Education*, 790 S.W.2d 186, 60 Ed. Law Rep. 1289 1989)

I quote the Kentucky decision at length to stress how far schools in twenty-first century America have come from nineteenth-century Boxford, Massachusetts. Sole responsibility for the maintenance and funding of Kentucky schools is placed not with local school districts but with the legislature. Instead of parents deciding what their children's education should impart, central authority defines the nine characteristics that schools need to have, and the seven capacities with which children are supposed to graduate.

The Kentucky decision also demonstrates a shift in the focus of school finance litigation. The early cases, such as *Serrano,* concentrated on equity in finance. Solutions involved shifting money from rich districts to poor ones—although even that is not as straightforward as it sounds. Later cases switched from asking for an equitable division of resources to an adequate education, an exponentially more complex issue. Defining adequacy is an elementary task compared to having to measure it. Legislators and school officials are left scratching their heads over what it means for a school to be "available"—is a 20-minute bus ride close enough?— or "substantially uniform;" or exactly how to measure students' self-knowledge of their "physical wellness." But measure they must in order to demonstrate that schools are doing what the court asked them to do. Finally, once adequacy is defined and reduced to quantifiable measures, legislators must determine the financial resources needed to reach the performance level deemed adequate.

THE EFFECTS OF CENTRALIZATION

American educators have always had to comply with silly regulations and the seemingly incomprehensible caprices of higher-ups. State rules in Oregon once required that students write from the bottom of the page to the top (Tyack 1974, 17). The wave of centralization that hit public schools in the 1960s and 1970s had a much greater impact than a few more bureaucrats and regulations. Matters that were once solely local concerns became subject to the decisions of ever-higher authorities.

The increasing interference of higher authority was accompanied by a substantial shift upward in the responsibility for funding schools as well. At the end of the 1920s, 83 percent of school revenue came from local sources, 16.5 percent from state governments, and less than 1 percent from the federal government. Stress on local finances due to the Depression caused a significant shift toward state responsibility, so that by 1940, 68 percent of funding came from local sources, and 30 percent came from the state capitols. This trend continued until, by the beginning of the 1980s, a milestone was reached: a greater share of funding came from the state government than from local districts. By 1997, 45 percent of school funding came from local sources, 48 percent from the state, and 7 percent from the federal government (U.S. Department of Education 2002, 48).

In addition to the vertical encroachment of higher levels of government into the domain of those below them, there was also a horizontal encroachment as the judiciary assumed functions properly belonging to the legislative branch. Legislative bodies—where the public itself or through elected representatives meets, deliberates, and votes—are the proper forums for deciding the purpose, necessary features, and level of funding for any public service. Legislative bodies are more representative of various interests and sentiments comprising the public will than a single judge, a panel of judges, or an agency chief. Legislatures are the proper place to balance the lofty sentiments expressed in laws and constitutions against competing uses for limited resources.

Perhaps the most spectacular example of judicial overreach is the case of the Kansas City, Missouri, school district. In the 1970s, the Kansas City school district was the archetype of a crumbling inner-city school system. The student body was 73 percent nonwhite; the electorate was largely older and white. Research has found that elderly electorates are reluctant to fund the education of youths of a different race: Kansas City was no different. In the 20 years after African Americans became the majority in 1969, the electorate voted down 19 straight tax increases for the schools. It was widely agreed that the schools were in a deplorable state: test scores were falling; violence was on the rise; the buildings were decaying; and books were in tatters. Visitors to the schools left with tears in their eyes (Ciotti 1998).

In 1977, members of the school board, district residents, and school-children brought suit in federal court alleging that the state of Missouri was causing racial segregation in the district. After 8 years of preliminaries and trial, Judge Russell Clark decided to almost literally throw money at the problem. The plaintiffs were given free rein to create the ideal school system, with the state and local taxpayers picking up the tab. The goal was not only to help children in the district, but also to build a system so attractive that it would lure white children out of private schools and back from the suburbs. Per-pupil spending became the highest in the nation; teacher salaries were increased; and 15 new schools were built. The district also adopted such amenities as "an Olympic-sized swimming pool with an underwater viewing room, television and animation studios, a robotics lab, a 25-acre wildlife sanctuary, a zoo, a model United Nations with simultaneous translation capability, and field trips to Mexico and Senegal" (Ciotti 1998, 1).

The state of Missouri paid for 75 percent of this extravagance, putting a strain on its resources. At one point, an estimated 44 percent of the state's education budget went to the Kansas City district, and other districts in the state had to fire personnel and cut back on extracurricular activities and maintenance due to a decline in state aid. In the face of steadfast refusal by local voters to raise taxes, Judge Clark ordered two increases in the property tax and a 1.5 percent tax on the income of suburban residents who worked in Kansas City. The power of an unelected federal judge to order a local government to increase taxes was upheld five to four by the Supreme Court.

Despite the best facilities in the nation and its production of one Rhodes Scholar, the Kansas City experiment was a failure. Test scores did not increase, and white children did not come flocking back. Aside from being a classic experiment testing the relationship between spending and achievement, the Kansas City case demonstrated the problems that arise when local schools become accountable to higher authorities—in this case a judge, but this is true of state legislatures and federal agencies as well. Since the entire premise of Judge Clark's intervention was desegregation, the district was harried persistently for evidence—such as counts of white kids, black-white ratios, and estimates of a disparity index—that the program was working. The district found it easier to meet the targets by letting black students drop out than by attracting white ones, so in the beginning nothing was done about the district's high dropout rate. Meanwhile, the unquantifiable attributes of public schools—their place in the community, the attachment of parents—were neglected.

As Wise (1979) points out, greater intrusion by higher authorities into the affairs of local school districts inevitably leads to a quantification of school outputs. Judges need disparity indices; departments of education want to see test scores. At the capitol, schools become another state department having to develop and track the quantitative performance measures favored by government budget agencies. This quantification leads to a narrowing of the mission of schools as attention becomes riveted on what is measurable.

A handful of studies have looked at the effect of school district bureaucracy on student achievement. Anderson, Shughart, and Tollison (1991) found that bureaucracy, as measured by the number of nonteaching personnel per student, had a negative impact on test scores and graduation rates. A 1 percent increase in the number of nonteaching staff per student lowered achievement test scores 11.5 to 13.8 percent—a tremendous, but barely statistically significant, effect. Edwin West and Halldor Palsson (1988), on the other hand, found that administrative costs in public schools have a negative effect on private school enrollment—that is, high administration expenses somehow cause parents to choose public schools. West and Palsson offer two possible explanations for this. The first, a bit of a reach, is that more administrators make teachers work harder at teaching. The second explanation is that large numbers of public school administrators is an indicator of enough political clout to impose sufficient regulations on private schools to make them relatively unattractive. A third explanation for West and Palsson's finding, which I offer here, is that even a well-done statistical analysis will occasionally produce a freakish, counterintuitive result. Finally, Wong and Shen's (2001) examination of district takeovers found that the takeover of a school district by the mayor led in some cases to academic improvement in the lowest-performing schools, as measured by test scores, and to better fiscal management. Takeover by the state, however, had mixed results on both student and fiscal performance.

John Chubb and Terry Moe (1990) offer a thorough examination of how school organization, broadly defined, influences student achievement. More than a mere study of the effects of the growth of school bureaucracy and centralization since the 1960s, Chubb and Moe's *Politics, Markets, and America's Schools* is an assault on the way public schools have been governed and organized since the Progressive reformers kicked the political machines out of the schoolhouse. By school organization, Chubb and Moe mean more than simply the district's organizational chart and procedural rules. For them, organization included the numerous qualities, from written procedures to more ineffable qualities such as teacher morale, that have been suspected to be influences on school effectiveness. Chubb and Moe condensed these numerous features into a "school organization index." The index served as a composite measure of school characteristics in four dimensions: goals, leadership, personnel, and practice. School attributes in each dimension were determined by several qualitative and quantitative measures—for example, graduation requirements, principal's emphasis on teaching, teacher absenteeism, teacher collegiality, percentage of students on an academic track, and homework assignments.

Chubb and Moe found that school organization plays as large a role in students' success as do the socioeconomic characteristics of their parents. In turn, school organization was affected by school size, student commitment to learning and behavior, parents' socioeconomic status and involvement, and bureaucratic constraints on principals from both the central district office and the teachers' union. Student characteristics—behavior and willingness to learn—had by far the largest impact on school organization. For behavior alone, if other school characteristics are held equal, a school among the 25 percent suffering most severely from student misbehavior would have an organizational effectiveness 52 percentage points lower than a school among the 25 percent of schools with the best-behaved students. Bureaucratic constraints were the second most important factor affecting school organization. Excessive central office control over curriculum, instructional methods, and hiring and firing of teachers and above-average union control over personnel policy had an adverse impact equivalent in size to an ill-disciplined student body (Chubb and Moe 1990, chap. 5).

Economists have conducted numerous studies of the effects of initiatives to equalize school finance. In addition to the obvious question of whether equalization schemes actually equalize spending, there is the logical follow-up question about whether the additional money improved school quality and student performance. Finally, since equalizing spending undermines the local control necessary to Tiebout competition, there are interesting questions about how equalization schemes affect the sorting of families among neighborhoods.

Although equalizing spending may seem like a straightforward matter of a state government's levying taxes and cutting checks to poor districts, the reality is not so simple. A state legislature could solve the equalization problem by completely abolishing school districts within the state, levy a statewide tax, and send the funds directly to schools based on some per-pupil formula. However, Hawaii is presently the only state with what is essentially one giant statewide school district. In seeking to comply with—or head off—a judicial mandate, legislatures in other states have attempted to equalize funding while trying to preserve some semblance of the traditional district system. This has involved developing plans to redistribute funds among districts while still allowing districts to tax themselves. The result has been complex formulas for the distribution of state funds among districts. The most common type of equalization, foundation aid, guarantees each district in the state a fixed level of spending per pupil; districts remain free to levy additional taxes if they wish to spend more than the minimum amount. The second form of equalization is the "power equalization" or "guaranteed tax revenue" scheme. Guaranteed tax revenue equalization attempts to ensure that individual districts raise equal funds for equal tax effort. That is, districts with the same tax rate will have the same revenue regardless of differences in property valuation.

Equalization formulas can affect the incentives faced by local taxpayers. For example, under a simple foundation aid formula, if local taxpayers wish to levy a tax on themselves to increase spending above the foundation level, their school will receive one dollar for every additional tax dollar raised. The case of guaranteed tax revenue schemes is much more complex. In California, all local property taxes raised for schools are thrown into a common pot and redistributed equally among districts. Thus, if taxpayers in a district choose to raise their taxes, their school will receive much less than a dollar in return. Thus, there is no incentive for taxpayers to raise their school property taxes above the state-mandated minimum. Not all guaranteed tax revenue schemes are like California's. In New Jersey, taxpayers in districts with a property value per student below a given amount can see spending increase by more than one dollar for every tax dollar raised. Thus, depending on the specific formula used by a state, voters may choose to raise or lower spending on education (Hoxby 1998a).

Furthermore, equalization formulas can affect the ability of districts to raise revenue through capitalization of school quality in property values. For example, suppose parents—through an active PTA—are successful in implementing some policy that raises the quality of their school. We know that Tiebout competition will cause property values to increase, since a high-quality school will increase the demand for houses in the district.

Higher property values mean higher property taxes, but this is no problem under a locally controlled system, since voters may choose to lower the tax rate so their overall bill is the same, or they may simply choose to let the additional tax revenue flow to the local school. Under an equalization formula, however, some of this extra tax revenue is siphoned off by the state and given to other districts. Thus, equalization imposes a tax on local efforts to improve school quality. Indeed, as Hoxby (1998a) points out, under a foundation aid system, housing values will drop in districts that are net contributors to state equalization, and values will rise in districts that are net takers of state aid. Since status as a contributor or taker depends on property values, capitalization can undo the effects of equalization.

Equalization can have other effects on taxpayer incentives. While the property tax is deductible from federal and state taxes, state income taxes are deductible only at the federal level, and sales taxes are not deductible at all. Thus, if a state government uses revenue from income or sales taxes to equalize revenue, the effective tax price of education in the state will go up. As with the price of shoes and gasoline, if the tax price of a government service goes up, taxpayers will vote for less of it. Second, property taxes are also paid by commercial, industrial, and agricultural property as well, meaning that parents in effect are receiving a subsidy for their children's education from these sources. Again, if other taxes are used for equalization, then the tax price faced by voters may increase.

Equalization may also undo the benefits of Tiebout sorting that aided in the rise of public education in the first place. Local control allowed areas wanting more education to move ahead without being held back by regions that were poorer or more skeptical of public education. Equalization throws decisions about spending on education into the state legislature, where schools have to battle against police, prisons, and roads for funding; where small districts are at the mercy of large districts that have more representatives and can hire lobbyists; and where poor regions can resist tax increases.

We have seen that 20 years of toil and trouble have succeeded in only in nudging down spending inequality among school districts nationwide. Murray, Evans, and Schwab (1998) found that court-ordered plans to equalize spending reduced inequality within states by 19 to 34 percent by raising spending in poor districts. David Card and Abigail Payne (1998) similarly found that equalization raised spending in poor districts. Hoxby (1998a) found that poor districts benefited in states where the equalization formulas did not cause a great disincentive for taxpayers. However, spending in poor districts dropped in states like California, whose formulas imposed severe tax prices. Thomas Downes (1992), when looking solely at California, found that *Serrano* did cause a convergence in spending between rich and poor districts, but *Serrano* has also been linked to lower per-student spending overall in the state. From 1970 to 1990, per-pupil spending fell by 23 percent; Fabio Silva and Jon Sonstelie (1995) estimated that half of that drop was due to *Serrano*.

The philosophy behind spending equalization assumes that communities would spend more on education if they could, and the only thing holding them back is lack of income. However, Tiebout sorting assumes that differences between communities in education spending are due to a differing taste for education as well as variations in income. So a district may be spending less on education simply because it chooses to. Hence, if state aid is given to a low-spending district, residents may decide to lower their own tax burden and free-ride to some extent on state taxpayers. Jonathan Guryan (2001) found evidence of this in Massachusetts. He estimated that every dollar in state aid resulted in only a net increase of 50 to 75 cents in spending on education.

It is also true, but often not remembered, that not all poor children live in property-poor districts. So even though spending in low-revenue districts may have increased, it does not necessarily follow that there was a net benefit to the poor. School finance reform in California did not direct more revenue to poor families, and indeed made some worse off. Richmond, California, a community with a largely low-income African American population, was considered a property-rich district because of oil refineries located there. Under California's school finance equalization scheme, it became a net contributor to the state's equalization fund (Fischel 1998). Equalization of funding in California did not equalize school quality either. Sonstelie, Brunner, and Ardon (2000) found premiums in home values based on the school district in which they were located still existed, a significant clue that quality differences existed as well. Premiums ranged from +45 percent to –24 percent compared to the baseline school district used.

School finance equalization has had mixed effects on student achievement. Thomas Downes (1992) found that equalization of funding did not lead to a convergence of test scores in California. Sonstelie, Brunner, and Ardon (2000) conclude that there is tentative evidence that *Serrano* adversely affected student achievement in the state. Student performance in California declined during the 1980s and compares poorly to student performance in other states even after adjusting for economic and demographic differences. In Massachusetts, equalization caused an increase in average test scores for fourth graders. Equalization may have reduced inequality in achievement for eighth graders as well, but in a less than desirable fashion. While test scores for low-achieving students rose, performance by high-achieving students fell. These changes roughly offset one another, so that the overall average score for eighth graders was unchanged (Guryan 2001).

Nationwide, the effects have been mixed as well. Card and Payne (1998) found that equalization led to a modest convergence between children from different family backgrounds. Their strongest result is a 5 percent decline in the gap in SAT scores between children with highly educated and poorly educated parents. Thomas Downes and David Figlio (1998) found that the effect of an equalization plan depends upon its motivating force. Plans done to comply with a judicial mandate had a positive but statistically insignificant effect on achievement, while equalization plans constructed by legislatures without the explicit prodding of a judge raised achievement in mathematics about 1 percent for children in districts at the average spending level. Although, equalization done at the behest of the courts was statistically insignificant, it had a positive effect for schools at all spending level. Equalization plans with solely a legislative origin may have lowered the test scores in high-spending districts while increasing scores in low-spending districts. Finally, Caroline Hoxby (1998a) finds tentative evidence that equalization can affect the dropout rate. Dropout rates are higher in states with what she refers to as "anti-spending" equalization reforms—those states whose equalization formulas create a disincentive for local communities to raise taxes.

An alternative way to test for the effect of equalization on school quality is to look at what happens to enrollment in private schools in states that have enacted equalization schemes. If equalization causes school quality to decline due to the reduction in competition, or if parents are unhappy with the loss of control that comes with greater centralization of funding, parents may head for the exit and enroll their children in private schools. Thomas Downes and David Schoeman (1998) link an increase in private school attendance in California to the effects of *Serrano*. From 1970 to 1990, the proportion of California children in private schools increased from 8.5 percent to 10.2 percent; at the same time nationwide, private school market share was falling. Most of this increase came among the wealthiest families. Private school enrollment for children from the 10 percent of families with the highest incomes increased from 14 percent to 21 percent between 1970 and 1990. Over the same two decades, private school enrollment increased from 10 to 14 percent for children from families in the second 10 percent of the income distribution. Private school attendance remained unchanged in the lower 60 percent of families (Sonstelie, Brunner, and Ardon 2000). This compares to a nationwide private school enrollment rate of 11 percent. Downes and Schoeman estimate that 44 percent of the increase in total private school enrollment from 1970 to 1980 was a result of California's equalization efforts. Nationwide, Hoxby (1998a) again finds that the more anti-spending a state's plan is, the higher private school enrollment.

If equalization of spending across school districts narrows the gap in school quality between rich and poor districts—because the quality of

poor schools increases, the quality of wealthy schools declines, or both—
it will also narrow the gap in property values. This reduces the incentive
for families to engage in Tiebout sorting based on finding a good school
for their children. Since the net benefit from moving to a rich district is
smaller, families that formerly would have moved out of districts with
poor schools may elect to stay to enjoy other amenities—a short com-
muting distance or cultural attractions—that the communities offer. Thus,
equalization may cause communities to be more diverse. Few studies have
looked for this effect. Daniel Aaronson (1999) found little evidence that
court-ordered reform changed the composition of neighborhoods. In
states where the courts found the funding system constitutional, the fraction of low-income individuals increased in low-income districts. However, yet another analysis by the team of Downes and Figlio (1999) found
evidence that more low-income, less-educated families moved into more-
exclusive communities, enabled by a decrease in the housing premium
attributed to the local schools. They linked equalization plans to a reduction of growth in the average and a decline in the fraction of residents
with a college degree in high-spending districts. Furthermore, there is
evidence that equalization attracted high-income, more educated individuals into public schools in the central cities of metropolitan areas. The
household income and education of parents of public school students is
higher in cities where equalization policies have been implemented. This
is even truer for private school students in these communities. So equalization may reduce the incentive to flee to the suburbs, but the parents
who remain may send their children to private schools instead of to the
possibly improved public ones.

By reducing Tiebout competition, equalization also undermines popular support for its foundation, the property tax. Many features of the property tax tend to make it unpopular. The tax bill is received in one generally
significant lump sum. The blow is not softened by withholding, as is the
case of the income tax, or by being taken in numerous, small amounts, as
is the case with the sales tax. Second, in addition to housing prices being
sensitive to the quality of local public services, they also rise due to other
market forces and inflation. This can become a burden if incomes do not
rise as well. Nevertheless, homeowners have been fierce defenders of the
property tax. Over two decades, Michigan voters rejected 12 straight ballot
proposals to shift the burden of school finance away from the property
tax (National Research Council 1999b, 88). Voter support for the property
tax has proven to be broad-based, and resistance to lessening its importance is not due to the political influence of wealthy districts (Campbell
and Fischel 1996).

The reader familiar with the history of the last quarter-century should
be able to recall a counterexample to the assertion that the public loves
the property tax. In 1978, California voters passed, by a two-to-one mar-

gin, Proposition 13, which froze property tax rates on individual property at 1 percent and reduced assessments to their 1975 levels. However, a keen insight by William Fischel (1989) explains how Proposition 13 was the exception that proves the rule. In the years leading up to Howard Jarvis's taxpayer revolt, attempts by the California legislature to meet the judicial mandates of *Serrano* eroded the connection between the property tax paid by a homeowner and funding received by the neighborhood school. In 1977, in response to *Serrano II*, the legislature passed the equalization plan described above, completely severing property taxes from the quality of local schools. Property tax revenue over the state-mandated minimum was shipped to Sacramento to be spread around the state to comply with the judicial wish for nearly absolute equality in spending. As Caroline Hoxby (1998a) points out, since local homeowners did not benefit directly from property tax rates over the minimum or from the quality of local schools capitalized in their property values, it was rational for them to roll back both. It is no coincidence that the Proposition 13 ceiling is equal to the state minimum property tax rate. Fischel also sees a connection between voter unrest in Massachusetts and New Jersey and equalization efforts in those states (Fischel 1998).

In *Savage Inequalities*, his book on the vast disparities in education spending in the United States, Jonathan Kozol links the same chain of events in California. Kozol quotes a state legislator who called Proposition 13 "the revenge of wealth against the poor" (Kozol 1992, 220). Kozol then continues with a pessimistic conclusion about Americans' commitment to equality, fairness, and racial harmony. However, Proposition 13 won in both rich and poor communities, including a whopping 70 percent "yes" vote in Baldwin Park—a municipality named by Kozol as a victim of the inequitable allocation of school funds (Fischel 1998). What Kozol and others overlook is an equally strong American belief, for better or worse, in local control.

CONCLUSION

This chapter has provided a sketch of the 200-year history of attempts to increase central control over community schools in the United States. Although it has attempted to be frank regarding the drawbacks of local control, the chapter has sought to underscore the often-overlooked benefits of local control. The belief in the right of parents to raise their children as they see fit is deeply ingrained in the American psyche. Small, locally controlled schools are more amenable to the voice of parents than are large or remote authorities. Thus, undermining local control undermines support for public schools. Local control promotes Tiebout competition, which like competition in the markets for private goods, leads to both allocative and productive efficiency. Schools are more aligned with the preferences of parents, and give more bang for the buck. In addition, bigness in school districts leads to other problems, which adversely affect students.

The greater effectiveness of voice and exit in small communities, the greater affinity people feel for a local community, the discipline of competition, and awkwardness of large organizations are as close to being social facts as anything can be. No matter how much frustrated reformers view these principles as cantankerous and archaic tribalism or the pottering of free-market or individualistic fanatics, they are facts with which centralizing efforts have had to deal for over 200 years, and will still have to face in the future.

CHAPTER 5

Reforming American Education

Before discussing where American public schools should go in the next millennium, let us recap the several trajectories they followed in the previous century. Aided by its decentralized system of school control, the United States has been among the world leaders in education for the past two centuries both in terms of the resources devoted to schooling and the proportion of its children who have been educated. Already one of the leaders in primary education during the nineteenth century, the United States pushed farther ahead of other nations at the beginning of the twentieth by opening up secondary education to the majority of adolescents. As the century progressed, by every measure the nation devoted ever more resources to public education. The portion of national income given to schools increased. Despite growing enrollment, per-pupil spending increased and class sizes fell, and, despite the increasing demand for teachers, the teaching corps became more highly trained. During the last decades of the twentieth century, attention turned to more equally dividing the resources devoted to education. Legal discrimination was abolished, but efforts to make the quality of schools more uniform by redistributing funding met with only limited success.

The opening up of the American high school sparked a debate that still continues. As high school enrollment started to explode, education leaders and theorists argued over whether to require the new students to take traditional academic subjects, or to expand the high school curriculum to offer classes supposedly more relevant to the needs and problems of the new students and modern society. In keeping with the American egalitarian ethic and the new theories of pedagogy emanating from universities, Americans rejected the creation of separate secondary schools for vocational and academic subjects, and instead created a system of internal choice within high schools. Students chose, or were directed toward, separate tracks depending on whether they were heading to college, the office, or the shop floor. Nevertheless, they remained within the same building.

The evidence regarding student achievement before WWII is so sparse and problematic that it is dangerous to draw any conclusions about trends in performance. Despite the usual grumbling from old-timers and the dissent of some academics over the new curriculum, the nation was apparently largely satisfied with what students were learning. All this changed after WWII. Questions about the effectiveness of public schools in preparing American children for citizenship and the job market were pushed onto the national stage by the Cold War and the baby boom. The new science of mass aptitude and achievement testing allowed policymakers and critics to track student performance on a large scale. Beginning in the mid-1960s, student scores on a broad range of standardized tests began to plummet, and concern over the quality of American education seemed justified. Student performance hit bottom in the mid-1970s. In some subjects—science and math—test scores have gained back the losses and are now better than ever. In reading, however, student achievement has remained essentially flat for 30 years. Aside from trends, other indicators of achievement worry many observers. Internationally, American students are in the middle of the pack in terms of achievement, and large segments of the population do not seem to be learning skills adequate enough to allow them to earn a middle-class living.

The post–WWII era also saw a significant change in the governance of public schools. Throughout the history of public schools in the United States, there had been tension between forces wishing to standardize schools and centralize control on one side, and parents and local authorities wanting to retain a voice in school policy. This conflict was only one manifestation of the larger struggle between national and local forces that has been a continuous theme of American history. After WWII, the centralization of authority brought about by war and depression and the flowering of the civil rights movement tipped the balance in education, as in other policies, toward centralization. A large share of the responsibility for funding schools was transferred from local districts to state governments, and along with the funding went a large measure of control. The federal government started playing a larger role in order to help racial minorities, the poor, the disabled, and women. In addition to legislators, judges at all levels took a more active role in school policy.

Thus, compared to the beginning of the twentieth century, public schools at the beginning of the twenty-first have more of practically everything: more resources divided more equally, more children, more types of classes, more responsibilities, more interference from higher levels of government, and more stakeholders with more powerful voices. What has not increased at an equal pace has been student achievement and public confidence. During the last half of the twentieth century, public schools were almost continually buffeted by successive waves of reform to ameliorate a multitude of ills. Critics on the left saw public schools as racist and impersonal, if not cruel, institutions. Critics on the right saw them as academically flabby and ideologically suspect.

The plans of reformers on all sides are to continue public education along some of these trajectories and reverse course along others. There is a continued effort by many to devote more resources to public schools, make sure the resources are divided more equally, and sweep away what are viewed as archaic and oppressive teaching methods. Many others want to restore rigor to the curriculum, boost academic achievement, and give parents greater voice and choice in the schooling of their children.

This chapter argues for the creation of a system to give parents greater power and flexibility in choosing the school to which to send their children. The adjective *greater* should be noted. In the United States, parents have always had choice to some extent. Even after the establishment of the common school system, Tiebout competition provided some degree of choice for parents. As such, education has been only nominally free, with the price of housing in the better school districts serving as a barrier to those with lower incomes. For over 40 years, government policy has sought to increase the educational opportunities of less fortunate children through reforms that have tended to centralize the school system. This has led to inefficiency, lower achievement, and the alienation of parents. School choice can square this circle by providing greater equity through a decentralized system that returns to parents the voice in school governance that has been steadily chipped away over the past decades.

FORMS OF REFORMS

The numerous reforms of public education that have been placed on the table for the past 30 years can be usefully classified into two categories: accountability reforms and establishment reforms. Accountability reforms are based on the premise that public school teachers, administrators, and students lack the proper incentives to meet the education goals desired by parents and society. As employees of a public monopoly, the reasoning goes, school administrators and teachers do not face the same market discipline and incentives to perform well that managers and employees of private organizations do. Except in the most egregious cases, neither the positions nor the salaries of public school employees are affected by how well they perform their jobs. Civil service and union contracts make it difficult to fire the incompetent. Salary schedules ensure that the incapable and apathetic teacher is paid as much as the energetic and effective one. The option of exit can be exercised only imperfectly. Dissatisfied parents may move or put their children in private schools, but both are costly options. Furthermore, competition has been reduced by centralization and consolidation of school districts. In 1937, there were 119,000 school districts and nearly 250,000 schools in the United States. By 2000, there were approximately 15,000 districts and 90,000 schools (U.S. Department of Education 2002, table 89).

Accountability reforms seek to put into place incentives to induce public school administrators and teachers to meet selected objectives. To do this, accountability reforms need two features. First, they require an inventory of selected objectives. Second, they need some authority outside of the schools that evaluates the schools' success and failure in meeting the objectives and, based upon that evaluation, has the power to mete out rewards and punishments to schools.

Depending upon how these two components are configured, accountability reforms can be divided into two types: centralizing reforms and decentralizing reforms. Under centralizing accountability reforms, the objectives and incentives come from a government agency above the local school district. Centralizing accountability reforms generally consist of a curriculum and standards mandated by the higher authority, large-scale testing to measure student progress toward meeting the standards, and some reward or punishment for schools based on the success of their students. Examples of centralized accountability reforms are school report cards and schemes that pay teachers and principals based on student performance.

Decentralizing accountability reforms seek to transfer to parents the authority both to set standards and to reward or punish schools. Under a decentralizing accountability reform, the objectives of a school depend upon the individual preference of parents. It is assumed that parents will sort themselves into schools whose goals fit most closely with their own. It is the responsibility of parents to ensure that schools meet these goals; if not, punishment takes the form of exit: the parent withdraws the child from the school and enrolls him or her in an alternative. Examples of decentralizing accountability reforms are open enrollment that removes the traditional school attendance boundaries, charter schools, and various tax and cash subsidies to make it easier for parents to send their children to private schools. Centralizing and decentralizing accountability reforms are not mutually exclusive. It is often imagined that the testing and standards of a centralized plan would aid parents in making informed decisions in selecting schools for their children.

An establishment reform is any plan to improve public schools that is not an accountability reform. Establishment reforms include school finance equalization schemes, initiatives to reduce class sizes, attempts to increase parent involvement, and curriculum reform. This may seem like a vague and unwieldy category, but the items in it have two things in common. First, while accountability reforms assume that public agencies, by nature or as a result of recent history, lack the proper incentives to perform well, establishment reforms do not assume that the system of governance of public schools is flawed in a fundamental way. Injustice, red tape, and backwardness may exist, but they are not the result of inherent defects in the way public schools are organized and governed. Second, establishment reforms are often advocated by supporters of public education—hence the label "establishment reforms." Supporters of establishment reforms are frequently skeptical of, if not downright hostile to, accountability reforms, which they view as attacks on the system.

Unlike the supporters of each type of reform, the substance of establishment reforms and accountability reforms are not opposed to one another. Indeed, since many establishment reforms do not directly speak to school governance, one might question why they are discussed here. I examine establishment reforms solely through the lens of school control. So, for example, I do not discuss the merits of proposed curriculum reforms in terms of whether they teach what children need or should know. However, I do touch on curricular and other establishment reforms in terms of trying to bring about change in a school system made up of fallible and self-interested human beings situated in a diverse society governed by a federal system.

ESTABLISHMENT REFORM PLANS

Human nature, seldom being satisfied for long, always seeks to improve things. One area of endeavor that has been the topic of constant scrutiny, search for progress, and advice has been instruction of the young. The ancient Greek Menander declared: "The man who has never been flogged has never been taught." Subsequent thinkers from Rousseau through Pestalozzi, Montessori, Dewey, and more have offered their theories on how to improve the education of children—with a pronounced deemphasis on flogging that has grown over time. Many establishment reforms follow in this tradition, calling for changes in curriculum and teaching methods. Berliner and Biddle, for example, call for throwing away what they characterize as the traditional and archaic curriculum of "pumping bits of knowledge from the past into passive students." The old methods, they assert, require drill, rote learning, and tests. They, on the other hand, believe that, to be properly educated for the twenty-first century, a student must be able to do many things, including work independently and in groups, evaluate people and products, reason, train others, communicate and plan, solve problems, "engage in metacognition," and function in multicultural settings. This requires teaching methods that allow for more student participation, cooperative learning, self-aware thinking, and multicultural education. All this, they hold, is supported by the latest in psychological research (Berliner and Biddle 1995, 298–303).

In addition to being the latest torchbearers in the long search for better methods of teaching, establishment reformers are also the heirs and defenders of the legacy of Horace Mann, Henry Barnard, and other common-school advocates. Establishment reformers are strong believers in an egalitarian school system, and as a consequence are frequently vehemently opposed to tracking that segregates students by ability. They are also against public support for private schools. The common-school advocates' belief that religion in school should be limited to a bland, nondenominational Christianity has evolved in establishment reformers into complete opposition of teaching religion in schools, and sometimes open hostility to what they view as radical sects.

Establishment reforms range in scope from changing the way teachers teach to transforming the politics and economy of the entire nation. At the top of Berliner and Biddle's list is ameliorating social problems such as poverty and racial prejudice that have a negative impact on schools. They call for measures to redistribute income by raising the minimum wage, reducing the workweek, mandating benefits for part-time work, and providing tax-supported jobs. They are less specific about how to eradicate racial prejudice. Lawrence Stedman also sees addressing larger issues in the society as necessary to help American schools (Stedman 1996). Other reforms advocated by establishment reformers are aimed more directly at schools: equalization of funding; reducing school size; reform of the curriculum, teaching practices, and methods of evaluating students; greater involvement in schools by parents and the community; early childhood education; and higher professional status for educators.

Barriers to Establishment Reforms

Supporters of certain establishment reforms are well into their second century of trying to get their ideas widely adopted. The reader would not be the first one to ask why—if the proposed reforms are clearly beneficial, are consistent with enlightened and humane thinking, and are supported by the latest and best research—they have not yet been fully incorporated into the public schools. David Tyack and Larry Cuban, in their book *Tinkering Toward Utopia* (1995), attempted to answer this vexing question. Tyack and Cuban reviewed 100 years of school reform, including ideas ranging from merit pay to replacing teachers with televisions and computers. They observed four characteristics of successfully adopted reforms. First, successful reforms were natural extensions of procedures and programs already in place and did not upset other aspects of school operations. For example, a program for free breakfast is an obvious next step after a free lunch program. The second characteristic was that reforms were not controversial and did not go beyond the public's beliefs of what a school should be. The third characteristic was that the reforms created a constituency powerful enough to defend their continued existence (Tyack and Cuban 1995, 57–58).

These three characteristics are standard ingredients of political success: don't upset currently existing interest groups, and create new, influential ones to support your efforts. The fourth common feature identified by Tyack and Cuban was that successful reforms tended to be mandated by the law and easily monitored. Realistically, then, the set of feasible reforms is not limited by the imagination of researchers and reformers, but rather by constraints imposed by politics, the structure of organizations, and the limits of policy instruments. It is important to emphasize that Tyack and Cuban's fourth identified characteristic has as much an objective basis as the first three. This point might not appear immediately obvious to many. It may seem that once the first three characteristics are met and the galaxy of interest groups aligned properly, then a legal mandate would immediately follow. However, it is important to realize that not all reforms can be transformed into workable laws and that not all levels or branches of government are able to implement the same types of reforms. Just as the novelty of a reform, or the strength and passion of its opponents or supporters can be weighed, albeit imperfectly, the ability of various policy authorities to effectively accomplish specific reforms can also be evaluated.

I refer to the various official government entities that have the power to enact policies that govern American public schools as "policy authorities." The school principal is the most immediate policy authority; above him are the superintendent and the school board; and above them are the state legislatures and departments of education. Higher still are the U.S. Department of Education and Congress. Also included is an assortment of judges. This entire structure I refer to as the "governing pyramid."

The set of feasible policies available to any policy authority—whether a principal, school board, legislature, or judge—is bounded by a policy frontier. This frontier is determined by the budget and constitutional constraints, social norms, the expertise of the authority, the problem of controlling large organizations of human beings, and the limits of written laws and policies when confronted by the diversity and uncertainty of the real world. The budget available to a policy authority is perhaps its most prominent, immediate, and continual limitation. The legislature or agency that is flush enough with resources to satisfy all the interest groups importuning is rare indeed. Constitutional provisions also limit the actions of policy authorities. The First Amendment of the U.S. Constitution is believed by many to prohibit school vouchers that may be used to attend religious schools. The Blaine amendments, constitutional prohibitions against public support of religious schools, in many states apply a more specific ban. Constitutions ostensibly place limits on the types of actions each branch of government may take. Under the traditional separation of powers, executive, legislative, and judicial bodies have delimited boundaries setting apart their powers and responsibilities—although these boundaries have become blurred in recent times. It is the responsibility of legislators to write policy into law and decide how much taxpayer money to spend in implementation. Executive agencies do the actual implementing within their allotted budgets. Judges settle disputes that arise from implementing the policies adopted by the legislature.

Often intertwined with constitutional limits are social and political norms. The federal structure of government in the United States has a constitutional foundation, but in education there has traditionally been a great deference to local control above that found in the state and federal constitutions. Local control can be objectively justified as helping make school operations more efficient through Tiebout competition. However, Americans did not spend over 200 years fighting against centralizing authorities for control of their schools in anticipation of Tiebout's economics article. The deference to local control is based on a belief in local autonomy—whether of an individualistic Jacksonian sort or in a collective form as Shain would have it—that has very deep roots in the American psyche.

Policy authorities are also limited by their lack of knowledge and expertise about issues. Executive officials such as principals, superintendents, and department chiefs are intended to be knowledgeable about the aspects of policy that are their responsibilities. However, judges and legislators from school boards on up to the U.S. Congress are laymen and may lack expertise. They may be ignorant of the history of an issue, and they may only vaguely understand the rules and regulations already in place. School funding schemes are devilishly complex and require some familiarity with the tax code. Legislators and judges may be unfamiliar with academic research on a topic, and they often lack the technical training in the social sciences to judge the merits of the dueling studies frequently issued by groups on either side of a controversy. They may not know some of the more arcane technical jargon such as *norm-referenced tests*, *average daily enrollment*, or *power equalization*.

There are ways for legislators to overcome lack of knowledge about the technical aspects of an issue. They can rely on their staffs, agency employees, and lobbyists for outside interest groups for some instruction. Following the advice of Adam Smith, they can seek to increase their productivity through specialization and division of labor by forming committees of jurisdiction to govern specific issues. Legislators sitting on committees become experts to the extent they are able on the topics under their purview. Note that this is only a partial solution, since the majority of legislators who are not on specific committees must to some extent trust the recommendations and legislation that come from the committee's members. Policy authorities can mitigate to some extent their lack of expertise, but they cannot wholly eliminate it.

Above all, policy authorities are limited by the tools they have at hand. Aside from the occasional photo opportunity in a political campaign, legislators, governors, and presidents rarely roll up their sleeves and step in front of a classroom. Judges, too, are rarely found in the halls of the local school. Principals are present on campus, and school board members and superintendents can be frequent visitors, but even they cannot be at every school and in every classroom. To put their wishes into place, policy authorities universally employ written instructions: policy manuals, resolutions, laws, regulations, and orders. They then must rely on subordinates to ensure that their instructions are put into effect as originally intended.

Simply by handing down a law or regulation, a policy authority is making two findings. The first is that the subordinate policy authorities have been deficient in addressing the matter of concern. A policy authority and the subordinates may agree on priorities, and the deficiency may merely be due to a lack of resources. The new policy may then just need additional funding for the mutually shared goals to be carried out. Alternatively, subordinates may have different priorities than the policy authority. The subordinates may be using what is viewed as an ineffective curriculum, failing to provide certain services, or the children under their jurisdiction may not be saying the Pledge of Allegiance often enough. In the case of differing priorities, the new policy is an imposition of the higher authority's preferences onto those below. The second finding explicit in any policy is the method preferred by the issuing authority to remedy the deficiency. The remedy may be laid out with a high degree of specificity. For example, the federal law regulating the education of disabled children spelled out the procedural rights available to disabled children and mandated that their education be integrated as much as possible with that of other children.

Both findings imply that a policy is a movement toward uniformity of objectives and uniformity of methods. It follows that any policy is born with a potential conflict among Tyack and Cuban's list of features of successful reforms. In order to make reforms more palatable, those responsible for implementing them should have the discretion to alter the new policies to make them more amenable to local preferences and circumstances. However, since legislative mandates—along with judicial orders, regulations, and other written policy instruments—are predicated on uniformity, it is impossible to completely avoid conflict with local conditions. The tension between inherently rigid and uniform policy instruments and the immense diversity of conditions and preferences against which they are applied helps to delineate the policy frontier. This constraint becomes more acute higher up on the governing pyramid. Whereas a school board has merely to confront the situation faced by a dozen or so schools scattered over several square miles, Congress must set policies to be followed by thousands of schools from Alabama to Alaska.

The policy frontier is also limned by the fact that the instructions of policy authorities must be carried out by agents. Since legislators are unable to go into the classrooms themselves, they have to rely on executive agencies to transfer their policy wishes to the schools under their jurisdiction. This opens the possibility that policies may be altered or thwarted. A major development in the study of organizations over the past several decades has been the recognition that bureaus and agencies are not staffed by worker bees striving single-mindedly for the good of the hive. Rather, government organizations employ individuals who have as much self-interest as their counterparts in the private sector. This self-interest may manifest itself in minor shirking, such as taking an extra half-hour for lunch, but the reader should not confuse self-interested bureaucrats with lazy or corrupt bureaucrats. Self-interest may take the form of believing that one should do right and that what is right may conflict with what immediate or remote superiors want done. Like the policy authorities that give them their orders, agency heads and their deputies are unable to read minds or see through walls. Consequently, they must rely upon their subordinates to faithfully carry out their wishes. Every delegation of authority is a fissure of hairline width or larger that may transform or undermine a policy structure.

Paul Hill (2003) vividly describes the organization of state education agencies and local school districts as geological rather than logical. Every wave of education reform—the vocational movement, the desegregation effort, initiatives to help the poor and handicapped—leaves behind a bureau or division supported by federal funds and staffed by persons who believe in and are committed to their work. Rather than petrify quietly into fossils, these bureaus make continual and sometimes contradictory demands of those below them:

[A]s most superintendents discover, the bureaucracies do not work for them. Their nominal subordinates have firm political and economic bases—control of categorical funds, alliances with elected officials, support in local community or ethnic organizations, close ties with the teachers' union, etc. The business of such bureaucracies is not to promote school quality, but to isolate problems and diffuse responsibility. (Hill 2003, p. 3)

In short, any organization made up of human beings must be monitored in order to ensure that it fulfills the mission it is given, but monitoring is never perfect. Of course, there are super bureaucrats such as Frank Rigler, the superintendent of schools in the city of Portland from 1896–1913, who serve as examples of overcoming the difficulty of monitoring self-interested agents. To ensure that his teachers stuck to the established curriculum, Rigler met with them every Saturday to go through the textbooks. He instructed them on the questions they should ask and the answers they should accept. It was said that Rigler, ensconced in his office, knew the exact page that was being studied simultaneously in every school in Portland (Tyack 1974, 48). However, even Rigler seems unimpressive next to the formidable Hippolyte Fortoul, the French Minister of Ecclesiastical Affairs and Public Education from 1851 to 1856. Minister Fortoul once bragged to a visitor, after looking at his watch, that he knew the passage of Virgil being studied at that moment by every student in the nation's lycées (Coulson 1999, 102).

Presently, the spirit of Frank Rigler and Minister Fortoul lives on in what are known as direct instruction or teacher-centered programs—policies that have met with some success. Direct instruction is a teaching program in which teachers follow scripted lesson plans to ensure that "every kid in every class learns the same material at the same time." Direct instruction has proven useful with highly mobile student populations because it ensures that teachers know exactly to what material the new students in their classes have been exposed, and it has also been credited with raising test scores. However, direct instruction is the exception that proves the rule. It is the type of reform that can be imposed from even the loftiest heights in the governing pyramid, since it specifically aims to limit the discretion of those at the bottom. Also, its measure of performance is precisely the type that may be expected from such a rigid program: average student scores on standardized tests. Direct instruction is the classic recipe for a reform that a bureaucracy can successfully implement: limited discretion for subordinates combined with a narrow performance measure. Such reforms would likely fail in meeting a wider range of objectives. Worker satisfaction, for example, is one goal that direct instruction has failed to achieve. Teachers dislike what they call the "drill and kill" of direct instruction and say their creativity is stifled by "military-style lesson plans." Also left out are those students who are not average. Because it limits discretion and focuses on average test scores, direct instruction necessarily gives teachers the incentive to teach to the middle student, with the risk of losing those with skills above or below average (Brice 2002).

It would take a great deal of naïveté, however, to believe entirely in the legend of Superintendent Rigler or the braggadocio of Minister Fortoul. A sick child in a Portland classroom or a tardy professor in Lyon would have been enough to upset the clocklike precision of their plans. To state the problem more generally, even the most well meaning of agents, fully trying to carry out stated policy to the letter, will confront circumstances unforeseen by their superiors when drafting the policy. Policy authorities may try to plan for contingencies, but to list every possible contingency and describe the action to be taken in every circumstance would require a document of impossible length. Consequently, policymakers have no choice but to give some discretion to their agents and hope that unplanned-for circumstances are addressed in the spirit of their intentions. Furthermore, the variability of local conditions give subordinates an advantage over their superiors, since the subordinates are likely privileged with information unknown to those above them. The deputy can strategically withhold or misrepresent the information to excuse failure, push for a more preferred alternative, or achieve other goals. An agent's ability to selectively inform those above has few limitations. The November 8, 2002, *Arizona Republic* reports that the superintendent of the Deer Valley district in Arizona hid a $1.6 million deficit from his school board. As one moves up the hierarchy, the amount of information about local conditions and unforeseen problems grows, making it more difficult for those on the next level to digest. Thus, difficulty in monitoring increases the higher one goes on the governing pyramid.

The severity of the constraints that make up the policy frontier can grow or diminish as one moves up or down the governing pyramid. As one moves up the pyramid, the budget constraint lessens; governments with greater regional scope can call upon more resources. Redistribution meets with weaker political opposition toward the top of the pyramid because there is less chance that individuals will be taxing themselves to provide a benefit. More resources also means larger staffs and bureaus, which helps ameliorate the expertise problem. However, the higher one travels up the governing pyramid, the more difficult for written policy instruments to address fully unforeseen circumstances and the diversity of local conditions. It also becomes harder to monitor the increasing layers of agents. Since these problems increase for policy authorities higher up the governing pyramid, the higher the authority the smaller the menu of available policies.

These limits on the actions of policymakers are not found in the simple missionary model of reform. In the missionary model, agents of the policy authority set out, armed with the carrots of funding and the sticks of regulatory enforcement, for the hinterlands, where the new reform has not been adopted due to either ignorance or a lack of resources. Once the natives see that the new ways are supported by a consensus of all competent researchers and, it is to be hoped, sufficient funds, then they will implement them without hesitation. Even real missionaries struggle against a scarcity of resources, the obtuseness of the home office, and the hostility of the natives and local shamans.

Increasing Inputs

Efforts to increase the resources devoted to schooling are the most common and seemingly most straightforward way to improve education.

They have an intuitive appeal: why can't more teachers and more money make schools better? Unless they are drastic programs, such as initiatives to overhaul school finance, input-based reforms are so sensitive and preserving of the status quo that one hesitates to call them reforms at all. Input reforms also seem to lie well within the power of most policy authorities. Per-pupil spending is clearly within the scope of most policy authorities. All legislatures can hand out money, and some judges have ordered lawmakers to do so. Counting dollars and teachers is also quite easy.

However, seeing that money flows to enhancing certain aspects of education, such as reducing class sizes or improving the qualifications of teachers, is still problematic. Policy authorities higher up on the governing pyramid may have their priorities crossed with those below them. The state may want smaller classes, but the school board wants new computers, and the principal needs a new math teacher. Since money is fungible, the higher authority must hand down funding with strings and restrictions attached to see that it is put to the intended use.

Furthermore, input reforms are one-dimensional. The policy authority tries to reduce class sizes or hire better trained teachers with little consideration of the interaction between the policy lever being pushed and other parts of the system. This is in part due to the still-crude nature of research on the education production function. The school system still largely remains a black box to researchers in this area: money, teachers, and master's degrees are put into the hopper at one end, and better educated students are supposed to come out the other end. Although researchers are increasingly dissatisfied with this state of affairs, the problem would not be entirely resolved even if more sophisticated models were developed. The implementation of policy through bureaucratic hierarchies still requires policy authorities to hand down straightforward directives to their agents, and agents to hand back up simple measures to show that they are complying with orders. Neither legislators nor bureaucrats are able to explore all the nuances and interactions in their laws and reports. School operations are thus reduced to numbers on a graph or pie chart.

California's attempt to reduce class size on a large scale is an instructive example of the barriers even an apparently simple reform can face. Reducing the number of students per class would seem to put a check next to every item on Tyack and Cuban's list. It is a natural extension of existing procedure with an obvious intuitive appeal. Fewer students per teacher implies that teachers will be able to spend more time with individual students. Extra personal attention and individual instruction lead to higher student achievement. The average parent would probably view the effect of smaller classes in this straightforward way. Academic researchers, it should be no surprise, have vastly complicated the issue. They have not settled how large an impact—if any—reducing class sizes may have, or exactly how smaller classes improve student achievement. Nevertheless, parents value smaller class sizes. Class size frequently appears as a statistically significant influence on parental choice of private schools. In addition, teachers supposedly approve of smaller classes because managing smaller classes requires less work. Teachers' unions like reducing class sizes because schools must hire more teachers to do so.

Several carefully controlled model programs and field tests, such as Tennessee's Project STAR and Wisconsin's Project SAGE, have found positive results from reducing class sizes. These results inspired California, awash in tax revenue gleaned from the Internet boom, to implement class size reduction on a large scale. In 1996, the legislature passed SB 1977, which established a voluntary program that paid schools an extra $850 for every student in kindergarten through third grade who was placed in a class with 20 or fewer students. This implied a reduction of 30 percent in the average class size statewide.

The immediate impact of the California initiative was a scramble for teachers for the increased number of classes, which led to a rapid rise in the number of inexperienced and less-credentialed teachers. In the 1995–96 school year, before the reform took effect, 1.8 percent of kindergarten through third-grade teachers in California lacked full credentials. By 2000, this had increased to 13.3 percent. The effect cascaded to other grade levels. Before the reform was implemented, 1.8 percent of teachers of grades seven and eight did not have full credentials. By 2000, 16.5 percent did not (Stecher and Bornhstedt 2002). The effect was greater on schools serving nonwhite and low-income students, as more certified and experienced teachers were lured away by affluent and white schools. Before the initiative, there were only moderate differences in the teaching corps of nonwhite and low-income schools and other schools. In 1999, 25 percent of African American students in schools with at least 75 percent of the student body enrolled in subsidized lunch programs had a teacher who was in his or her first or second year, and 30 percent had a teacher who was not fully certified. By contrast, 12 percent of white students in schools with a small fraction taking a subsidized lunch had a teacher with two years of experience or less, and 5 percent had a teacher who was not fully credentialed (Jepsen and Rivkin 2002).

By 2000, the initiative had succeeded in placing over 95 percent of kindergarten through third-grade students in classes of 20 or fewer. The impact, however, has been disappointing. The positive impact that smaller class sizes had on student achievement has been offset by the adverse effect of the new teachers. It is not clear what characteristics of the newly hired teachers led to poor student performance. The link between certification and student performance was weak. There was a much stronger effect due to experience, but it did not fully explain the negative impact of the new teachers. Jepsen and Rivkin speculate that other unobserved characteristics of the newly hired teachers offset the effect of smaller class sizes. Furthermore, class size reduction led to a reallocation of resources as schools shifted funding from facility maintenance, music and arts, computers, sports, libraries, and other school programs. Tighter budgets after the bursting of the Internet stock bubble and recession have caused schools to consider cutting back on the class size reduction program (Sack 2002).

The disappointing results from California show the pitfalls that lie between ideas with intuitive appeal that are supported by interest groups and backed by academic research and a successfully implemented policy. The initiative ran straight into an unanticipated resource constraint: the lack of qualified teachers. Although Biddle and Berliner contend that the money was not sufficient, the initiative caused every school district in the state to begin hiring during one of the tightest labor markets in decades. The resources needed to overcome this hurdle would have been much more than the $1.6 billion the state budgeted each year for the program. Added to the unintended consequences are the resources bled from other school programs. The net benefit for California students, especially for the poor and nonwhite, is probably negative.

Biddle and Berliner acknowledge the tremendous resources in both personnel and facilities needed to reduce class sizes. They list resource requirements as one of the reasons there have been no government mandates requiring smaller classes despite what they view as the overwhelming research consensus regarding the benefits of such a mandate. They express some faith that once the American public knows the full truth about the benefits of smaller classes, the public's sense of fairness and egalitarianism will cause them to devote the funding necessary. Interestingly, Biddle and Berliner focus only on a federal role. The emphasis seems somewhat misplaced, since the federal government still plays only a small role in funding schools. In addition, the federal government has yet to fully fund its mandates on special education and accountability, so there is little reason to believe that it would provide sufficient funding for a mandate reducing class size. Consequently, as in California, a federal mandate would probably lead to the cannibalization of other school functions—the priorities of a higher policy authority would once again have overridden local preferences.

As policy measures go, class size reduction is relatively simple. It requires a legislature only to mandate a number, provide appropriate funds, and arrange for a procedure to ensure that the funding is indeed causing classes to get smaller, rather than the library or gym to get larger. The California experience shows that reducing class size is instrumentally within the policy frontier of a state legislature. SB 1977 was successful in placing children in significantly smaller classes. The results were nevertheless disappointing. In addition, state or federal mandates can roll over local priorities. School boards, after looking at California's experience, may prefer to spend extra funds on ensuring that large classes have competent teachers rather than having small classes taught by inexperienced ones. The improvement on standardized tests may be less important to parents than arts or sports. The California example, combined with the advisability of deferring to local priorities, leads to the conclusion that decisions regarding class size and many similar input reforms should probably be left to a policy authority no higher than the local school board.

"Soft" Reforms

Input reforms are relatively easy for a policy authority to implement compared to "softer" establishment reforms. Take, for example, the following recommendations for improving teaching methods:

- Present new material in small steps to [sic] that the working memory does not become overloaded.
- Help students develop an organization for the new material.
- Guide student practice by supporting students during initial practice, and providing for extensive student processing. (Rosenshine 2002)

These suggestions were taken from a review of the research on classroom teaching methods that was part of a larger omnibus evaluation of school reforms, ranging from early childhood education through teachers' unions and professional development to vouchers and charter schools. Although all are reforms in the sense that they are suggestions for how to change public schools for the better, they are vastly different in terms of which policy authority, if any, would be most effective in implementing them. The above precepts seem more at home on the blackboard in a college of education than in a school board resolution, state regulation, or federal legislation. How might a policy authority at any level encourage teachers to use them? Backers might start at the top, envisioning a grant program for professional development paid for by the state or federal government. But who should be responsible for defining precisely what "sufficiently small steps" are, or specifying ways to help students organize? Legislators could roll up their sleeves and write legislation of nearly unprecedented length and specificity, and then hope that everyone from agency chiefs down to teachers has sufficient respect for the requirements—they are the law of the land, after all—to adhere to them as the lawmakers intended. More than likely, however, legislators would not have the time or expertise to resolve such issues. The enabling legislation might mention "promoting effective teaching methods" and possibly throw in the requirement that they be "research-based" in an effort to ward off lending support to other methods that may be viewed as popular quackery. It would then be up to agency heads to decide what teaching methods are worth promoting. They may agree that research points undeniably to the teaching methods mentioned above, or they may not.

Like all reformers, advocates of establishment education reforms hope for universal adoption of their ideas. This naturally leads to gravitation toward the higher levels of government, since there lie the resources and power for universal adaptation. However, many soft establishment reforms, like the teaching precepts above, are unsuited as policy for authorities in the higher reaches of the governing pyramid, and inappropriate as policy for an authority at any level. Unlike input-based reforms, soft establishment reforms lack the hard measures of inputs and outputs beloved of policymakers and bureaucrats. Policymakers need some measure to gauge the extent of their reform efforts. Progress in reducing class sizes can be reported up the chain of command to a legislative committee in the form of a statewide average class size. The numbers can be broken down by district to detect laggards, and reported by school to find disparities. Teacher salaries and teacher credentials are similarly easy to aggregate and digest. But how can legislators and the agency delegates measure the extent to which teachers are allowing "pacing that gives students time to think," or "sustained involvement with a small number of topics, rather than superficial coverage of many topics," or "treating students' ideas and contributions with respect" (Berliner and Biddle 1995, p. 305)? A researcher attempted to measure the extent to which schools adopted progressive teaching in the 1930s through 1950s by examining whether schools bought fixed or movable desks. The idea was that the ability to move furniture into circles or groups could serve as an indirect indicator of schools' adoption of nontraditional methods (Zilversmit 1976). Legislatures and agencies similarly can resort only to imperfect surrogate measures to track the adoption of soft reforms.

The same is true of the outputs of soft reforms. How are policymakers supposed to track whether students are more thoughtful or cooperative, demonstrate initiative, or are tolerant? Although many complain that test scores reflect a narrow, reductionist, and utilitarian view of education, test scores can be collected on a mass scale and compared through time and across jurisdictions. In an era when every public agency from sanitation agencies to fire departments is asked to set performance goals and accountability measures, soft education reforms are at a disadvantage if they are unable to produce such material for policymakers.

Soft education reforms are more suited for adoption by local levels of authority such as school boards and principals. Since implementation and performance do not have to be reported through several levels of bureaucracy, they can be easily tracked without resorting to stark numerical measures. In addition, because soft reforms often deal with how classrooms are run or what is taught, they run the danger of crossing Tyack and

Cuban's second criterion for successful reforms. Soft reforms may not square with the beliefs of parents and teachers regarding how a "real school" should be run or what it should teach. Imposing or encouraging a soft reform from the state or federal level not only runs the risk of failure, but also contravenes the principles of deference to local values and preferences that has been central to the American system of education.

The general uncertainty of social science research also calls for decentralized implementation of soft reforms. Despite over a hundred years of trying, reformers have been unable to eradicate individual testing, memorization, and drill from American classrooms. This is partly because many parents feel that schools should be operated in a structured, "back-to-basics" way. Although reformers claim to have the latest and best research on their side, the latest and best research has a way of changing. In the first half of the twentieth century, the latest and best research supported separating students into different courses of study based on IQ tests. Today, research supposedly shows that tracking is harmful. Given the uncertain nature of social science and its history of justifying harmful and shameful practices, reformers should exercise some humility and deference to the diverse local views of the proper way schools and classrooms should be run.

Pushing soft reforms through mandates from a central authority is unnecessary. If the reforms are indeed improvements, schools would adopt them once presented with evidence of their superiority, without the need of a mandate. The decentralized diffusion of ideas allows for experimentation and adaptation to local circumstances. Without a central mandate, the reform will not become entrenched and protected by vested interests. If it proves ineffective or is discredited by the latest research, or if an even better idea comes along, local authorities can change policy without waiting for the law to be changed or devising ways to circumvent it. America's decentralized system of governing public schools has been crucial to the expansion of public schools and innovation within them. It should be allowed to continue in the future.

CENTRALIZING ACCOUNTABILITY REFORMS

If policymakers cannot directly control school quality, they may be able to foster it indirectly through a system of incentives. This is part of the logic behind centralizing accountability reforms. The ostensible attraction of an accountability system is that policymakers do not have to worry about or meddle extensively with the way schools operate. Rather, in a centralizing accountability system, policymakers set a standard, provide the incentives, and let educators determine the most effective way of meeting the goals. Schools may raise teacher pay, reduce class sizes, teach reading through phonics or whole language—it does not matter, as long as the schools meet the standards.

Centralizing accountability schemes can be usefully classified in three dimensions. The first is who is accountable. Some plans hold the student accountable by requiring him or her to pass a test before moving up a grade or graduating. This is consistent with over 100 years of educational practice and social norms, which held that students were primarily responsible for their academic success (Ravitch 2002). Alternatively, and in keeping with more contemporary mores, the school—administrators, principals, and teachers—are held accountable.

The second dimension along which an accountability plan may be gauged is its severity. The incentives used by centralizing accountability systems pinch to varying degrees. For students, failure to pass a test may mean no diploma. A less draconian measure would be to award honors diplomas, or to award diplomas to students who have passed a test and certificates of completion to those who have simply put in the required seat-time. For schools, the accountability measures most often take the form of school report cards and designations as "failing" or "A+" schools. Depending on the program, failing schools may face various carrots and sticks, including takeover by the state, additional resources, or the possibility of losing students because their pupils become eligible for a school choice program. The rewards for successful schools can be a flag, a payment to the school, or bonuses for staff. We have already seen that grades on school report cards can be reflected in housing prices, so even published rankings, without immediate financial penalties, can have a large impact on a school district.

The final dimension of a centralizing accountability reform is the instrument used to evaluate those to be held accountable. It should be no surprise, since these plans are centralizing, that the measures of student and school performance rely heavily on standardized and quantifiable measures: most commonly student scores on standardized tests. Tests are the traditional measure of educational attainment, and they are cheap. The average testing system costs less than $20 per pupil, much less than the typical input-based reform. Even if accountability tests had a modest impact on student achievement, their cost-effectiveness would likely be much higher than input-base reforms (Hoxby 2002a). In 2003, of the states using tests to assess high school students, 49 used multiple-choice questions; 26 used short-answer questions; and 42 used essay questions. Only 2 used portfolios of students' work. Of the states creating school ratings, 12 used only test scores; 18 used test scores combined with other numerical measures such as dropouts, attendance, or graduation rates; and 3 used site visits (*Quality Counts 2003* 2003).

The idea of increasing the accountability of American public schools has been floating on the winds of reform since at least the beginning of the twentieth century. The more recent wave of accountability began washing over public schools in the early 1970s. By 1974, state legislatures had passed at least 73 separate laws intended to increase school accountability that knitted together the latest fads in education and management. Schools were ordered to set standards and objectives, monitor progress with tests, evaluate the cost-effectiveness of programs, and gather and report information about performance to parents, legislators, and the general public. All this was to be done in the name of efficiency and adequacy. The laws meddled extensively in school operations by handing down far-reaching mandates regarding school management and planning. Texas passed requirements on how schools should budget; California specified the criteria on which districts should evaluate teachers. The Ohio legislature, in creating the state's system for "educational management information and accountability capabilities," made sure to specify that the state department of education would "utilize the technology of the computer." Most of these laws required districts to set the standards and monitor progress. Others were more ambitious. Rhode Island's 1973 law called for the state's Board of Regents to develop a master plan for education covering elementary schools through universities, both public and private. Although the calls for standards, performance, and efficiency were extensive, the laws contained no penalties for failure (Wise 1979, 2, 12–23).

In the mid-1970s, states began implementing minimum competency tests. The Great Test Score Decline prompted a back-to-basics movement as state and federal governments pushed schools to emphasize instruction in basic skills. To monitor the progress of schools in ensuring that all students attained minimum skills, and to identify and direct remedial resources to students who did not reach the minimum standards, states introduced minimum competency tests. By 1978, 33 states had minimum competency tests in place (Wise 1979). Although the tests were originally intended as diagnostic measures, many states converted them into requirements for graduation (Cohen 1996).

The publication of *A Nation at Risk* under the Reagan administration signaled a significant change in the emphasis of the accountability movement. Instead of ensuring that students met a minimum level of skills, the push was on for "excellence"—rigorous curricula based in fundamental subjects, and high standards for student performance. By the end of the 1980s, a Republican president, George H. W. Bush, was offering a plan for national education standards. Toothless standards were eventually put into place under Bill Clinton as Goals 2000. In 1994, the same year Goals 2000 passed, Congress included in the reauthorization of Title I—the primary federal statute covering education programs for disadvantaged children—requirements for states to set high academic standards, put performance goals to meet those standards into place, develop means to measure progress, and hold schools and districts accountable for the results (Cohen 1996). As of April 2002, only 19 states had measures that fully complied with the 1994 laws, yet states were already facing even more stringent standards under the 2002 reauthorization (Robelen 2002).

The increasing role of the federal government in holding local schools accountable continued with the 2002 reauthorization of the Elementary and Secondary Education Act, President George W. Bush's No Child Left Behind Act. The act requires states to set up a testing system to evaluate students and determine a minimum proficiency level, and it requires that *all* students in the state meet the set level by 2014. This has caused some states to contemplate lowering their previously set levels to make it easier to meet the federal mandate (Emerson 2002).

While federal efforts have been heavy on standards and light on incentives, several states and local districts have put into place full-blown accountability systems that include incentives to meet performance goals. South Carolina was the first in 1984 with its Educational Improvement Act. The law spent additional money on teacher pay and capital improvements; stiffened the criteria for graduating from high school by increasing the course requirements and implementing a basic skills exit exam; put into place local school councils; and created an incentive program for schools. Schools received a cash award—in addition to a flag—based on student gains on standardized reading and mathematics tests, student and teacher attendance, and the school's dropout rate. The entire package necessitated a 20 percent increase in the state's education budget (Clotfelter and Ladd 1996). States with low student achievement and a high proportion of residents who are poor, nonwhite, or lack high school diplomas have been more aggressive creating accountability systems during the accountability drive that followed *A Nation at Risk* (Betts and Costrell 2001). By 2003, 17 states had accountability systems that provided rewards to high-performing schools. With respect to sanctions for underperformance, 11 states had provisions to close schools; 12 allowed students to transfer; 6 had provisions for turning the school over to private management; and 3 could sanction schools by withholding funds. With respect to student accountability, 5 states made promotion contingent on passing an exam, while 19 required students to pass an exam to graduate (*Quality Counts 2003* 2003).

As Robert Maranto (2001) points out, accountability and other school reforms are part of the broader "reinventing government" movement. Government reinventors seek to improve the efficiency and lower the cost of public services by imposing marketlike incentives on their providers. This can be done through straightforward privatization of government functions, contracting out public services to private providers, public-private competition in which private and public agencies compete for contracts for public services, and performance incentive schemes for public agencies. The motto of reinventing is, of course, accountability, and a great emphasis is put on contracts, specific performance measures, and incentives for meeting service objectives. The reinventing government initiative has received bipartisan support.

Outside of education, reinventing government initiatives have tended to be internal reforms, brought about by reforming mayors or city managers. No public institution in the United States has been under as much pressure to reinvent itself as public schools. I can offer no reasons for why this might be the case. Crime waves rise and fall, and crime and punishment are subject to the same liberal-conservative clash in values as education. Yet the critiques of public police forces and research examining the effectiveness of resources devoted to policing have not received the public attention, the debates have not reached the pitch or volume at a national level, and the proposed reforms have been less radical than the debates over public education. There have been no significant efforts by state and federal governments to interfere with municipal police departments. Cities have become as dysfunctional as the schools they encompass, but they have been left, by and large, to sort it out for themselves. Future research will have to determine why.

The Impact of Centralizing Accountability Reforms

Research on the impact of centralizing accountability has not yet approached the volume of the studies that examine the effectiveness of education inputs. There is tentative evidence that standards and incentives have had a positive effect on student achievement. David Grissmer and his coauthors (2000) found that NAEP scores of students in North Carolina and Texas are higher than would be expected, given their demographic profile and level of education inputs, and cautiously attribute this to the accountability systems in those states. The Texas Education Agency and some scholars have an even more positive view regarding the effects of the Texas system, but others are more doubtful (Ladd 2001; Murnane and Levy 2001). Clotfelter and Ladd (1996) find some evidence that the Dallas program had a positive effect.

Students perform better on standardized tests in states with minimum competency tests and states that have systems that sanction and reward schools based on student performance. The effect, however, is small—typically less than one-half of a grade-level equivalent (Bishop et al. 2001). Minimum competency tests have a much larger impact on the earnings of students after they have graduated. Students graduating from schools in states with such tests earn 5 to 11 percent more than graduates in states without them. Students in testing states are also more likely to go to college, although the effect here is small as well (Bishop and Mane 2001; Bishop et al. 2001). One worry regarding standards and testing accountability systems is that students will become discouraged and drop out. While some studies support this claim (Catterall 1989; Lillard and DeCicca 2001), others find more subtle results. Bishop and Mane (2001) found that, while testing did not increase dropout rates as a whole, it did raise the fraction of students who stayed an extra year before graduating and the number of students who obtained a GED. Below-average students were more likely to drop out in testing states or need an extra year to earn a regular diploma.

The minimal effect on test scores combined with the larger impact on wages indicates that, while students may not be learning more in testing states, employers place a greater value on high school diplomas. The need for some students to stay in school longer might also have a positive impact on wages. It is a robust finding of the research that more time spent in school leads to higher earnings. Betts (1997) argues that keeping students in school longer by requiring them to pass minimum competency tests before they graduate or drop out would have just such a positive effect on earnings.

Stronger evidence for a positive effect from centralized accountability systems comes from other countries. Many other countries—either at the national or provincial level—require students to pass what John Bishop refers to as a curriculum-based external exit exam or CBEEE (pronounced see-bee). CBEEEs are based on standards developed by a central authority outside the schools, and are required of almost all secondary students. Instead of being pass-fail, CBEEEs return scores showing differing levels of achievement. Wossmann (2000) found that students in countries with centralized standards and testing perform better. This result was seconded by Bishop (1997), who found that students in countries with CBEEEs scored about one grade level higher in mathematics and 1.2 grade levels higher in science on the Third International Mathematics and Science Study. On the 1991 International Assessment of Educational Progress (IAEP), students from CBEEE countries scored about two grade levels higher in math but did no better in science. In Canada, students from provinces with CBEEEs scored roughly four-fifths of a grade level higher in mathematics and three-fifths of a grade level higher in science on the IAEP. Bishop also found that the behavior of students, parents, and educators was different in CBEEE provinces. Students reported spending more time reading for fun and watching science shows on television. Parents tended to talk more with their children about their classes. Schools had more hours of instruction in science and math and assigned more homework. The schools also had better labs, and their students did more experiments. Math and science teachers were more likely to have studied the subject in college.

Problems with Centralizing Accountability Reforms

Centralizing accountability reforms have been controversial and have received strong opposition from surprising quarters. The first question to ask is whether the increase in test scores represents a real increase in cognitive ability or is a spurious result.

Judging schools primarily by their test scores has been criticized for causing teachers to narrow what they teach in class to conform with the test, and to teach students strategies to game the test and to even cheat (Berliner and Biddle 1995, 196–98; Darling-Hammond and Wise 1985). Jacob (2002) found that gains in test scores on the high-stakes exams used by the Chicago public school system were due to increases in test-specific skills and student stamina. Students on high-stakes tests remained diligent to the ends of the tests instead of flagging on the last questions. There was no comparative increase in performance on a low-stakes test also taken by Chicago students. Jacob also found that teachers responded to incentives by placing more students in special education, retaining students, and not teaching subjects, such as science and social studies, that were not tested. Figlio and Winicki (2002) found that Virginia schools facing sanctions under that state's accountability system increased the calories served to students in their lunchrooms on testing days.

For some idea of other outcomes we might expect, it is useful to look at the effect of performance incentives in other government programs. The programs created by the Job Training Partnership Act to provide job training for the disadvantaged have operated under a performance standards system since 1983 (Heckman, Heinrich, and Smith 1997). Courty and Marschke (1996) found that training centers did game the incentives. Heckman, Smith, and Taber (1996), on the other hand, found that despite the incentives, training center employees did not engage in "cream-skimming" but rather admitted the most disadvantaged to the program. Heckman and his coauthors speculate that cream-skimming might not be such a bad thing, since it would ensure that the program has the greatest impact per dollar spent. They believe that the relative indifference of training center workers to incentives is due to the fact that those choosing to work in the field have a preference for helping the more disadvantaged. They go on to conjecture that hiring people with a taste for social work allows the social service agencies to pay less and creates an inertia that makes bureaucracies resistant to change. Both of these outcomes, they grant, may have advantages. A more expensive bureaucracy that is hypersensitive to political winds may be worse.

Accountability systems might have the same effect on those choosing to enter education. People may choose to be teachers in large part because of the autonomy they have in the classroom, and they may be willing to accept lower pay in exchange. Accountability systems may create an environment that is more favorable for more responsive, and more expensive, workers.

Beyond this, it is worth asking exactly what benefits students and society receive from higher scores on standardized tests—a question that comes rather late in this book. Until now, we have used test scores to evaluate the performance of public schools over the past three decades and to judge the impact and worth of various policies and trends. This is because, as mentioned before, test scores are an easy output to measure, track through time, and compare across schools, states, and nations. Is improving performance on standardized tests something to which society should devote a large amount of money and effort?

The answer to this question is yes, up to a point. Scores on standardized tests are useful predictors of the probability of a student's continuing high school, attending college, and finding a job. Above all, test scores are useful in predicting earnings of students once they enter the job market. Scores on standardized tests partially help explain earnings differences between college graduates and those without college degrees, the differences in earnings between blacks and whites, and wage inequality in the United States and internationally (Blau and Kahn 2001; Grogger and Eide 1995; Neal and Johnson 1996). On the macroeconomic level, scores on international achievement tests partially account for differences in economic growth among nations (Hanushek and Kimko 2000).

However, while test scores may explain in part differences in earnings, they actually explain only a small part. For example, test scores account for only 5 to 15 percent of differences in wage inequality between the United States and other nations. Indeed, research has only limited success in explaining why people earn what they do. Taken together, age, race, sex, schooling, test scores, occupation, experience, and parents—all factors repeatedly examined by research—are typically able to account for only 25 to 33 percent of earnings differences (Bowles, Gintis, and Osborne 2001). The effect of education on the economic prosperity of nations is similarly small (Bils and Klenow 2000; Hendricks 2002).

Meanwhile, researchers have been examining how noncognitive factors influence earnings. Surveys of managers repeatedly find that they value characteristics such as proper attitude, honesty, and communications skills above academic achievement. One survey conducted by the Census Bureau asked managers to rate various traits of potential job candidates on a scale of 1 to 5, with 5 being the most important. Academic performance and scores on employer tests ranked 2.5. Attitude was the most important at 4.6, followed by communications skills at 4.2 (Berliner and Biddle 1995, 89; Bowles, Gintis, and Osborne 2001).

Research has confirmed the importance of noncognitive skills. Although students who earn GEDs have significantly higher cognitive ability than other high school dropouts, they earn little more than other dropouts and

10 percent less than what would be predicted by their cognitive skills and the other characteristics—such as race and sex—typically considered by researchers when studying earnings. Employers evidently value the motivation and discipline needed to stay in school more than just the credential itself. In addition to motivation, employers also value good looks. Women and men considered attractive receive an earnings premium of 9 to 14 percent respectively (Bowles, Gintis, and Osborne 2001). How clean a person keeps his or her house significantly predicts earnings, the probability that his or her children will complete school, and what the children will earn 25 years later (Dunifon, Duncan, and Gunn 2001). Apparently, spending time in school teaching grooming and housekeeping does have some value for students.

Schools foster traits other than cognitive ability that provide an advantage in the labor market. Cognitive development as measured by test scores accounts for no more than 20 percent of the earnings impact of educational attainment. On the other hand, both teachers and work supervisors rate higher and reward individuals who are "perseverant," "dependable," "consistent," "punctual," and "tactful" and who "empathize." Both teachers and supervisors place rate lower and penalize those who are "creative" and "independent." So much for the new pedagogy and curriculum intended to foster creativity and independence in students (Bowles, Gintis, and Osborne 2001).

Thus, the standardized achievement tests used by centralizing accountability systems are able to measure only a part of the results of schooling valued by employers. In addition, we have seen in the previous chapter that academics are only part of what parents value in schools. It should be no surprise, then, that centralized accountability systems, especially testing, have met with resistance from parents, who have organized movements to boycott or have filed lawsuits challenging tests. Some of the strongest objections come from affluent parents who dislike the pressure testing puts on their children, and the time and resources it takes away from more preferred activities in and out of school (Betts and Costrell 2001; Gottlieb 2002; Traub 2002).

Like all centralized reforms, testing induces movement toward the mean. In below-average schools, testing may induce discipline and attention to the fundamentals that—even though taught in a way to cause John Dewey to roll in his grave—improve the basic skills of students. For above-average schools, however, competence in the basics is taken for granted, and testing requires spending time and resources to meet standards that are actually lower than those set by schools and parents. To go straight to the top for an example, the science labs in the public schools in wealthy Scarsdale, New York, are equipped with the latest in digital lab equipment. The standards set by the state of New York require children to be familiar with the less-than-state-of-the-art triple-beam balances.

This requires Scarsdale schools to take the triple-beams out of mothballs and teach their students how to use them (Traub 2002).

Like so much of education policy, testing to measure the performance of students, teachers, and schools is nothing new. Neither are the problems that come with it. In 1874, Samuel King, the first superintendent of public schools in Portland, Oregon, implemented districtwide tests to measure student progress. To inform parents and give teachers and students incentives, each child's score was published in the local paper. At first, the results were abysmal. In 7 out of 21 classrooms, no children passed; only in 6 classrooms did more than half the students score well enough to move on to the next grade. Although results improved in later rounds, angry parents and apprehensive teachers joined together to obtain King's resignation three years later. His successor, Thomas Crawford, abolished the tests, at the same time making observations on the pernicious effect of excessive competition and rivalry (Tyack 1974, 47–48).

Internationally, in 1862 the British Parliament passed a full-blown centralized accountability system with testing and incentives that came to be known as the Payment by Results program. The program placed the financial well-being of the schools in the hands of government inspectors, who paid schools based on student achievement and attendance. In response to the incentives of the program, teachers cut back on the subjects they taught, providing instruction only on the items and skills the inspectors tested. Teaching methods heavily emphasized practice tests and memorization without comprehension. Schoolmasters ensured that all the seats were full on the day the inspector arrived—to the point of compelling gravely ill and contagious children to be present—in order to obtain the full allocation based on attendance. The mechanical teaching methods, pinched curriculum, and generally adverse impact of the Payment by Results program was condemned by a government commission and by notable figures including scientist T. H. Huxley and the poet, social critic, and school inspector Matthew Arnold (Coulson 1999, 90–91).

Centralizing accountability reforms are the latest clash in the continuous fight between central and local authorities over control of American schools. It is ironic that the effort to push centralized accountability was sparked by the *Nation at Risk* report released under a Republican president who campaigned on abolishing the federal Department of Education, and culminated under another Republican president in the No Child Left Behind Act. It may be said that Republicans are returning to their Whig roots. Both the reforms of Horace Mann and Henry Barnard and the efforts to implement centralized accountability reforms are premised on the belief that the local authorities are unable and unwilling to run their schools properly. In the comments of modern advocates of standards such as Diane Ravitch and Bill Bennett can be heard the Whig call for a national culture.

Centralizing accountability reforms, by definition, are supposed to be within the policy frontier of authorities high on the governing pyramid. However, there are strong arguments against centralized accountability being implemented by an authority that is too central. The Whig reformers did not have the benefit of modern political science, so they attributed the faults of the local systems to ignorance, parsimony, and the tribalism of German immigrants, among other motives. However, with the principles of public choice theory in mind, we can critically examine the basis of centralized accountability reforms and even speculate about their eventual effectiveness. Centralized accountability reforms are based on the premise that school districts lack strong incentives to boost student achievement and use taxpayer dollars efficiently. This may be because schools, like all public agencies, lack the market discipline faced by private firms, or it may be because control over schools has been captured by interest groups such as teachers' unions that are interested in benefits for their members. In any case, these groups have been able to seize control over local schools from parents and taxpayers, and run them to their benefit and to the detriment of students.

However, it is not clear how the problems of the local political arena can be solved by moving authority and control up to an even larger political arena. Indeed, doing so may make matters worse. The higher authority, whether at the state capitol or in Washington, D.C., is even more remote from local communities. Well-organized interest groups—the teachers, the administrators, the textbook publishers, the victims' advocates—are at an even greater advantage in the larger, more remote arenas than in the smaller ones. They can lodge themselves permanently in offices down the street from the legislature or department of education, and hire full-time, paid lobbyists for a constant presence in front of policymakers.

The immediate difficulty this poses is that centralized accountability is rarely implemented in its pure form. Recall that the elegance of an accountability system is that policymakers merely had to establish standards and let schools figure out the best way to meet them. Policymakers did not have to specify management or pedagogical techniques, or for the most part have to worry about inputs such as teacher qualifications. However, the logrolling involved with producing a bill usually results in accountability reforms that are accompanied by other mandates and programs. The No Child Left Behind Act, in addition to its testing requirements, also contained language designed to promote the use of phonics to teach reading, to increase the number of certified teachers, and to ensure the Boy Scouts access to school facilities. The long-term problem facing centralized accountability reforms is that the permanent presence of hostile interest groups will cause constant pressure to erode the reforms, reducing the standards and taking the edge off of the incentives.

Centralizing accountability systems, therefore, lack a fundamental justification for overriding local control. If parents and taxpayers are at a disadvantage in school board meetings, they will be at an even greater disadvantage in the legislature or in Congress. This, along with the possible perverse effect of incentives, the fact that performance measures only partially capture what employers and parents value about schools, and the principle of deference to local control, argues against the use of centralizing accountability systems.

DECENTRALIZING ACCOUNTABILITY REFORMS

Decentralized accountability reforms—school choice, in other words— seek to free the incentives facing schools from the web of political influence woven by the many interest groups involved in public education. Instead of voice being the primary means of control, as with centralizing accountability and establishment reforms, control through exit is the foundation upon which decentralized reforms are based. Decentralized accountability plans attempt to make schools answer primarily to parents rather than to the orders of ever-higher authorities on the governing pyramid. This, it is hoped, will at least allow parents to obtain a higher quality of education and make schools more efficient. This hope, which lightly jumps from choice to efficiency and high quality, is based on an analogy to the market. Schools seeking to attract students will supposedly not dabble with pedagogical fads or politically radical propaganda that takes away from learning. Since the school's owners will be able to appropriate any monetary surplus, they will have an incentive to operate more cost-effectively.

The purest form of school choice is to abolish publicly operated schools altogether and rely solely on private schools to supply education. This does not preclude a role for government. As in the country's youth, government may still provide aid to parents to help pay for their children's education. This aid can be in the form of a cash grant, a voucher, or a tax incentive. Government aid may be targeted at the needy or provided universally. A second form of school choice is through charter schools. These are independent, often privately owned and operated schools that are granted a charter by a public agency. In return for abiding by the terms of the charter, the school receives public funds for serving students. The largest school choice program in the nation as of this writing is Arizona's system of charter schools. In 2000, 5.5 percent of Arizona children attending a publicly supported school went to a charter school (Arizona Superintendent of Public Instruction 2002).

School choice is commonly thought of as an item on the conservative-libertarian-right-wing agenda. The most famous intellectual father of school vouchers is Milton Friedman (1955), the Nobel laureate economist and noted advocate of free markets . However, school choice and vouchers have strong roots on the left of the political spectrum as well. John Coons and Stephen Sugarman, who laid the legal and intellectual foundation for the school finance equalization movement, also authored a monograph advocating school vouchers (Coons and Sugarman 1978). Their advocacy of financial equality led them directly to vouchers.

Just as centralizing accountability reforms are an offshoot of the reinventing government movement that has led to the development of accountability measures for government services at all levels, decentralizing accountability measures are also cousin to a broader range of reforms of government services. There are two general avenues through which the government may provide benefits to the public. The first avenue is the traditional supply-side methods in which a government agency itself is the supplier. Public education, public housing, federal veterans hospitals, and public transportation are examples. The second method is the provision of government subsidies to the public through vouchers or tax credits, allowing individual beneficiaries to choose to obtain the service from a private provider. Food Stamps, the GI Bill and other support of college students, and Medicare are examples of demand-side subsidies.

Demand-side subsidies are founded on two advantages of private-sector markets. Competition and the profit motive induce private-sector organizations to be more cost-efficient. Because they are free from government procurement and civil service rules, and because they sometimes operate as for-profit entities, private providers are thought to be more flexible, creative, and cost-effective. Second, the private sector is more deferential to consumer sovereignty—the belief that, in a free society, the needs of individual consumers should hold the greatest sway in determining the nature of the goods and services provided. Competition for government-subsidized beneficiaries is supposed to make providers more customer-friendly than the traditional bureaucracy. Demand-side subsidies, then, are thought to allow the government to stretch its tax dollars farther and better satisfy beneficiaries.

Who Would Choose to Choose?

Although some libertarian thinkers may contemplate dismantling the entire public school system, school choice—either through vouchers or charter schools—is more often seen as an adjunct to the present system. Rather than continue to batter directly at the school gates to achieve change as with establishment or centralizing reforms, school choice seeks to influence schools indirectly through competition. The possibility of losing students and the funding that accompanies them will induce public schools to become more effective.

If a system of school choice is grafted on to the presently existing public school system, who will choose to choose? Since public schools are an institution crafted by majority-rule politics, it is logical to conclude that the majority deem public schools adequate. Consequently, those most likely to take advantage of school choice are minorities of some sort: the deeply religious, racial and ethnic groups that are a local minority, the dissenters, and the square pegs. This conclusion would immediately be disputed by those steeped in public choice theory and practical politics, who know that majority-rule politics can be manipulated to the advantage of special interests. In the case of public education, interest groups such as teachers' unions can triumph in political arenas from the local school board to the U.S. Congress, winning policies that benefit their members at the expense of children and taxpayers.

Strong testimony for the indifference of the majority toward school choice can be found in the numerous school choice ballot initiatives that have invariably crashed in flames. In 1993, Proposition 174 in California, which would have created an unconditional $2,600 voucher, lost by 70 percent to 30 percent. A second attempt in 2000 lost by 71 percent to 29 percent. In Oregon in 1990, a tax credit initiative was defeated by a two to one margin. In Colorado, a 1992 voucher initiative lost by 67 percent to 33 percent, and a 1998 tax credit plan went down with 59 percent of voters opposing. In 1996, a voucher initiative was defeated 66 percent to 34 percent in the state of Washington, and in Michigan a 2000 voucher plan lost by 69 percent to 31 percent (Moe 2001). Terry Moe attributes the slaughter to the peculiar nature of the campaigns surrounding ballot initiatives. Fischel (2002) hypothesizes that resistance to school choice is a result of parents' valuing their local school's role in producing social capital. This is not the typical argument that schools play a role in socializing children. Rather, sporting events, pageants, and PTA meetings are a way for *parents* to meet one another and interact. Brunner, Sonstelie, and Thayer (2001) suggest that opposition may be homeowners protecting the value of their property. School choice through direct subsidies undermines the geographically based school choice system now in place, and hence could erode the premium in housing prices enjoyed by homeowners living in good school districts. Indeed, Brunner, Sonstelie, and Thayer found that opposition to California's Proposition 174 was correlated with property values. However, since high property values are correlated with school quality, it may simply be that voters in districts with quality schools—as measured by local property values—were more inclined to vote against vouchers. In an examination of the voting patterns of renters, Brunner and his coauthors were unable to say which reason might be the case.

In their examination of the effect of Minnesota's tax deduction for private school tuition, Kirby and Darling-Hammond (1988) found that high-income parents with children in public schools would be less likely to switch to private schools if given a subsidy than parents with lower incomes. Wealthier individuals are more likely to consider school quality when choosing a home. For them, too, housing prices are less of a barrier to moving into the neighborhood of a good school. This result is seconded by Moe (2001), who found that parents who are better able to select schools through Tiebout choice are more satisfied with their local schools. Kirby and Darling-Hammond's findings question the effectiveness of tax subsidies for school choice. Poor parents do not have the income to fully take advantage of income tax deductions or credits, while rich parents who are able to buy housing in areas with good public schools would be relatively indifferent to choice.

Qualitative evidence that school choice is more appealing to those in the minority comes from Arizona's charter school movement. The charter school system in Arizona is in essence equivalent to a voucher program. Parents are able to send their children to a wide variety of privately operated schools, with no restrictions on the number or type of children who may choose. The schools are paid, for all intents and purposes, on a per-child basis similar to a voucher. The major differences between Arizona's charter school system and the voucher system as it is typically advocated have to do with regulations that, although significant, could easily be added onto a voucher plan. First, entry into Arizona's charter school market is regulated by the state. It is not difficult to imagine that the government would limit the use of vouchers to schools approved in a manner similar to the process used for Arizona charters. Second, the funding formula for charter schools is more complex than a straightforward cash grant. However, it is conceivable, and likely, that the political process will transmogrify the voucher's simple elegance in this aspect as well. Differential vouchers based on income or a student's special needs are the most obvious modification. Antifraud provisions to ensure that the vouchers are being used to send real children to real schools will also likely complicate matters. Finally, Arizona's charter schools are not entirely free of government regulation. They may not engage in selective admissions, for example. However, again it is not hard to imagine the acceptance of voucher-supported children being contingent on submitting to similar regulations. Even with this level of regulation, Arizona is still considered the Wild West in terms of school choice, yet less than 6 percent of children who attend public schools in the state attend charter schools.

Advocates of school choice point to the large outpouring of demand and waiting lists in some of the pilot school choice programs. In the first year of Cleveland's voucher program, 6,000 applications were received for 2,000 scholarships. In Milwaukee, 578 students applied for 406 seats. Some private scholarship programs have experienced the same level of response. In New York, 20,000 students applied for 1,200 scholarships offered by the School Choice Scholarship Foundation. In Washington,

D.C., 7,500 applied for 1,000 scholarships (Gill et al. 2001, p. 123). There has also been strong parental interest in the choice options created by the No Child Left Behind Act (MacDonald 2002).

These cases, however, lend support to the contention that the potential market for school choice is small and particular. Private and public school choice programs have been primarily focused on low-income African American parents living in especially disadvantaged school districts in northern cities. These are precisely the groups that Moe (2001) finds tend to support school choice. Whether this demand can be generalized to a majority of American parents remains in question.

Statistical analyses and models of the demand for choice yield a wide range of results. Buddin, Cordes, and Kirby's (1998) examination of private school demand found that families are insensitive to tuition costs. They concluded that school vouchers would cause few families to switch from public to private schools. Hoxby (1996a) estimated that a $1,000 voucher (in 1994 dollars) would cause the fraction of children attending private schools nationwide to increase from 10 percent to 14 percent. Cohen-Zada and Justman (n.d.) calculated that a voucher equal to 20 percent of public school spending per pupil would increase the fraction of children attending private schools by 4 percent. This result is consistent with the model developed by Nechyba (2000). However, Nechyba found that the magnitude of demand depends on the quality of the local school. He estimated that subsidies on the order of 20 percent of public school spending would cause 23 percent of children living in low-quality districts to move to private schools, but would have no effect on children in average and high-quality districts. If the voucher was of a sufficient size—60 percent of public school spending—all children would elect to attend private schools. Epple and Romano (1998) found that 100 percent private school attendance would occur with a more generous voucher equivalent to the minimum average public school spending per pupil.

If such vouchers were implemented, it is unknown how fast the private sector could expand to absorb all these children. The potential supply of schools for parents deciding to leave public schools has barely been examined by researchers. A small handful of studies have looked at what factors affect the opening, closing, and location of private schools, but have had little success in finding a set of factors consistently related to private school formation (Downes and Greenstein 1996; Barrow 2001). A survey of private schools in Michigan found enough capacity for 3 percent of the state's public school students, and a willingness among many schools to consider expansion (Brouillette 1999). Only Arizona's experience with charter schools lends more than theoretical support to the idea that the private sector will be able to absorb a significant number of students. Much more needs to be done before we will have a clear picture of the impact of school choice.

Choice, Achievement, and Public School Quality

Advocates and researchers of school choice look to three streams of research for clues and support regarding the impact of school choice on student achievement: studies comparing public and private schools, empirical research of Tiebout competition, and examinations of current school choice programs. We have already reviewed the first two areas of research. Research on achievement at private schools leads us to expect a positive impact of school choice on achievement for nonwhite urban children. The extensive literature on the effects of Tiebout competition implies that school choice will have a broader effect. The evidence of Tiebout competition's positive impacts on student outcomes and efficiency is convincing enough to draw acknowledgement from known skeptics of school choice (Belfield and Levin 2001).

Studies of the modest voucher and the larger charter school programs have also found a positive impact. Studies of these programs confronted the same difficulty that hampered research comparing private and public schools: potential bias in the estimates of impacts due to the possibility that parents choosing to choose are more motivated, wealthier, or have other advantages not enjoyed by parents who keep their children in public schools. Howell et al. (2001), in a study of voucher programs in Washington, D.C., New York, and Dayton, Ohio, benefited from being able to assign student subjects randomly to voucher and nonvoucher groups. Their results mirror those of the private-public school literature. While choice had no effect on most students, it significantly raised achievement among African American students able to use vouchers. The effect was significant: a 0.26 standard deviation increase in reading scores and a 0.30 standard deviation increase in math scores after two years. This was twice the impact estimated for the centralizing accountability systems of Texas and North Carolina, and only slightly smaller than the estimated impact of Tennessee's program to reduce class sizes.

Studies of voucher programs in Milwaukee and Cleveland have suffered from a scarcity of data and more problematic controls. Nevertheless, research has tended to find a positive impact on achievement. Examinations of student achievement have found that, for the most part, charter schools do as well as public schools, sometimes do better, and occasionally do worse (Gill et al. 2001).

The overwhelming evidence is that school choice has a positive effect on customer service by schools and parental satisfaction. Charter schools in Washington, D.C., were found to be physically cleaner and more attractive than their public counterparts. They also radiated a greater sense of safety and excitement. Parents felt that charter school staffs treated them with greater courtesy and were more responsive than the employees of public schools (Teske et al. 2001). Parents able to participate in a voucher program professed significantly greater satisfaction than parents with children in public schools. In Dayton, 47 percent of voucher parents gave their schools a grade of A, compared to 8 of their counterparts with children attending public schools. In Washington, D.C., the margin was 46 percent to 15 percent. Only 38 percent of voucher parents gave their children's school an A in more demanding New York. This was still over four times the fraction of public school parents who gave their child's school the same score. In Milwaukee, the fraction of voucher parents who declared themselves very satisfied with the academics, safety, and other aspects of their children's school was consistently two to three times greater than the fraction of public school parents saying they were very satisfied with the same features (Gill et al. 2001, 128–34).

As proponents of school choice had hoped, choice often has a positive impact on schools faced with competition. Public school districts in Arizona competing with charter schools provide more services, such as all-day kindergarten, and take greater pains to keep parents informed. Principals provide more support for teachers, and teachers have a greater say in scheduling, discipline, and curriculum (Maranto et al. 2001). These effects, however, are found only in public schools that already have a cooperative atmosphere between the principal and faculty. Dysfunctional schools remained dysfunctional despite competition (Hess, Maranto, and Milliman 2001). Choice induces schools to hire teachers who are more proficient in math and science and who display greater effort and independence (Hoxby 2000b). Student performance improved in public schools in Milwaukee, Michigan, and Arizona confronted with competition due to vouchers and charter schools, with an increase of the order of 1 to 2 points in the percentile ranking on national tests (Hoxby 2002b).

School Choice and Social Cohesion

After the glowing review in the previous section, we now turn to some of the concerns and objections many have regarding school choice. Supporters of American public schools have been hostile toward private schools since the common-school movement (Kaestle and Vinovskis 1980, 33–34, 100). Private schools cream off the best students and their parents, who are often the most wealthy, educated, and influential members of a community. Hirschman (1970) believed that the exit of such individuals should be blocked in order to prevent public institutions from losing important resources and leadership. Under a system of school choice, many worry, taxpayers will subsidize havens for white flight and nests of dangerous sectarians, and the public schools left behind will be even more feeble and starved for resources. However, as Paul Hill and Kacey Guin (2002) admonish, the potential undesirable outcomes of school choice should not be compared to the common-school ideal, but rather to the actual conditions found in American public schools.

Theoretical models (Epple and Romano 1998), the experience of other countries (Fiske and Ladd 2001; Winkler and Rounds 1996), and evidence from choice programs in the United States (Schneider and Buckley 2002) raise the concern that choice would lead to the stratification and fragmentation of America's schoolchildren, soon followed by the stratification and fragmentation of American society. This objection is based on the presumption that children of all races, creeds, and means rub shoulders in today's American public schools, and that education dollars are allocated equally among all students. However, American public schools suffer from inequality not only among states or between inner-city and suburban districts, but also within school districts and individual schools (Roza and Miles 2002). Simply being an institution governed by politics and voice does not mean that all voices are equal. Wealthy and more-educated parents tend to have more influential voices and are able to steer resources toward their children. More experienced, and hence better-paid, teachers are able to take advantage of seniority rules and cluster in schools with more pleasant working environments. Hence, per-pupil spending tends to be greater in these schools as well (Hill and Guin 2002; Roza and Miles 2002). A balancing of the costs and benefits of public education indicates that public education redistributes income from the poor and nonwhite to the rich and white (Grubb 1971). High housing prices can serve as well as tuition and entrance examinations to exclude the disadvantaged. The racial makeup of public schools can be more homogeneous not only than that of society as a whole, but also than that of the surrounding neighborhood (Hill and Guin 2002). Clubs and sports teams tend to be more segregated than their schools (Clotfelter 2001).

Actual choice programs in the United States give ample indications that children from all segments of society will take advantage of the opportunity to choose. Education entrepreneurs in Arizona have been willing to open schools to serve disadvantaged populations For example, PPEP TEC High School, an operator of 14 charter school sites throughout Arizona, including 3 near the border with Mexico, primarily focuses on the children of migrant and seasonal farmworkers and students who have dropped out of school. Charter schools in the central Phoenix area served by the Phoenix Union High School District are able to draw students from a broad geographic area. Since Phoenix Union is under a desegregation order, students must seek a variance to leave the school. Eighty-one percent of the students who sought such permission to attend a charter school were minority students (Gifford, Ogle, and Solmon n.d.). The exodus of minority students helps Phoenix Union meet the racial balancing goals of its desegregation order. In Texas, charter schools are disproportionately nonwhite and low-income. In the 2000–2001 school year, 41 percent of charter school students were African American, compared to 14 percent in public schools overall; 37 percent of charter school students were Hispanic, compared to 41 percent overall; and 54 percent were economically disadvantaged, compared to a little over 50 percent for the state (Texas State Board of Education. 2002). The racial composition of private school classrooms is often more representative of the nation than the racial makeup of public school classes. Racial mixing has been found to be more frequent in private schools as well (Greene 2000a).

By weakening the link between geographic location and school quality, school finance equalization reform has led to somewhat greater integration in local neighborhoods. School choice, by further disconnecting the location of the home from the location of the school, can increase integration by race and income in the surrounding neighborhoods and remove a significant disincentive for families to move to the central cities (Glaeser, Kolko, and Saiz 2000; Nechyba 2000).

This is not to say that schools of choice will uniformly be small melting pots. Many charter schools are designed to serve specific ethnic and racial groups. Hawaii has charter schools in which students are taught in the Hawaiian language, learn about native customs and traditions, and learn academic subjects through the lens of native culture—astronomy for ocean navigation, for example (Buchanan and Fox 2003).

For Whig common-school reformers and their modern heirs, public schools are important applicators of the values and culture that are supposed to cement American society together. In public schools, children are supposed to be taught common values, customs, language, and morals that are to make them good citizens and pleasant neighbors. Here again, there is a divergence between the ideal and the real. American public school systems have historically been rather sloppy masons in applying social cement. Schools serving immigrants and urban workers were starved of resources. Parents were allowed to flout compulsory attendance and child labor laws in order to take advantage of their children's ability to earn income (see chapter 3).

Families in the United States and elsewhere are not passive bricks upon which the elite may trowel their doctrines, customs, and language at will. However eager some groups have been to homogenize society, the American ethic of freedom has allowed ethnic and racial groups to form their own tax-exempt churches and societies, publish books and newspapers and broadcast radio and television programs in their native languages, and send their children to private schools (Ravitch 1978, p. 70). The Supreme Court has upheld the right of parents to send their children to private schools. Although states may regulate private schools, the Court has upheld the schools' right to teach in foreign languages (Van Geel 1976). In the past, ethnic minorities have demanded that *public* schools teach in their own languages. San Francisco had cosmopolitan schools that taught children in French, German, and English. The superintendent stated that students should be able to study subjects such as math and geography in their native languages. At the end of the nineteenth century, students of German origin in Cincinnati divided their time evenly between an English and a German teacher (Tyack 1974, 106–9). Despite the "multiculturism" of today's public schools, they still exist in a monocultural desert caused by the nativist wave that followed WWI.

Ethnic and racial groups have been willing and able to resist assimilation efforts that they believe will destroy values they consider important (Ravitch 1978, 70), and schools have proven unable to force assimilation when their subjects are unwilling. The attempts of the government-supported Indian schools to eradicate the indigenous culture of Native American children and integrate them into white society ended in failure, and are now looked on as an episode of national shame.

The values schools attempt to impart are shaped by political give and take and compromise among various interest groups. The nineteenth century fight between Protestants and Catholics over teaching religion in school demonstrates how this process of give and take between elite reforms and popular will forms the institutions meant to weld society together—although "give and take" is a rather mild phrase for controversy that sometimes led to rioting, arson, and bloodshed. Calvin Stowe could believe in a nonsectarian Christian education. Horace Mann could recommend in his *Twelfth Report* that schools not teach controversial issues, and claim that the school board could choose suitably sterilized books. However, the nation's growing Catholic population saw public school classrooms as much less neutral and benign. Catholics complained that schools used a Protestant rather than Catholic version of the Bible and that scriptural instruction was carried out in the Protestant manner: simple reading without commentary or instruction. Textbooks cast slurs on Catholics and the Catholic Church (Kaestle 1983, 80, 168–71; Nasaw 1979, 70–172).

In response to complaints from Catholic parents and competition from Catholic schools, school and government officials tried to make some accommodations. When he was governor of New York, William Seward— an otherwise staunch Whig and supporter of common schools—called for schools in which Catholic children could be taught in their own languages by teachers sharing their faith (Kaestle 1983, 157). In 1840, in response to what Cubberly called Seward's "dangerous proposal," Catholics in New York City asked that their schools once again receive the public funding that had been revoked 15 years earlier. Their petition was supported by a Jewish congregation and the Scotch Presbyterian Church. Other Protestant sects, however, opposed the division of public support among religious schools (Cubberly 1919, 178). The resulting debate led to the demise of the private philanthropic Public School Society and the placement of control firmly in public hands. The ward system that was created, however, had enough flexibility to allow the use of the Catholic Douay Bible in Catholic-dominated wards, although Bible instruction was still to be done in the Protestant manner. A similar attempt at compromise led to more tragic results in Philadelphia. In 1843, a school board decision that allowed Catholic children use the Douay Bible and excused them from other religious instruction led to an escalation of animosity and misunderstanding that exploded in the Bible riots of 1844. After the smoke had cleared, 13 lives had been lost and a church destroyed by fire (Kaestle 1983, 168–70).

In his 1875 message to Congress, President Ulysses S. Grant asked that the U.S. Constitution be amended to require states to support nonsectarian common schools, and that states be prohibited from supporting religious schools. James G. Blaine, one of those hoping to succeed Grant as president, introduced such an amendment. It made it through the House, but the Democratic majority in the Senate, understanding it to be an anti-Catholic measure, defeated it. The majority of states, however, added so-called Blaine amendments to their own constitutions, prohibiting public support of religious schools (Peterson 1985, 42). By the end of the nineteenth century, the continuing controversy had eroded away the overtly religious and mostly Protestant Christian features of public education. Public school students in a minority of states still prayed and read the Bible. Also widespread were references to a generic higher power and Christmas pageants. Taking the place of the metaphysical religion was a civic religion whose trappings consisted of icons of Washington and Lincoln, patriotic hymns, and flag salutes (Fraser 1999).

Public schools, however, cannot force children to partake of even the mildest aspects of civic culture. Two Supreme Court decisions only three years apart dramatize the steady corrosion of public education as an instrument of social cohesion. In *Minersville School District v. Gobitis* (1940), the Court backed a school district's expulsion of two children of Jehovah's Witnesses for refusing to salute the flag. A free society, it stated, needed to be bound together by common traditions. The Constitution did not prevent schools from inculcating unifying feelings and beliefs. In 1943, in *West Virginia State Board of Education v. Barnette*, the Court reversed itself and ruled that a compulsory flag salute was unconstitutional. No public officials, including school officials, could impose conventions in religion, politics, nationalism, or any other matter (Sandel 1996, 53–54).

Today, public schools are accused of lacking the will, let alone the authority, to pass on a common culture (Ravitch 2001; Sorokin 2002). Instead of social cement, public schools see themselves as applying social grease to alleviate friction among the sharp edges and rough surfaces of the many parts of American society: "Community means an attitude of 'Live and let live' more than of people working together" (Powell, Farrar, and Cohen

1985, 58). The public education establishment has become an easy target for cultural critics. The first-year anniversary of the September 11 terrorist attacks was marked by a predictable exchange between the National Education Association and conservative critics over what to tell children. Conservatives disparaged the NEA's suggested lesson plans as being nonjudgmental and focusing excessively on students' emotions about the attack. Defenders of the curriculum, on the other hand, implied that their critics were disguised bigots who wanted to ignore the nation's own sins and scare children (Zernike 2002).

Public schools, then, are overrated as means of social cohesion. The alternative, however, is not the fragmentation of society. Individuals and families recognize the advantages of being able to move in a larger society (Lazear 1999), and Americans have been willing to sew society together not only through schools both public and private, but also through fraternal societies, philanthropic organizations, and bowling leagues (Putnam 2000). The important feature of this process is that it has been voluntary and rises up from the bottom more than it is pushed down from the top. In the decades around the beginning of the twentieth century, immigrant communities put great faith in schools both public and private to turn their children into Americans. Private schools, rather than being places to flee from the larger society, emphasized how they were able to integrate children into American society more efficiently by building upon family and cultural traditions. At the Hebrew Institute in New York, children memorized the Declaration of Independence in both Hebrew and English (Tyack 1974, 242).

In short, if the values needed to be a good citizen are as important to parents as the skills needed to be a productive worker, private schools should impart both. However, if society is falling into pieces, it is fruitless to attempt to put it together in the public school classroom. Evidence backs the assertion that private schools can be as effective, if not more effective, in creating social capital. Students in Catholic schools score higher than students in assigned public schools on five measures of civic education, including community service, political knowledge, and political tolerance. Students in public magnet schools score no better in these areas than their assigned peers. Students in non-Catholic private schools do not demonstrate as broad a superiority, although they still tend to outscore assigned public school students. Only students in non-Catholic religious schools show greater political intolerance (Campbell 2001). College students educated in private schools also tend to be more politically tolerant (Wolf et al. 2001). Parents participating in a choice program among public schools displayed greater participation in the PTA and voluntary activities. They were also more likely to have greater contact with other parents and to have expressed trust in their children's teacher (Schneider et al. 1997). The vast majority of parents (85 percent) with children in Arizona charter schools were aware of the dates and times of the meetings of their school's governing board; 90 percent had participated in board meetings (Gifford and Ogle 1998). The same percentages are unlikely to be found in the typical public school district.

CONCLUSION

This chapter has surveyed the myriad reforms, plans, proposals, and schemes to alter the several trajectories American public schools have been following for the past 50 years. Establishment reforms have roots reaching back into nearly 200 years of effort to improve American schools. Many establishment reforms hold the promise of improving American schools; however, many establishment reformers suffer from a blind spot about the unintended political, social, and educational effects of their plans. In their eagerness to make schools more equitable or more enlightened, establishment reforms have contributed to the greater bureaucratization and centralization of American schools. Using Paul Hill's vivid metaphor, the various agencies responsible for public education have become geologic monuments, with each layer representing a past reform initiative. These accretions have made the system larger and less responsive. Centralization has alienated parents and voters from the system, making them more likely to send their children to private schools and less likely to support public schools with their taxes.

Centralizing and decentralizing reforms are more aware of the importance of the structure of school governance and incentives. They are widely seen in the reform movement as complementary, with the centralizing measures providing information and a quality guarantee to parents as they select schools. A choice policy that allows parents to remove their children from schools deemed to be failing by the measures of the central authorities is frequently used as a stick in centralizing accountability plans (Finn 2002).

Yet, aside from their call for greater accountability, the two streams of reform are quite different, and in some aspects are in direct conflict. As I emphasize with the labels I use to classify them, they differ fundamentally in where they locate power over schools. Centralizing reforms continue the trend of the past two centuries of increasing the power of higher levels of government over local schools. Decentralizing reforms, on the other hand, seek to partly undo the accumulation of control by central authorities and return a greater say to parents, where it has traditionally rested. Second, centralizing accountability reforms, like the establishment reforms, override local preferences and tend to make schools more uniform. The more schools have to hew to standards handed down by central authorities, the less significant differences among schools become and the less meaningful choice becomes.

Finally, decentralizing accountability reforms are consistent with the premises of the model upon which they are based. Decentralizing reforms assume that the voice as a means of school governance has malfunctioned; that interest groups have captured the schools and run them, according to their self-interest, to the detriment of parents, children, and taxpayers. Decentralizing accountability reforms solve this problem by moving the way of governing schools away from a voice toward an exit. Centralizing reforms are also based on the belief that interest groups are operating schools to suit their interests rather than those of children and society. However, while decentralizing reforms seek to outflank these interests by moving school governance to a field where they are less dominant, centralizing reforms seek to vanquish them head-on in the arena of voice. In the state legislatures and the U.S. Congress, centralizing reformers seek laws to implement the standards and accountability measures they believe will bring all interests to serve greater student achievement. At bottom, the agenda of centralizing reformers is based on the premise that the wrong sort are in control, but they offer no reason why this is the case. So, although centralizing reformers may assemble a coalition to enact their program, it remains vulnerable to the shifting sands of politics. The same interest groups are out there, still as powerful as before, looking to water down standards and soften accountability measures. The long-term effectiveness of centralizing reforms is always in doubt.

The evidence reviewed in this chapter shows that both centralizing and decentralizing accountability reform can be effective, as measured by increases in standardized test scores. However, other factors lend superiority to decentralizing reforms. First, centralizing reforms accentuate the control of higher levels of government over local schools, a trend that has, on balance, been detrimental to schools. Second, because they focus accountability upward, centralizing reforms concentrate on quantitative measures of performance that are only part of what parents and society expect from their schools. As we saw in this chapter, although high test scores are associated with higher earnings, other factors play a larger role in success after graduation. Third, decentralizing reforms promote a level of parental engagement that can lead to enhanced social capital not found in centralizing reforms. In centralizing reforms, parents are passive consumers who are told by higher authorities whether their schools measure up to the authorities' standards. Parents play a little role in creating the school improvement plans that are often required by centralizing systems. School choice, on the other hand, directly engages parents in important decisions about their children's education and has been shown to foster greater formation of social capital.

The evidence reviewed above shows that decentralized reforms have the potential to improve the paths of student achievement and efficiency that schools have followed for the past decades. By increasing the power given to parents, decentralized reforms can significantly reverse the course toward greater centralization. A voucher system can bring about public support per student that is exactly equal. This would require a system of taxation and distribution of education funds that is much more centralized than currently exists. The fact that a more-decentralized system of parental choice needs an even more centralized system of school funding is, perhaps, the concept's Achilles' heel.

Establishment reformers will continue to plod forward with the sincere hope that an institution governed by majority-rule politics will be sensitive to the needs of minorities and responsive to parents increasingly accustomed to being provided with high-quality goods and services that are closely fitted to their personal preferences. Centralizing accountability reforms, if not immolated in the immediate future by public opposition, will settle down to become another stratum of school reform, nestled among the other fossils. In the end, decentralizing reforms hold the greatest promise of altering the path followed by American public schools in the direction of equity, diversity, increased achievement, greater efficiency, and freedom.

Bibliography

Aaronson, Daniel. 1999. "The Effect of School Finance Reform on Population Heterogeneity." *National Tax Journal* 51 (March): 5–29.

Access Education 2002. "Finance Litigation." www.accessdnetwork.org.

Achilles, C. M. 1996. "Students Achieve More in Smaller Classes." *Educational Leadership* February: 76–77. Quoted in Verstegen, Deborah A., and Richard A. King. 1998. "The Relationship between School Spending and Student Achievement: A Review and Analysis of 35 Years of Production Function Research." *Journal of Education Finance* 24 (fall): 243–62.

Altonji, Joseph G., Todd E. Elder, and Christopher R. Taber. 2002. "Selection on Observed and Unobserved Variables: Assessing the Effectiveness of Catholic Schools." Unpublished.

American Consumer Satisfaction Index. www.theasci.org (visited May 2, 2002).

American Textbook Council. 2000. "Report 2000: History Textbooks at the New Century." www.historytextbooks.org/2000.htm (visited December 2, 2002).

Anderson, Gary M., William F. Shughart II, and Robert D. Tollison. 1991. "Educational Achievement and the Cost of Bureaucracy." *Journal of Economic Behavior and Organization* 15: 29–45.

Arizona Superintendent of Public Instruction. 2002. *Annual Report: Fiscal Year 2000–2001.* Phoenix, Ariz.: Arizona Department of Education.

Augenblick, John G., John L. Myers, and Amy Berk Anderson. 1997. "Equity and Adequacy in School Funding." *The Future of Children* 7: 63–78.

Bailyn, Bernard. 1960. *Education in the Forming of American Society.* New York: W.W. Norton & Company.

Ballou, Dale. 1996. "Do Public Schools Hire the Best Applicants?" *Quarterly Journal of Economics* 111 (February): 97–133.

———. 1999. "The New York City Teachers' Union Contract: Shackling Principals' Leadership." Manhattan Institute Civic Report 6.

Ballou, Dale, and Michael Podgursky. 1995a. "Education Policy and Teacher Effort." *Industrial Relations* 34 (January): 21–39.

———. 1995b. "Recruiting Smarter Teachers." *Journal of Human Resources* 30: 326–38.

———. 1998. "Teacher Recruitment and Retention in Public and Private Schools." *Journal of Policy Analysis and Management* 17: 393–417.

Barrow, Lisa. 2001. "Private School Location and Neighborhood Characteristics." *Economic Perspectives 3Q,* Federal Reserve Bank of Chicago, 13–30.

Baugh, William A., and Joe A. Stone. 1982. "Teachers, Unions, and Wages in the 1970s: Unionism Now Pays." *Industrial and Labor Relations Review* 35 (April): 368–76.

Baumol, William J., 1967. Macroeconomics of Unbalanced Growth: The Anatomy of Urban Crisis. *The American Economic Review* 57 (June): 415–26.

Beard, Robert, and Paul J. J. Payack. 2002. "Presidential Debates Mirror Long-Term School Decline." www.yourdictionary.com/library/presorts.html.

Becker, Gary S., and Kevin M. Murphy. 1988. "The Family and the State." *Journal of Law and Economics* 31 (April): 1–18.

Belfield, Clive R., and Henry M. Levin. 2001. "The Effects of Competition on Educational Outcomes: A Review of U.S. Evidence." National Center for the Study of Privatization in Education, Columbia University Teachers College Occasional paper 35.

Berger, Mark C., and Eugenia F. Toma. 1994. "Variation in State Education Policies and Effects on Student Performance." *Journal of Policy Analysis and Management* 13: 477–49.

Berliner, David C., and Bruce J. Biddle. 1995. *The Manufactured Crisis.* Reading, Mass: Perseus Books.

Betts, Julian R. 1995. "Does School Quality Matter? Evidence from the National Longitudinal Survey of Youth." *Review of Economics and Statistics* 77 (May): 231–49.

———. 1996. "Is There a Link between School Inputs and Earnings? Fresh Scrutiny of an Old Literature." Pp. 141–90 in *Does Money Matter?* ed. Gary Burtless. Washington, D.C.: Brookings Institution Press.

———. 1997. "The Two-Legged Stool: The Neglected Role of Educational Standards in Improving America's Public Schools." *FRBNY Economic Policy Review* (March): 97–116.

Betts, Julian R., and Robert M. Costrell. 2001. "Incentives and Equity under Standards-Based Reform. Pp. 9–74 in *Brookings Papers on Education Policy 2001,* ed. Diane Ravitch. Washington, D.C.: Brookings Institution Press.

Betts, Julian R., and Robert W. Fairlie. 2001. "Explaining Ethnic, Racial and Immigrant Differences in Private School Attendance." *Journal of Urban Economics* 50: 26–51.

Biddle, Bruce J., and David C. Berliner. 2002. "What Research Says about Small Class Sizes and Their Effects." Education Policy Studies Laboratory, College of Education, Arizona State University, EPSL-0202-101-EPRP.

Bils, Mark, and Peter J. Klenow. 2000. "Does Schooling Cause Growth?" *American Economic Review* 90 (December): 1160–83.

Bishop, John H. 1989. "Is The Test Score Decline Responsible for the Productivity Growth Decline?" *American Economic Review* 79 (March): 178–97.

————. 1990. "Incentives for Learning: Why American High School Students Compare So Poorly to Their Counterparts Overseas." *Research in Labor Economics* 11: 17–51.

————. 1997. "The Effect of National Standards and Curriculum-based Exams on Achievement." *American Economic Review* 87 (May): 260–64.

Bishop, John H., and Ferran Mane. 2001. "The Impacts of Minimum Competency Exam Graduation Requirements on High School Graduation, College Attendance and Early Labor Market Success." *Labour Economics* 8: 203–22.

Bishop, John H., et al. 2001. "The Role of End-of-Course Exams and Minimal Competency Exams in Standards Based Reforms." Pp. 267–345 in *Brookings Papers in Educational Policy 2001*, ed. Diane Ravitch. Washington, D.C.: Brookings Institution Press.

Black, Sandra E. 1999. "Do Better Schools Matter? Parental Valuation of Elementary Education." *Quarterly Journal of Economics* May: 577–99.

Blair, John P., and Sam Staley. 1995. "Quality Competition and Public Schools: Further Evidence." *Economics of Education Review* 14: 193–98.

Blair, Julie. 2002. "Teachers Take Bids for Power to Legislatures." *Education Week.* (June 12).

Blau, Francine D., and Lawrence M. Kahn. 2001. "Do Cognitive Test Scores Explain Higher U.S. Wage Inequality?" National Bureau of Economic Research, Working Paper 8210.

Bogart, William T., and Brian A. Cromwell. 1997. "How Much More Is a Good School District Worth?" *National Tax Journal* 50: 215–32.

Bolick, Clint. 1993. *Grassroots Tyranny: The Limits of Federalism.* Washington, D.C.: Cato Institute.

Borland, Melvin V., and Roy M. Howsen. 1992. "Student Academic Achievement and the Degree of Market Concentration in Education." *Economics of Education Review* 11: 31–39.

Botstein, Leon. 1999. "It Is Time to Abolish Our High Schools." *Arizona Daily Star* (May 20).

Bowles, Samuel, Herbert Gintis, and Melissa Osborne. 2001. "The Determinants of Earnings: A Behavioral Approach." *Journal of Economic Literature* 39 (December): 1137–76.

Brasington, David M. 1998. "School District Consolidation, Student Performance, and Housing Values." Unpublished.

————. 1999. "Which Measures of School Quality Does the Housing Market Value?" *Journal of Real Estate Research* 18 (November-December): 395–413.

Breneman, David W. 1998. "Remediation in Higher Education: Its Extent and Cost." Pp. 359–83 in *Brookings Papers on Education Policy.* Washington, D.C.: Brookings Institution.

Brice, Jessica. 2002. "High-Poverty Schools That Succeed Share Common Teaching Programs." Associated Press (September 25).

Brinig, Margaret F., and F. H. Buckley. 1996. "The Market for Deadbeats." *Journal of Legal Studies* 25 (January): 201–32.

Brouillette, Matthew J. 1999. "Unused Capacity in Privately Funded Michigan Schools." Mackinac Center for Public Policy, S99-02.

Brown University. 2002. "Horace Mann, Class of 1819." www.brown.edu/web master/about/history/mann.shtml.

Brunner, Eric, Jon Sonstelie, and Mark Thayer. 2001. "Capitalization and the Voucher: An Analysis of Precinct Returns from California's Proposition 174." *Journal of Urban Economics* 50: 517–36.

Buchanan, Nina K., and Robert A. Fox. 2003. "To Learn and to Belong: Case Studies of Emerging Ethnocentric Charter Schools in Hawai'i." *Education Policy Analysis Archives* 11 (8). (Retrieved February 24, 2003, from http://epaa.asu.edu/epaa/v11n8/.)

Buddin, Richard J., Joseph J. Cordes, and Sheila Nataraj Kirby. 1998. "School Choice in California: Who Chooses Private Schools?" *Journal of Urban Economics* 44: 110–34.

Business Wire Inc. 2000. "*Training* Magazine Releases Annual Industry Report Findings." (November 17).

Campbell, Colin D., and William A. Fischel. 1996. "Preferences for School Systems: Voters Versus Judges." *National Tax Journal* 49 (March): 1–15.

Campbell, David E. 2001. "Making Democratic Education Work." Pp. 241–67 in *Charters, Vouchers, and Public Education*, ed Paul E. Peterson and David E. Campbell. Washington, D.C.: Brookings Institution Press.

Campbell, Jay R., Catherine M. Hombo, and John Mazzeo. 2000. *NAEP 1999, Trends in Academic Progress*. Washington, D.C.: U.S. Department of Education, National Center for Education Statistics, NCES 2000-469.

Cannell, J. J. 1987. *Naturally Normed Elementary Achievement Testing in America's Public Schools: How All 50 States Are Above the National Average*. 2nd ed. Daniels, W. Va.: Friends for Education.

Card, David, and Alan B. Krueger. 1992. "Does School Quality Matter? Returns to Education and the Characteristics of Public Schools in the United States." *Journal of Political Economy* 100 (February): 1–40.

———. 1996. "School Resources and Student Outcomes: An Overview of the Literature and New Evidence from North and South Carolina." *Journal of Economic Perspectives* 10 (autumn): 31–50.

Card, David, and A. Abigail Payne. 1998. "School Finance Reform, the Distribution of School Spending, and the Distribution of SAT Scores." National Bureau of Economic Research, Working Paper 6766.

Catterall, James S. 1989. "Standards and School Dropouts: A National Study of Tests Required for High School Graduation." *American Journal of Education* (November): 1–34.

Chall, Jeanne S. 1996. "American Reading Achievement: Should We Worry?" *Research in the Teaching of Reading* 30 (October): 303–10.

Chall, Jeanne S., and Sue S. Conard, with Susan Harris Sharples. 1991. *Should Textbooks Challenge Students?* New York: Teachers College Press.

Chambers, Jay G. 1977. "The Impact of Collective Bargaining for Teachers on Resource Allocation in Public School Districts." *Journal of Urban Economics* 4: 324–39.

———. 1995. *Public School Teacher Cost Differences Across the United States*. Washington, D.C.: U.S. Department of Education, National Center for Education Statistics, NCES 95-758.

Chubb, John E., and Terry M. Moe. 1990. *Politics, Markets, and America's Schools*. Washington, D.C.: Brookings Institution Press.

Ciotti, Paul. 1998. *Money and School Performance: Lessons from the Kansas City De-*

segregation Experiment. Washington, D.C.: Cato Institute, Policy Analysis 298.

Cizek, Gregory J. 1999. "Give Us This Day Our Daily Dread: Manufacturing Crises in Education." www.pdkintl.org/kappan/kciz9906.htm (visited September 9, 1999).

Clotfelter, Charles T. 2001. "Interracial Contact in High School Extracurricular Activities." Terry Sanford Institute of Public Policy, Duke University, Working Paper SAN01-09.

Clotfelter, Charles T., and Helen F. Ladd. 1996. "Recognizing and Rewarding Success in Public Schools." Pp. 23–63 in *Holding Schools Accountable*, ed. Helen F. Ladd. Washington, D.C.: Brookings Institution Press.

Cohen, David K., 1996. "Standards-Based School Reform: Policy, Practice, and Performance." Pp. 99–127 in *Holding Schools Accountable*, ed. Helen F. Ladd. Washington, D.C.: Brookings Institution Press.

Cohen-Zada, Danny, and Moshe Justman. n.d. "The Political Economy of School Choice: Linking Theory and Evidence." National Center for the Study of Privatization in Education, Teachers College, Columbia University. Occasional Paper 57.

Coleman, James S., et al. 1966. *Equality of Educational Opportunity*. Washington, D.C.: U.S. Government Printing Office.

Coleman, James S., Sally Kilgore, and Thomas Hoffer. 1981. *Public and Private High Schools*. Washington, D.C.: National Center for Education Statistics.

Congressional Budget Office. 1986. *Trends in Educational Achievement*. Washington, D.C.: Congress of the United States.

Coons, John E., and Stephen D. Sugarman. 1978. *Education by Choice*. Berkeley: University of California Press.

Coons, Martha, John W. Jenkins, and Carl Kaestle. 1980. "Education and Social Change in Two Nineteenth-Century Massachusetts Communities." Pp. 139–85 in *Education and Social Change in Nineteenth-Century Massachusetts*, ed. Carl F. Kaestle and Maris A. Vinovskis. Cambridge, UK: Cambridge University Press.

Coulson, Andrew J. 1996. "Schooling and Literacy over Time: The Rising Cost of Stagnation and Decline." *Research in the Teaching of English* 30 (October): 311–27.

———. 1999. *Market Education, The Unknown History*. New Brunswick, N.J.: Transaction Publishers.

Courty, Pascal, and Gerald R. Marschke. 1996. "Moral Hazard under Incentive Systems: The Case of a Federal Bureaucracy." Pp. 157–90 in *Advances in the Study of Entrepreneurship, Innovation, and Growth*, ed. G. Libecap. Greenwich, Conn.: JAI Press.

Cousin, Victor. 1930 [1836]. "Report on the State of Public Instruction in Prussia." Pp. 115–240 in *Reports on European Education*, ed. Edgar W. Knight. New York: McGraw-Hill.

Crawford, John, and Sharon Freeman. 1996. "Why Parents Choose Private Schooling: Implications for Public School Programs and Information Campaigns." *ERS Spectrum* (summer): 9–16.

Cubberly, Ellwood P. 1919. *Public Education in the United States: A Study and Interpretation of American Educational History*. Boston: Houghton Mifflin.

Darling-Hammond, Linda, and Arthur E. Wise. 1985. "Beyond Standardization: State Standards and School Improvement." *Elementary School Journal* 85 (January): 315–36.

Dembner, Alice. 1996. "Colleges Consider Intensive Training: 'Boot Camp' Eyed for Remedial Aid." *The Boston Globe* (December 23).

Downes, Thomas A. 1992. "Evaluating the Impact of School Finance Reform on the Provision of Public Education: The California Case." *National Tax Journal* 45 (December): 405–20.

Downes, Thomas A., and David N. Figlio. 1998. "School Finance Reforms, Tax Limits, and Student Performance: Do Reforms Level-Up or Dumb Down?" Department of Economics, Tufts University, Discussion Paper 98-5.

———. 1999. "Economic Inequality and the Provision of Schooling." *FRBNY Economic Policy Review* (September): 99–110.

Downes, Thomas A., and Shane M. Greenstein. 1996. "Understanding the Supply Decisions of Nonprofits: Modelling the Location of Private Schools." *RAND Journal of Economics* 27 (summer): 365–90.

Downes, Thomas A., and David Schoeman. 1998. "School Finance Reform and Private School Enrollment: Evidence from California." *Journal of Urban Economics* 43: 418–43.

Downes, Thomas A., and Jeffrey E. Zabel. 1997. "The Impact of School Characteristics on House Prices: Chicago 1987–1991." Unpublished.

Dunifon, Rachel, Greg J. Duncan, and Jeanne Brooks Gunn. 2001. "As Ye Sweep, So Shall Ye Reap." *American Economic Review* 91 (May): 150–54.

Duplantis, Malcolm M., Timothy D. Chandler, and Terry G. Geske. 1995. "The Growth and Impact of Teachers' Unions in States without Collective Bargaining Legislation." *Economics of Education Review* 14: 167–78.

Eberts, Randall W. 1984. "Union Effects on Teacher Productivity." *Industrial and Labor Relations Review* 37 (April): 346–58.

Eberts, Randall W., and Timothy J. Gronberg. 1990. "Structure, Conduct, and Performance in the Local Public Sector." *National Tax Journal* 43 (2): 165–73.

Eberts, Randall W., and Joe A. Stone. 1986. "Teacher Unions and the Cost of Public Education." *Economic Inquiry* 24 (October): 631–43.

———. 1987. "Teacher Unions and the Productivity of Public Schools." *Industrial Labor Relations Review* 40 (April): 354–63.

Edson, C. H. 1982. "Schooling for Work and Working at School: Perspectives on Immigrant and Working-Class Education in Urban America, 1880–1920." Pp. 145–87 in *The Public School Monopoly*, ed. Robert B. Everhart. San Francisco: Pacific Institute for Public Policy Research.

Education Law Center. 2002. www.edlawcenter.org.

Elson, W. H., and C. Keck. 1910. *Grammar School Reader, Book Three.* Chicago: Scott, Foresman. Quoted in Andrew J. Coulson. 1996. "Schooling and Literacy over Time: The Rising Cost of Stagnation and Decline." *Research in the Teaching of English* 30 (October): 311–27.

Emerson, Adam. 2002. "Schools May Lower Standards to Stay off Federal Watch List." *Lansing State Journal.* October 24.

Epple, Dennis, and Richard E. Romano. 1998. "Competition between Private and Public Schools, Vouchers, and Peer-Group Effects." *American Economic Review* (March): 33–62.

Evans, William, and Robert Schwab. 1995. "Finishing High School and Starting College: Do Catholic Schools Make a Difference?" *Quarterly Journal of Economics* 110: 947–74.

Evers, Williamson M., and Herbert J. Walberg, eds. 2002. *School Accountability.* Stanford, Calif: Hoover Institution Press.

Fernandez, Raquel, and Richard Rogerson. 1997. "The Determinants of Public Education Expenditures: Evidence from the States, 1950–1990." National Bureau of Economic Research, Working Paper 5995.

Figlio, David N., and Maurice E. Lucas. 2002. "What's in a Grade? School Report Cards and House Prices." Unpublished.

Figlio, David, and Jens Ludwig. 2000. "Sex, Drugs and Catholic Schools: Private Schooling and Non-Market Adolescent Behaviors." National Bureau of Economic Research, Working Paper 7990.

Figlio, David N., and Joe A. Stone. 1999. "Are Private Schools Really Better?" *Research in Labor Economics* 18: 115–40.

Figlio, David N., and Joshua Winicki. 2002. "Food for Thought: The Effects of School Accountability Plans on School Nutrition." National Bureau of Economic Research, Working Paper 9319.

Finn, Chester E., Jr. 2002. "Real Accountability in K–12 Education: The Marriage of Ted and Alice." Pp. 23–46 in *School Accountability,* ed. Williamson M. Evers and Herbert J. Walberg. Stanford, Calif.: Hoover Institution Press.

Fischel, William A., 1989. "Did Serrano Cause Proposition 13?" *National Tax Journal* 42 (December): 465–73.

———. 1998. "School Finance Litigation and Property Tax Revolts: How Undermining Local Control Turns Voters away from Public Education." Lincoln Land Institute, Working Paper.

———. 2002. "An Economic Case against Vouchers: Why Local Public Schools Are a Local Public Good." Department of Economics, Dartmouth University Working Paper 02-01.

Fiske, Edward B., and Helen F. Ladd. 2001. "Lessons from New Zealand." Pp. 59–79 in *Charters, Vouchers, and Public Education,* ed. Paul E. Peterson and David E. Campbell. Washington, D.C.: Brookings Institution Press.

Flores v. Arizona. 2000. United States District Court, District of Arizona, CIV 92-596 TUC ACM.

Flyer, Fredrick, and Sherwin Rosen. 1997. "The New Economics of Teachers and Education." *Journal of Labor Economics* 15 (January, part 2): S104-S139.

Fowler, William J., Jr., and Herbert J. Walberg. 1991. "School Size, Characteristics, and Outcomes." *Educational Evaluation and Policy Analysis* 13 (summer): 189–202.

Fraser, James W. 1999. *Between Church and State.* New York: St. Martin's Press.

Friedkin, Noah E., and Juan Necohea. 1988. "School System Size and Performance: A Contingency Perspective." *Educational Evaluation and Policy Analysis* 10 (fall): 237–49.

Friedman, Milton. 1955. "The Role of Government in Education." In *Economics and the Public Interest,* ed. Robert A. Solo. New Brunswick, N.J.: Rutgers University Press.

Fun with Dick and Jane: A Commemorative Collection of Stories. 1996. San Francisco:

CollinsPublishers. Quoted in Diane Ravitch. 2000. *Left Back*. New York: Simon and Schuster, 253.

Galbincea, Barb. 2001. "Many College Freshmen Not Ready, Report Finds." *Cleveland Plain Dealer,* December 12.

Galley, Michelle. 2002. "Research: Boys to Men." *Education Week,* January 23.

Gallup International. 2000. *The Gallup Poll Monthly* 418 (July): 44–45.

Gamoran, Adam. 1987. "The Stratification of High School Learning Opportunities." *Sociology of Education* 60 (July): 78–94.

———. 1992. "The Variable Effects of High School Tracking." *American Sociological Review* 57 (December): 812–28.

Gehring, John. 2002. "N.Y. Appeals Court Rebuffs Lower Court's School Aid Ruling." *Education Week,* July 10.

Gemello, John M., and Jack W. Osman. 1984. "Estimating the Demand for Private School Enrollment." *American Journal of Education* 92 (May): 262–79.

Gewertz, Catherine. 2003. "Bathroom Blues." *Education Week.* February 12.

Gifford, Mary, and Melinda L. Ogle. 1998. *Focus on the Parents: Parents Talk about Charter Schools*. Phoenix, Ariz.: Center for Market Based Education.

Gifford, Mary, Melinda Ogle, and Lewis Solmon. n.d.. *Who Is Choosing Charter Schools?* Phoenix, Ariz.: Center for Market Based Education.

Gill, Brian P., et al. 2001. *Rhetoric versus Reality*. Santa Monica, Calif: RAND.

Glaeser, Edward L. 1995. "The Incentive Effects of Property Taxes on Local Governments." National Bureau of Economic Research, Working Paper 4987.

———. 2001. "Public Ownership in the American City." Harvard Institute of Economic Research, Harvard University, Discussion Paper 1930.

Glaeser, Edward L., Jed Kolko, and Albert Saiz. 2000. "Consumer City." Harvard Institute of Economic Research, Discussion Paper 190.

Goldhaber, Dan D. 1996. "Public and Private High Schools: Is School Choice an Answer to the Productivity Problem?" *Economics of Education Review* 15: 93–109.

———. 1999. "School Choice: An Examination of the Empirical Evidence on Achievement, Parental Decision Making, and Equity." *Educational Researcher* December: 16–25.

Goldhaber, Dan D., and Dominic J. Brewer. 1997. "Why Don't Schools and Teachers Seem to Matter?" *Journal of Human Resources* 32: 505–23.

Goldin, Claudia. 1998. "America's Graduation from High School: The Evolution and Spread of Secondary Schooling in the Twentieth Century." *Journal of Economic History* 58 (June): 345–74.

———. 1999. "A Brief History of Education in the United States." National Bureau of Economic Research, Historical Paper 119.

———. 2001. "The Human Capital Century and American Leadership: Virtues of the Past." National Bureau of Economic Research, Working Paper 8239.

Goldin, Claudia, and Lawrence F. Katz. 1995. "The Decline of Non-Competing Groups: Changes in the Premium to Education, 1890 to 1940." National Bureau of Economic Research, Working Paper 5202.

———. 1997. "Why the United States Led in Education: Lessons from Secondary School Expansion, 1910 to 1940." National Bureau of Economic Research, Working Paper 6144.

———. 1998. "Human Capital and Social Capital: The Rise of Secondary Schooling in America, 1910 to 1940." National Bureau of Economic Research, Working Paper 6439.

———. 2001. "The Legacy of U.S. Educational Leadership: Notes on Distribution and Economic Growth in the 20th Century." *American Economic Review* 91 (May): 18–23.

Gottlieb, Rachel. 2002. "'A' Is for Anxiety." *Hartford Courant.* September 30.

Greene, Jay P. 2000a. "Choosing Integration." *Issues in School Choice* 4 (September).

———. 2000b. *The Cost of Remedial Education: How Much Michigan Pays When Students Fail to Learn Basic Skills.* Midland, Mich: The Mackinac Center for Public Policy.

Grimes, Paul W., and Charles A. Register. 1990. "Teachers' Unions and Student Achievement in High School Economics." *Journal of Economic Education* (summer): 297–306.

Grissmer, David W., et al. 1994. *Student Achievement and the Changing American Family.* Santa Monica, Calif.: RAND.

Grissmer, David W., et al. 2000. *Improving Student Achievement.* Santa Monica, Calif.: RAND.

Grogger, Jeff, and Eric Eide. 1995. "Changes in College Skills and the Rise in the College Wage Premium." *Journal of Human Resources* 30 (spring): 280–310.

Grubb, W. Norton. 1971. "The Distribution of Costs and Benefits in an Urban Public School System." *National Tax Journal,* 24 (March): 1–12.

Grundlach, Erich, Ludger Wossmann, and Jen Gmelin. 2001. "The Decline of Schooling Productivity in OECD Countries." *Economic Journal* 111 (May): C135–C147.

Guryan, Jonathan. 2001. "Does Money Matter? Regression-Discontinuity Estimates from Education Finance Reform in Massachusetts." National Bureau of Economic Research, Working Paper 8269.

Hall, W. Clayton, and Norman E. Carroll. 1973. "The Effect of Teachers' Organizations on Salaries and Class Size." *Industrial and Labor Relations Review* 26: 834–41.

Hamby, Alonzo L. 1992. *Liberalism and Its Challengers.* New York: Oxford University Press.

Hamilton, Bruce W., and Molly K. MacCauley. 1991. "Determinants and Consequences of the Private-Public School Choice." *Journal of Urban Economics* 29: 282–94.

Hanushek, Eric A. 1986. "The Economics of Schooling: Production and Efficiency in Public Schools." *Journal of Economic Literature* 24 (September): 1141–77.

———. 1997. "Assessing the Effects of School Resources on Student Performance: An Update." *Educational Evaluation and Policy Analysis* 19 (2): 141–64.

———. 2001. "Black-White Achievement Differences and Governmental Intervention." *American Economic Review* 91 (May): 24–28.

———. 2002. "The Failure of Input-Based School Policies." National Bureau of Economic Research, Working Paper 9040.

Hanushek, Eric A., John F. Kain, and Steven G. Rivkin. 1998. "Teachers, Schools, and Academic Achievement." National Bureau of Economic Research, Working Paper 6691.

Hanushek, Eric A., and Dennis D. Kimko. 2000. "Schooling, Labor-Force Quality, and the Growth of Nations." *American Economic Review* 90 (December): 1184–1208.

Hanushek, Eric A., and Javier A. Luque. 2002. "Efficiency and Equity in Schools around the World." National Bureau of Economic Research, Working Paper 8949.

Hanushek, Eric A., and Richard R. Pace. 1995. "Who Chooses to Teach and Why?" *Economics of Education Review* 14: 101–17.

Hanushek, Eric A., and Margaret E. Raymond. 2001. "The Confusing World of Educational Accountability." *National Tax Journal* 54 (June): 365–84.

Hanushek, Eric A., and Steven G. Rivkin. 1997. "Understanding the Twentieth-Century Growth in U.S. School Spending." *Journal of Human Resources* 32 (1): 35–68.

Harbaugh, Rick. 2002. "Achievement vs. Aptitude: The Incentive-Screening Trade-off in College Admissions.' Preliminary draft presented at the Public Choice Society Meeting, San Diego, Calif.

Haurin, Donald R., and David Brasington. 1996. "School Quality and Real House Prices: Inter- and Intrametropolitan Effects." *Journal of Housing Economics* 5: 351–68.

Hayes, Donald P., Loreen T. Wolfer, and Michael F. Wolfe. 1996. "Schoolbook Simplification and Its Relation to the Decline in SAT-Verbal Scores." *American Educational Research Journal*, 33 (summer): 489–508.

Heckman, James J., Carolyn Heinrich, and Jeffrey Smith. 1997. "Assessing the Performance of Performance Standards in Public Bureaucracies." *American Economic Review* 87 (May): 389–95.

Heckman, James J., Jeffrey A. Smith, and Christopher Taber. 1996. "What Do Bureaucrats Do? The Effects of Performance Standards and Bureaucratic Preferences on Acceptance into the JTPA Program." Pp. 157–90 in *Advances in the Study of Entrepreneurship, Innovation, and Growth*, ed. G. Libecap. Greenwich, Conn.: JAI Press.

Hedges, Larry V., Richard D. Laine, and Rob Greenwald. 1994. "Does Money Matter? A Meta-Analysis of Studies of the Effects of Differential School Inputs on Student Outcomes." *Educational Researcher* 23 (April): 5–14.

Hendricks, Lutz. 2002. "How Important Is Human Capital for Development? Evidence from Immigrant Earnings." *American Economic Review* 92 (March): 198–219.

Henry, William A., III. 1994. *In Defense of Elitism*. New York: Doubleday.

Herrnstein, Richard J., and Charles Murray. 1996. *The Bell Curve*. New York: Free Press.

Hess, Frederick M., Robert Maranto, and Scott Milliman. 2001. "Responding to Competition: School Leaders and School Culture." Pp. 215–38 in *Charters, Vouchers, and Public Education*, ed. Paul E. Peterson and David E. Campbell. Washington, D.C.: Brookings Institution Press.

Hill, Paul T. 2003. "School Boards: Focus on School Performance, Not Money and Patronage." Progressive Policy Institute.

Hill, Paul T., and Kacey Guin. 2002. "Baselines for Assessment of Choice Programs." Pp. 15–49 in *Choice with Equity*, ed. Paul T. Hill. Stanford, Calif.: Hoover Institution Press.

Hirsch, E. D., Jr. 1987. *Cultural Literacy: What Every American Needs to Know*. Boston: Houghton Mifflin Company.

Hirschman, Albert O. 1970. *Exit, Voice and Loyalty*. Cambridge, Mass.: Harvard University Press.

Hoff, David J. 2002. "Bush to Push for Math and Science Upgrade." *Education Week*, November 20.

Hofstadter, Richard. 1962. *Anti-intellectualism in American Life*. New York: Random House. Quoted in Diane Ravitch. 1978. *The Revisionists Revised: A Critique of the Radical Attack on the Schools*. New York: Basic Books, 4.

Howell, William G., et al. 2001. "The Effects of School Vouchers on Student Test Scores." Pp. 136–59 in *Charters, Vouchers, and Public Education*, ed. Paul E. Peterson and David E. Campbell. Washington, D.C.: Brookings Institution Press.

Hoxby, Caroline M. 1996a. "The Effects of Private School Vouchers on Schools and Students." Pp. 177–208 in *Holding Schools Accountable*, ed. Helen F. Ladd. Washington, D.C.: Brookings Institution Press.

———. 1996b. "How Teachers' Unions Affect Education Production." *Quarterly Journal of Economics* 111 (August): 671–718.

———. 1998a. "All School Finance Equalizations Are Not Created Equal." Unpublished.

———. 1998b. "How Much Does School Spending Depend on Family Income? The Historical Origins of the Current School Finance Dilemma." *American Economic Review* 88: 309–14.

———. 2000a. "Does Competition among Public Schools Benefit Students and Taxpayers?" *American Economic Review* 90 (December): 1209–38.

———. 2000b. "Would School Choice Change the Teaching Profession?" National Bureau of Economic Research, Working Paper 7866.

———. 2002a. "The Cost of Accountability." National Bureau of Economic Research, Working Paper 8855.

———. 2002b. "How School Choice Affects the Achievement of Public School Students." Pp. 141–77 in *Choice with Equity*, ed. Paul T. Hill. Stanford, Calif: Hoover Institution Press.

———. 2002c. "School Choice and School Productivity (or Could School Choice Be a Tide That Lifts All Boats?)." National Bureau of Economic Research, Working Paper 8873.

Hubisz, John L. n.d. "Review of Middle School Physical Science Texts." David and Lucile Packard Foundation.

Jacob, Brian A. 2002. "Accountability, Incentives and Behavior: The Impact of High-Stakes Testing in the Chicago Public Schools." National Bureau of Economic Research, Working Paper 8968.

James, Estelle. 1993. "Why Do Different Countries Choose a Different Public-Private Mix of Educational Services?" *Journal of Human Resources* 28 (summer): 571–92.

Jefferson, Thomas. 1786. "Letter to George Wythe." *The Writings of Thomas Jefferson: Memorial Edition* 5: 396.

———. 1814. "Letter to Joseph C. Cabell." *The Writings of Thomas Jefferson: Memorial Edition* 14: 84.

———. "Note to Elementary School Act." *The Writings of Thomas Jefferson: Memorial Edition* 17: 243.

Jepsen, Christopher, and Steven Rivkin. 2002. "Class Size Reduction, Teacher Quality, and Academic Achievement in California Public Elementary Schools." Public Policy Institute of California.

Kaestle, Carl F. 1976. "'Between the Scylla of Brutal Ignorance and the Charybdis of a Literary Education': Elite Attitudes toward Mass Schooling in Early Industrial England and America." Pp. 177–91 in *Schooling and Society,* ed. Lawrence Stone. Baltimore: Johns Hopkins University Press.

———. 1983. *Pillars of the Republic, Common Schools and American Society 1780–1860.* New York: Hill and Wang.

———. 1991a. "Studying the History of Literacy." Pp. 24–25 in *Literacy in the United States,* ed. Carl F. Kaestle. New Haven, Conn.: Yale University Press.

———. 1991b. *Literacy in the United States.* New Haven, Conn.: Yale University Press.

Kaestle, Carl F., and Maris A. Vinovskis. 1980. *Education and Social Change in Nineteenth-Century Massachusetts.* Cambridge, UK: Cambridge University Press.

Kafer, Krista. 2002. "A Small but Costly Step toward Reform: The Conference Education Bill." Heritage Foundation, WebMemo 66.

Kasper, Herschel. 1970. "The Effects of Collective Bargaining on Public School Teachers' Salaries." *Industrial and Labor Relations Review* 24: 57–72.

Keeves, J. P., and P. Soydhurum. 1991. *The IEA Study of Science III, Changes in Science Education and Achievement: 1970 to 1984.* Oxford: Pergamon Press.

Kirby, Sheila Nataraj, and Linda Darling-Hammond. 1988. "Parental Schooling Choice: A Case Study of Minnesota." *Journal of Policy Analysis and Management* 7 (3): 506–17.

Kleiner, Morris M., and Daniel L. Petree. 1988. "Unionism and Licensing of Public School Teachers: Impact on Wages and Educational Output." Pp. 305–19 in *When Public Sector Workers Unionize,* ed. Richard B. Freeman and Casey Ichniowski. Chicago: University of Chicago Press.

Koretz, Daniel. 1992. "What Happened to Test Scores and Why?" *Educational Measurement: Issues and Practice* Winter: 7–11.

Kozol, Jonathan. 1992. *Savage Inequalities.* New York: HarperPerennial.

Krueger, Alan B. 1998. "Experimental Estimates of Education Production Functions." Princeton University Industrial Relations Section, Working Paper 379.

———. 2002. "Economic Considerations and Class Size." National Bureau of Economic Research, Working Paper 8875.

Kurth, Michael M. 1987. "Teachers' Unions and Excellence in Education: An Analysis of the Decline in SAT Scores." *Journal of Labor Research* 8 (fall): 351–67.

Ladd, Helen F., ed. 1996. *Holding Schools Accountable.* Washington, D.C.: Brookings Institution Press.

———. 2001. "School-Based Educational Accountability Systems: The Promise and the Pitfalls." *National Tax Journal* 54 (June): 385–99.

Ladner, Matthew, and Christopher Hammons. 2001. "Special but Unequal: Race and Special Education." In *Rethinking Special Education for a New Century,* ed. Chester E. Finn, Jr., Andrew J. Rotherham, and Charles R. Hokanson,

Jr. Washington, D.C.: Progressive Policy Institute and The Thomas B. Fordham Foundation.

Lakdawalla, Darius. 2001. "The Declining Quality of Teachers." National Bureau of Economic Research, Working Paper 8263.

Landes, William M., and Lewis C. Solmon. 1972. "Compulsory Schooling Legislation: An Economic Analysis of Law and Social Change in the Nineteenth Century." *Journal of Economic History* 23 (March): 54–91.

Lankford, Hamilton, and James Wyckoff. 1992. "Primary and Secondary School Choice among Public and Religious Alternatives." *Economics of Education Review* 11 (4): 317–37.

———. 1995. "Where Has the Money Gone? An Analysis of School District Spending in New York." *Educational Evaluation and Policy Analysis* 17 (summer): 195–218.

———. 1996. "The Allocation of Resources to Special Education and Regular Instruction." Pp. 221–57 in *Holding Schools Accountable*, ed. Helen F. Ladd. Washington, D.C.: Brookings Institution.

———. 1997. "The Changing Structure of Teacher Compensation." *Economics of Education Review* 16: 371–84.

Laqueur, Thomas W. 1976. "Working-Class Demand and the Growth of English Elementary Education." Pp. 192–205 in *Schooling and Society*, ed. Lawrence Stone. Baltimore: Johns Hopkins University Press.

Lazear, Edward P. 1999. "Culture and Language." *Journal of Political Economy* 107 (6, part 2): S95–S126.

———. 2001. "Educational Production." *Quarterly Journal of Economics*, 116 (August): 777–803.

Lee, Valerie E., and Anthony S. Bryk. 1988. "Curriculum Tracking as Mediating the Social Distribution of High School Achievement." *Sociology of Education* 61 (April): 78–94.

———. 1989. "A Multilevel Model of the Social Distribution of High School Achievement." *Sociology of Education* 62 (July): 172–92.

Lehmann, Nicholas. 1999. *The Big Test*. New York: Farrar, Strauss, and Groux.

Levy, Frank, and Richard J. Murnane. 1992. "U.S. Earnings Levels and Earnings Inequality: A Review of Recent Trends and Proposed Explanations." *Journal of Economic Literature* 30 (September): 1333–81.

Lietz, Petra. 1996. *Changes in Reading Comprehension across Cultures and over Time*. Munster/New York: Waxmann.

Lillard, Dean R., and Phillip P. DeCicca. 2001. "Higher Standards, More Dropouts? Evidence within and across Time." *Economics of Education Review* 20: 450–73.

Lindert, Peter H. 2001. "Democracy, Decentralization, and Mass Schooling before 1914." Agricultural History Center, University of California, Davis, Working Paper 104.

Linn, Robert L., M. Elizabeth Graue, and Nancy M. Sanders. 1990. "Comparing State and District Test Results to National Norms: The Validity of Claims That 'Everyone Is above Average.'" *Educational Measurement: Issues and Practice* 10 (fall): 5–14.

Lott, John R., Jr. 1997. "Does Political Reform Increase Wealth?: Or Why the Difference between the Chicago and Virginia Schools Is Really an Elasticity Question." *Public Choice* 91: 219–27.

———. n.d. "Public Schooling, Indoctrination, and Totalitarianism." John M. Olin Law and Economics, University of Chicago Law School, Working Paper 64 [2nd Series].

Loveless, Tom, and Paul Diperna. 2000. *How Well Are American Students Learning?* Washington, D.C.: Brookings Institution.

Lynd, Robert S., and Helen Merrell Lynd. 1956. *Middletown, A Study in American Culture*. New York: Harcourt, Brace and World.

MacDonald, Mary. 2002. "Parents Eager to Use School Transfer Law." *Atlanta Journal-Constitution*. May 6.

Maddison, Angus. 1987. "Growth and Slowdown in Advanced Capitalist Economies: Techniques and Quantitative Assessment." *Journal of Economic Literature* 25 (June): 649–98.

Mandeville, Bernard. 1989 [1723]. *The Fable of the Bees*. London: Penguin Books.

Manno, Bruno V. 1995. "Remedial Ed, Far Too Many Students Begin College Unprepared." *San Diego Union-Tribune*. July 15.

Manzo, Kathleen Kennedy. 2002. "Texas Board Adopts Scores of New Textbooks." *Education Week*. November 27.

Maranto, Robert. 2001. "The Death of the One Best Way: Charter Schools as Reinventing Government." Pp. 39–57 in *School Choice in the Real World*, ed. Robert Maranto et al. Boulder, Colo.: Westview Press.

Maranto, Robert, et al. 2001. "Do Charter Schools Improve District Schools?" Pp. 129–41 in *School Choice in the Real* World, ed. Robert Maranto et al. Boulder, Colo.: Westview Press.

Martinez-Vazquez, Jorge, Mark Rider, and Mary Beth Walker. 1997. "Race and the Structure of School Districts in the United States." *Journal of Urban Economics* 41: 281–300.

Martinez-Vazquez, Jorge, and Bruce A. Seaman. 1985. "Private Schooling and the Tiebout Hypothesis." *Public Finance Quarterly* 13 (July): 293–318.

McGuire, Martin C., and Mancur Olson, Jr. 1996. "The Economics of Autocracy and Majority Rule: The Invisible Hand and the Use of Force." *Journal of Economic Literature* 34 (March): 72–96.

Mendoza, Monica. 2002. "Residents Lose Fight over Adult Bookstore." *Arizona Republic*, December 11.

Milkman, Martin A. 1997. "Teachers' Unions, Productivity, and Minority Student Achievement." *Journal of Labor Research* 18 (winter): 137–50.

Miller, Charles G. 1940. "The Background of Calvin E. Stowe's 'Report on Elementary Instruction in Europe' (1837)." *Ohio History* 49 (April): 185–90.

Moe, Terry M. 2001. *Schools, Vouchers, and the American Public*. Washington, D.C.: Brookings Institution Press.

Monk, David H. 1992. "Education Productivity Research: An Update and Assessment of Its Role in Education Finance Reform." *Educational Evaluation and Policy Analysis* 14 (winter): 307–32.

Morgan,, William R. 1983. Learning and Student Life Quality of Public and Private School Youth. *Sociology of Education* 56 (October): 187–202.

Murnane, Richard J. 1984. "A Review Essay—Comparisons of Public and Private

Schools: Lessons from the Uproar." *Journal of Human Resources* 19 (2): 263–77.

Murnane, Richard J., and Frank Levy. 1996. *Teaching the New Basic Skills.* New York: The Free Press.

————. 2001. "Will Standards-Based Reforms Improve the Education of Students of Color?" *National Tax Journal* 54 (June): 401–15.

Murnane, Richard J., John B. Willett, and Frank Levy. 1995. "The Growing Importance of Cognitive Skills in Wage Determination." *The Review of Economics and Statistics* 77 (May): 251–66.

Murnane, Richard J., et al. 2000. "How Important Are the Cognitive Skills of Teenagers in Predicting Subsequent Earnings?" *Journal of Policy Analysis and Management* 19 (4): 547–68.

Murray, Sheila E., William N. Evans, and Robert M. Schwab. 1998. "Education-Finance Reform and the Distribution of Education Resources." *American Economic Review* 88 (September): 789–812.

Nasaw, David. 1979. *Schooled to Order: A Social History of Public Schooling in the United States.* New York: Oxford University Press.

National Commission on Excellence in Education. 1983. *A Nation at Risk: The Imperative for Educational Reform.* Washington D.C.: U.S. Government Printing Office.

National Commission on the High School Senior Year. 2001. *The Lost Opportunity of Senior Year: Finding a Better Way.* Princeton, N.J.: Woodrow Wilson National Fellowship Foundation.

National Research Council. 1999a. *Grading the Nation's Report Card: Evaluating the NAEP and Transforming the Assessment of Educational Progress.* Commission on the Behavioral and Social Sciences in Education, ed. James W. Pellegrino, Lee R. Jones, and Karen J. Mitchell. Washington, D.C.: National Academy Press.

————. 1999b. *Making Money Matter.* Committee on Education Finance, ed. Helen F. Ladd and Janet S. Hansen. Washington D.C.: National Academy Press.

Neal, Derek. 1998. "What Have We Learned about the Benefits of Private Schooling?" *FRBNY Economic Policy Review* (March): 79–86.

Neal, Derek A., and William R. Johnson. 1996. "The Role of Premarket Factors in Black-White Wage Differences." *Journal of Political Economy* 104 (October): 869–95.

Nechyba, Thomas J. 2000. "Mobility, Targeting, and Private-School Vouchers." *American Economic Review* 90 (March): 130–46.

Nellor, David C. L. 1984. "Public Bureau Budgets and Jurisdiction Size: An Empirical Note." *Public Choice* 42: 175–83.

New York Times. 1994. "Industry's New Schoolhouse. Education Life Supplement," January 9.

Nickell, Stephen, and Brian Bell. 1996. "Changes in the Distribution of Wages and Unemployment in OECD Countries." *American Economic Review* 86 (May): 302–8.

Oates, Wallace E. 1969. "The Effects of Property Taxes and Local Public Spending on Property Values: An Empirical Study of Tax Capitalization and the Tiebout Hypothesis." *Journal of Political Economy* 77: 957–71.

————. 1985. "Searching for Leviathan: An Empirical Study." *American Economic Review* 75 (September): 748–57.

OECD (Organization for Economic Co-Operation and Development). 2000. *Education at a Glance*. Paris: Center for Educational Research and Innovation.

O'Neill, June. 1990. "The Role of Human Capital in Earnings Differences between Black and White Men." *Journal of Economic Perspectives* 4 (autumn): 24–45.

Peltzman, Sam. 1976. "Toward a More General Theory of Regulation." *Journal of Law and Economics* 19 (August): 211–40.

————. 1993. "The Political Economy of the Decline of American Public Education." *Journal of Law and Economics* 36 (April): 331–70.

————. 1996. "Political Economy of Public Education: Non-College-Bound Students." *Journal of Law and Economics* 39 (April): 73–120.

Peterson, Paul E. 1985. *The Politics of School Reform, 1870–1940*. Chicago: University of Chicago Press.

Peterson, Paul E., and David E. Campbell, eds. 2001. *Charters, Vouchers, and Public Education*. Washington, D.C.: Brookings Institution Press.

Poterba, James M. 1996. "Demographic Structure and the Political Economy of Public Education." National Bureau of Economic Research, Working Paper 5677.

Powell, Arthur G., Eleanor Farrar, and David K. Cohen. 1985. *The Shopping Mall High School*. Boston: Houghton Mifflin.

Putnam, Robert D. 2000. *Bowling Alone: The Collapse and Revival of American Community*. New York: Simon and Schuster.

Quality Counts 2003. 2003. Special issue. *Education Week*. 22 (17): 80–109.

Randall, E. Vance. 1994. *Private Schools and Public Power*. New York: Teachers College Press.

Ravitch, Diane. 1974. *The Great School Wars*. New York: Basic Books.

————. 1978. *The Revisionists Revised: A Critique of the Radical Attack on the Schools*. New York: Basic Books.

————. 1983. *The Troubled Crusade: American Education, 1945–1980*. New York: Basic Books.

————. 2000. *Left Back*. New York: Simon and Schuster.

————. 2001. "Ex Uno Plures." *Education Next* Fall: 27–29.

————. 2002. "Testing and Accountability, Historically Considered." Pp. 9–21 in *School Accountability*, ed. Williamson M. Evers and Herbert J. Walberg. Stanford, Calif: Hoover Institution Press.

Reese, William J. 1995. *The Origins of the American High School*. New Haven, Conn.: Yale University Press.

Register, Charles A., and Paul W. Grimes. 1991. "Collective Bargaining, Teachers, and Student Achievement." *Journal of Labor Research* 12 (spring): 99–109.

Rivkin, Steven G. 1995. "Black/White Differences in Schooling and Employment." *Journal of Human Resources* 30 (fall): 826–52.

Robelen, Erik W. 2002. "States, Ed. Dept. Reach Accords on 1994 ESEA." *Education Week*, April 17.

Robinson v. Cahill. 1973. New Jersey State Supreme Court, 62 NJ 473, 303 A.2d.373.

Robitaille, David F. 1990. "Achievement Comparisons between the First and Second IEA Studies of Mathematics." *Educational Studies in Mathematics* 21: 395–414.

Rosenbaum, James E. 1978. "The Structure of Opportunity in School." *Social Forces* 57 (September): 236–56.

Rosenshine, Barak. 2002. "Converging Findings on Classroom Instruction." In *School Reform Proposals: The Research Evidence*, ed. Alex Molnar. Tempe: Arizona State University, Education Policy Research Unit, EPSL-0201-101-EPRU.

Rothbard, Murray. 1974. "Historical Origins." Pp. 7–27 in *The Twelve Year Sentence: Radical Views of Compulsory Education*, ed. William F. Rickenbacker. San Francisco: Fox and Wilkes.

Rothstein, Richard. 1998. *The Way We Were? The Myths and Realities of America's Student Achievement*. New York: Century Foundation Press.

Rothstein, Richard, and Karen Hawley Miles. 1995. *Where's the Money Gone?* Washington, D.C.: Economic Policy Institute.

Roza, Marguerite, and Karen Hawley Miles. 2002. *A New Look at Inequities in School Funding*. Seattle: Center on Reinventing Public Education, University of Washington.

Rush, Benjamin. 2002 [1786]. "Thoughts upon the Mode of Education Proper in a Republic." www.schoolchoices.org/roo/rush.htm.

Sack, Joetta L. 2002. "Smaller Classes under Scrutiny in Calif. Schools." *Education Week*. February 27.

Sandel, Michael J. 1996. *Democracy's Discontent: America in Search of a Public Philosophy*. Cambridge, Mass.: Harvard University Press.

Sander, William. 1997. "Catholic High Schools and Rural Academic Achievement." *American Journal of Agricultural Economics* 79:1–12.

Sax, Linda J., et al. 1999. *The American Freshman: National Norms for Fall 1999*. Los Angeles: Higher Education Research Institute, UCLA.

Schleunes, Karl A. 1989. *Schooling and Society: The Politics of Education in Prussia and Bavaria 1750–1900*. Providence, R.I.: Berg.

Schmidt, Amy B. 1992. "Private School Enrollment in Metropolitan Areas." *Public Finance Quarterly* 20 (July): 298–320.

Schneider, Mark, and Jack Buckley. 2002. "What Do Parents Want from Schools? Evidence from the Internet." National Center for the Study of Privatization in Education, Teachers College, Columbia University, Occasional Paper 21.

Schneider, Mark, et al. 1997. "Institutional Arrangements and the Creation of Social Capital: The Effects of Public School Choice." *American Political Science Review* 91 (March): 82–93.

Schneider, Mark, et al. 1998. "School Choice and Culture Wars in the Classroom: What Different Parents Seek from Education." *Social Science Quarterly* 79 (September): 489–501.

Shain, Barry Alan. 1994. *The Myth of American Individualism*. Princeton, N.J.: Princeton University Press.

Simon, Curtis J., and Cheonsik Woo. 1995. "Test Scores, School Career Length, and Human Capital Accumulation." *Research in Labor Economics* 14: 91–140.

Silva, Fabio, and Jon Sonstelie. 1995. "Did *Serrano* Cause a Decline in School Spending?" *National Tax Journal* 48: 199–215.

Sirotnik, Kenneth A. 1983. "What You See Is What You Get—Consistency, Persistency, and Mediocrity in the Classrooms." *Harvard Educational Review* 53 (February): 16–31.

Skocpol, Theda. 1992. *Protecting Soldiers and Mothers: The Political Origins of Social Policy in the United States.* Cambridge, Mass.: Belknap Press.

Smith, George H. 1982. "Nineteenth-Century Opponents of State Education: Prophets of Modern Revisionism." Pp. 109–55 in *The Public School Monopoly,* ed. Robert B. Everhart. San Francisco: Pacific Institute for Public Policy Research.

Sonstelie, Jon. 1982. "The Welfare Cost of Free Public Schools." *Journal of Political Economy* 90 (4): 794–808.

Sonstelie, Jon, Eric Brunner, and Kenneth Ardon. 2000. "For Better or For Worse? School Finance Reform in California." Public Policy Institute of California, Report 129.

Sorokin, Ellen. 2002. "No Founding Fathers? That's Our New History." *Washington Times,* January 28.

Southwick, Lawrence, Jr., and Indermit S. Gill. 1997. "Unified Salary Schedule and Student SAT Scores: Adverse Effects of Adverse Selection in the Market for Secondary School Teachers." *Economics of Education Review* 16: 143–53.

Stecher, Brian M., and George W. Borhnstedt. 2002. "Class Size Reduction in California: Findings from 1999–00 and 2000–01." CSR Research Consortium.

Stedman, Lawrence C. 1996. "An Assessment of Literacy Trends, Past and Present." *Research in the Teaching of English* 30 (October): 283–301.

Stedman, Lawrence C., and Carl F. Kaestle. 1991a. "Literacy and Reading Performance in the United States from 1880 to the Present." Pp. 75–128 in *Literacy in the United States,* ed. Carl F. Kaestle. New Haven, Conn.: Yale University Press.

———. 1991b. "The Great Test Score Decline: A Closer Look." Pp. 129–145 in *Literacy in the United States,* ed. Carl F. Kaestle. New Haven, Conn.: Yale University Press.

Steelman, Lala Carr, Brian Powell, and Robert M. Carini. 2000. "Do Teacher Unions Hinder Educational Performance? Lessons Learned from State SAT and ACT Scores." *Harvard Educational Review* 79 (winter): 437–66.

Stevenson, Harold W., et al. 1990. "Mathematics Achievement of Children in China and the United States." *Child Development* 60:1053–66.

Stevenson, Harold W., and Shinying Lee. 1998. "An Examination of American Student Achievement from an International Perspective." Pp. 7–52 in *Brookings Papers on Education Policy.* Washington, D.C.: Brookings Institution.

Stowe, Calvin E. 1930 [1837]. "Report on Elementary Public Instruction in Europe." Pp. 243–316 in *Reports on European Education,* ed. Edgar W. Knight. New York: McGraw-Hill.

Teske, Paul, et al. 2001. "Can Charter Schools Change Traditional Public Schools?" Pp. 188–214 in *Charters, Vouchers, and Public Education,* ed. Paul E. Peterson and David E. Campbell. Washington, D.C.: Brookings Institution Press.

Texas State Board of Education. 2002. *Texas Open-Enrollment Charter Schools Fifth-Year Evaluation.* Austin: Texas Education Agency.

Tiebout, Charles M. 1956. "A Pure Theory of Local Expenditures." *Journal of Political Economy* 64 (October): 416–24.

Toma, Eugenia Froedge. 1983. "Institutional Structures, Regulation, and Producer Gains in the Education Industry." *Journal of Law and Economics* 26 (April): 103–16.

Traub, James. 2002. "The Test Mess." *New York Times Magazine.* April 7.

Troen, Selwyn K. 1976. "The Discovery of the Adolescent by American Educational Reformers, 1900–1920: An Economic Perspective." Pp. 239–51 in *Schooling and Society,* ed. Lawrence Stone. Baltimore: Johns Hopkins University Press.

Trotter, Andrew. 2002. "Digital Dilemma: Can Computers Sub for Teachers?" *Education Week,* October 16.

Tyack, David B. 1974. *The One Best System, A History of American Urban Education.* Cambridge, Mass.: Harvard University Press.

Tyack, David B., and Larry Cuban. 1995. *Tinkering toward Utopia.* Cambridge, Mass.: Harvard University Press.

Tyack, David B., Thomas James, and Aaron Benavot. 1987. *Law and the Shaping of Public Education, 1785–1954.* Madison, Wis.: University of Wisconsin Press.

Urquiola, Miguel. 1999. "Demand Matters: School District Concentration, Composition, and Educational Expenditure." Unpublished.

U.S. Census Bureau. 2002. *Statistical Abstract of the United States 2001.* Washington, D.C.: U.S. Government Printing Office.

U.S. Department of Education. 1996a. *Pursuing Excellence.* Washington, D.C.: National Center for Education Statistics, NCES 97-198.

———. 1996b. *Remedial Education at Higher Education Institutions in Fall 1995.* Washington, D.C.: National Center for Education Statistics, NCES 97-584.

———. 1997. *Pursuing Excellence: A Study of U.S. Fourth-Grade Mathematics and Science Achievement in International Context.* Washington, D.C.: National Center for Education Statistics, NCES 97-225.

———. 1998a. *Digest of Education Statistics 2001.* Washington, D.C.: National Center for Education Statistics.

———. 1998b. *The 1994 High School Transcript Study Tabulations.* Washington, D.C.: National Center for Education Statistics, NCES 98-532.

———. 1998c. *Pursuing Excellence: A Study of U.S. Twelfth-Grade Mathematics and Science Achievement in International Context.* Washington, D.C.: National Center for Education Statistics, NCES 98-049.

———. 2002. *Digest of Education Statistics 2001.* Washington, D.C.: National Center for Education Statistics.

Van Geel, Tyll. 1976. *Authority to Control the School Program.* Lexington, Mass.: Lexington Books.

Verstegen, Deborah A., and Richard A. King. 1998. "The Relationship between School Spending and Student Achievement: A Review and Analysis of 35 Years of Production Function Research." *Journal of Education Finance* 24 (fall): 243–62.

Vinovskis, Maris A. 1985. *The Origins of Public High Schools.* Madison, Wis.: University of Wisconsin Press.

Viscusi, W. Kip, John M. Vernon, and Joseph E. Harrington. 1992. *Economics of Regulation and Antitrust.* Lexington, Mass.: D.C. Heath and Company.

Wall Street Journal. 1992. "Sharpen Your Pencil, and Begin Now," June 9. Quoted in Richard J. Herrnstein and Charles Murray. 1996. *The Bell Curve.* New York: Free Press, 419.

Weimer, David L., and Michael J. Wolkoff. 2001. "School Performance and Housing Values: Using Non-Contiguous District and Incorporation Boundaries to Identify School Effects." *National Tax Journal* 54 (June): 231–53.

Weiss, Kenneth R. 1999. "Cal State Cracks Down on Remedial Students." *Los Angeles Times*, November 18.

Wesley, Edgar B. 1944. *American History in Schools and Colleges*. New York: The Macmillan Company.

West, E. G. 1967. "The Political Economy of American Public School Legislation." *Journal of Law and Economics* 10 (October): 101–28.

West, Edwin G., and Halldor Palsson. 1988. "Parental Choice of School Characteristics: Estimation Using State-Wide Data." *Economic Inquiry* 26 (October): 725–40.

Westbury, Ian. 1992. "Comparing American and Japanese Achievement: Is the United States Really a Low Achiever?" *Educational Researcher* (June–July): 18–24.

Whittington, Dale. 1991. "What Have 17-Year-Olds Known in the Past?" *American Educational Research Journal*, 28 (winter): 759–80.

Winkler, Donald B., and Taryn Rounds. 1996. "Municipal and Private Sector Response to Decentralization and School Choice." *Economics of Education Review* 15 (4): 365–76.

Wise, Arthur E. 1979. *Legislated Learning*. Berkeley: University of California Press.

Wolf, Patrick J., et al. 2001. "Private Schooling and Political Tolerance." Pp. 268–90 in *Charters, Vouchers, and Public Education*, ed. Paul E. Peterson and David E. Campbell. Washington, D.C.: Brookings Institution Press.

Wong, Kenneth K., and Francis X. Shen. 2001. "Does School District Takeover Work?" Prepared for the annual meeting of the American Political Science Association.

Wossmann, Ludger. 2000. "Schooling Resources, Educational Institutions, and Student Performance: The International Evidence." Kiel Institute of World Economics, Working Paper 983.

Wrinkle, Robert D., Joseph Stewart, Jr., and J. L. Polinard. 1999. "Public School Quality, Private Schools, and Race." *American Journal of Political Science* 43 (October): 1248–53.

Wynne, Edward A., and Mary Hess. 1986. "Long-Term Trends in Youth Conduct and the Revival of Traditional Value Patterns." *Educational Evaluation and Policy Analysis* 8 (fall): 294–308.

Zanzig, Blair. 1997. "Measuring the Impact of Competition in Local Government Education Markets on the Cognitive Achievement of Students." *Economics of Education Review* 16: 431–41.

Zernike, Kate. 2002. "Lesson Plans for Sept. 11 Offer a Study in Discord." *New York Times*, August 31.

Zilversmit, Arthur. 1976. "The Failure of Progressive Education, 1920–1940." Pp. 252–63 in *Schooling and Society*, ed. Lawrence Stone. Baltimore: Johns Hopkins University Press.

Zwerling, Harris L., and Terry Thomason. 1995. "Collective Bargaining and the Determination of Teachers' Salaries." *Journal of Labor Research* 16 (fall): 467–84.

Index

Diminishing returns to school inputs, 77

Earnings, and education, 52, 56, 113, 126
Elementary and Secondary Education Act, 162
Employer desired qualities of workers, 112–13, 127
England, 109, 137–38
Enrollment, 9, 145, 152; high school, 99–100; international, 99–100, 135
Equality of Educational Opportunity (Coleman Report), 15, 69, 160
Equalization formulas, 170–72
Establishment reforms, 20, 183; barriers to implementation, 184–90
Exit, as form of control, 11, 139

Great high school boom: economic growth and, 130; geographic origins, 114; local control and, 114. *See also* High schools
Great School Legend, 101–2
Great Test Score Decline, 6, 38, 43, 45; significance of, 46–47; reasons for, 47–48, 75

Hall, G. Stanley, 107, 119
Hanushek, Eric, 69–70
Higher education: expansion of enrollment, 127–28; effect on high school performance, 128
High schools, 17, 35, 98; and decentralization, 114, 133; and expansion of curriculum, 17–18, 59, 100, 116, 121
Hirschman, Albert O., 11, 134
Housing values and school quality, 140
Hyperrationalization, 162

Immigrants, 5, 36, 117, 151, 216
Input reforms, 190–91
Interest groups, and growth of education, 102–5

Jefferson, Thomas, 143

Kansas City, MO, 78, 168–69
Krueger, Alan, 70–71

Labor unrest, 109
Literacy rates, 145
Local control, 10–12, 114, 133–34, 142; and expansion of public schools, 134–35, 139, 158

Mann, Horace, 2, 136, 145–46, 148, 150, 151, 154
Massachusetts Board of Education, 149
"Middletown," 122
Minorities: achievement trends, 51–52, 76; inequality of resources, 4, 77; private schools, 90–91, 191

A Nation at Risk, 6, 52, 65, 123, 128
National Assessment of Educational Progress (NAEP), 14, 47, 49, 54, 67; performance of minorities, 51–52, 76
No Child Left Behind Act, 205, 206
Non-teaching school staff: effect on achievement, 169; growth of, 5, 68, 79, 16

Opportunity to learn, 61–62

Permissive laws, 151
Private schools, 88–95; cost of, 94–95; demand for, 91–92; international demand for, 134; as social control, 155; student performance, 89–90
Professionalization of public services, 158–59
Progressive education 111, 114, 118–19
Property tax, 139–40, 150, 171–72; public support for, 175
Proposition 13, 176
Prussia, 110, 135–37, 148–49
Public expectations of schools, 18, 77–78
Public satisfaction with schools, 13, 64–65

About the Author

ROBERT J. FRANCIOSI is currently a research associate with the Arizona Department of Education. He has published scholarly and popular articles on numerous topics including education.